Indigenous Modernities

What are the hallmarks of a 'modern' city? Must cities in Asia and Africa acquire architectural elements of modernism from Western convention in order to be 'modern'? How have regional architectural traditions and building cultures outside the West encountered modernity? Reflecting on the cultural processes underlying urban transformation, *Indigenous Modernities* investigates what happens when global modernity engages with a place, locality, or tradition. Recognizing that modernity and colonialism are fundamentally connected, Dr. Hosagrahar examines the way 'traditional' built forms metamorphose to 'modern' in the context of colonialism, and reveals that oppositions like 'traditional' and 'modern,' or 'West' and 'non-West,' prevalent in scholarship on the built environment, are culturally constructed.

The author examines Delhi, India, during the late nineteenth and early twentieth centuries as it developed from a walled city into a fragmented metropolis. The transformation was more a palimpsest of plural and contentious processes than a linear path from one well-defined form to another. Citizens and officials of the colonial empire shaped Delhi's landscape together. In the fractured urbanism that emerged from the encounters, the familiar and the new redefined the city.

The interpretation of one city reminds us that 'modern' Delhi is like any place reconciling the dominant narrative of an imagined ideal with insubordinate local realities. Premised as they are on 'difference,' are the indigenous modernities of Dublin, Prague, and New York less obvious and disquieting than those of Delhi?

Dr. Jyoti Hosagrahar is Director of Sustainable Urbanism International, an independent non-profit research and policy initiative. She advises on urban development, historic conservation, and cultural sustainability issues in Asia. She currently teaches at Columbia University, New York. She has previously taught at the University of Oregon, Eugene, and earned her doctorate from the University of California, Berkeley.

THE ARCHI*TEXT* SERIES

Edited by Thomas A. Markus and Anthony D. King

Architectural discourse had traditionally represented buildings as art objects or technical objects. Yet buildings are also social objects in that they are invested with social meaning and shape social relations. Recognising these assumptions, the **Architext** series aims to bring together recent debates in social and cultural theory and the study and practice of architecture and urban design. Critical, comparative and interdisciplinary, the books in the series will, by theorising architecture, bring the space of the built environment centrally into the social sciences and humanities, as well as bringing the theoretical insights of the latter into the discourses of architecture and urban design. Particular attention will be paid to issues of gender, race, sexuality and the body, to questions of identity and place, to the cultural politics of representation and language, and to the global and postcolonial contexts in which these are addressed.

Jyoti Hosagrahar

Indigenous Modernities

Negotiating architecture and urbanism

Routledge
Taylor & Francis Group

LONDON AND NEW YORK

First Indian Reprint 2005

First published 2005
by Routledge
2 Park Square, Milton Park, Abingdon, Oxon OX14 4RN

Simultaneously published in the USA and Canada
by Routledge
270 Madison Ave, New York, NY 10016

Routledge is an imprint of the Taylor & Francis Group

Typeset in Frutiger by Wearset Ltd, Boldon, Tyne and Wear
Printed and bound in India by Brijbasi Art Press Ltd.

British Library Cataloguing in Publication Data
A catalogue record for this book is available from the British Library

Library of Congress Cataloging in Publication Data
Hosagrahar, Jyoti .
    Indigenous modernities : negotiating architecture and urbanism / Jyoti Hosagrahar.
        p. cm. – (The Architext series)
    Includes bibliographical references and index.
    1. Architecture–India–Delhi–19th century. 2. Architecture–India–Delhi–20th century. 3. City planning–India–Delhi–History–19th century. 4. City planning–India–Delhi–History–20th century. 5. Delhi (India)–History. I. Title. II. Series. 6. Postcolonialism and architecture. 7. Postcolonialism India.
    NA1508.D5H67 2005
    720 .954 560904–dc22

ISBN 0-415-32375-4 (hbk)
ISBN 0-415-32376-2 (pbk)

Contents

Acknowledgments

This book is, in part, a journey of self-discovery: an effort to understand my own shifting and ambivalent identities and their geographies of inhabitation. I grew up in New Delhi. From the perspective of an ordinary resident, my upbringing was quintessentially 'modern.' I lived in one of the newer planned neighborhoods in South Delhi and attended a renaissance school that embraced ideals of nationalism and secularism. A vast cultural distance separated the historic quarters of Delhi from the rest of the city. I first visited some of the main bazaar streets of historic Delhi as a student of architecture but had not thoroughly explored the older parts until I began this research project. It was some of the faculty at the School of Planning and Architecture in New Delhi who sparked my interest in understanding India's 'traditional' built environments even as we trained to follow the great modern masters. It was during my field visits and early research projects there that I began to contemplate the contradictory spatial realities of chrome and glass creations on the one hand and vernacular settlements on the other. For this early education, I remain forever in debt.

From the moment of initial research to the final manuscript, this book has been many years in the making. During this time I have accrued many debts. Institutions, colleagues, libraries, archives and collections, family and friends, and of course, the people of Delhi have all given with generosity and collaborated in this project. Research for this work first began at the University of California, Berkeley. Dell Upton's input and his own high standards of scholarship have contributed to my intellectual development and the shape of this book. I am grateful for his questions that spurred me to seek answers and to clarify my thoughts. From his early seminars to his comments on the manuscript, Thomas Metcalf's support of the book has been invaluable as have been the lessons I learned from Galen Cranz and Nezar Alsayyad.

Anthony King's guidance and friendship has been crucial throughout the life of this project. Every time I thought I had stretched as far as I could go, Tony would encourage me to go further. As editors of the Architext series, I could not have asked for more meticulous, demanding, and tireless readers than Tony King and Tom Markus. They made the process of book-writing an enriching one. I have been fortunate to have the advice of many friends and colleagues who read and reread portions of the manuscript over the years in its many incarnations including Annmarie Adams, Tridib Banerjee, Thomas Bender, Sibel Bozdogan, Zeynep Celik, Swati Chattopadhyay, Howard Davis, Mia Fuller, Will Glover, Marta Gutman, Hilde Heynen, Andrew Lees, Kenneth Mostern, Gulsum Nalbantoglu, Gyan Prakash, Vikramaditya Prakash, Peter Scriver, Arijit Sen, Abigail Van Slyck, and Gwendolyn Wright. The intellectual input of Catherine Asher, Marshall Berman, Manuel Castells, Dana Cuff, Paul Groth, Mark Jarzombek, Setha Low, A. G. Krishna Menon, K. T. Ravindran, Michael Sorkin, Richard Walker, and Michael Watts has been invaluable in the development of the book. I am also grateful for the feedback from reviewers and participants at conference presentations, including the participants of the seminar on teaching architectural history organized by JSAH and CASVA at the National Gallery of Art, Washington, D.C., those at meetings of the Society for Architectural Historians, the Society for American City and Regional Planning History, the Association for the Collegiate Schools of Architecture, the Association for the Collegiate Schools of Planning, the South Asia Conference at Berkeley, the Vernacular Architecture Forum, and the City One Conference of Serai.

Numerous institutions and individuals supported my archival and field research on Delhi. Research and production of visuals for the book was supported by a grant from the Graham Foundation. The American Institute of Indian studies (AIIS) supported extensive research in India and in London with a Junior and a Senior Fellowship. In New Delhi, P. R. Mehendiratta of the AIIS facilitated my research. A grant from the National Endowment for the Humanities and support from the University of Oregon faculty grant programs paid for some travel and research. Support from the NEH grant, and time off from teaching at the University of Oregon gave me much needed writing time for the book. For their continued encouragement and support I am very grateful to Robert Melnick, Michael Fifield, and Michael Utsey at the University of Oregon. I am grateful also to Stanford Anderson for giving me an affiliation with MIT and for including me in the History Theory Criticism seminars during the year I spent at Cambridge. The Jawaharlal Nehru University and the School of Planning and Architecture provided institutional support for my work in New Delhi for which I owe a special thanks to Ashis Maitra.

Narayani Gupta's work on Delhi was my first introduction to the city. On my earliest research visit she encouraged my work and shared generously her knowledge of historic Delhi, and its archival sources and has since read and commented on my pieces. Tanveer Ahmad Alvi, Khaliq Anjum, Banashree Bannerjee, Malay Chatterjee, Urvashi Dalal, the late Maheshwar Dayal, Abhijit Dutta, Muni Ashish Ganju, Jagmohan, Gangadhar Jha, Kavas Kapadia, H. K. Kaul, D. D. Mathur, A. G. Krishna Menon, Philip Oldenburg, Veena Oldenburg, Syyed Shafi, Khushwant Singh, P. S. A. Sundaram, Nalini Thakur, Geeta Dewan Verma, and Kiran Wadhwa, gave generously of their time and knowledge of Delhi.

Over the years during my visits to the many neighborhoods of historic Delhi and the early residential developments, numerous residents received me with warmth, welcomed me into their homes and their communities, and shared their knowledge of local history and urban development with me. I am grateful for the trust they placed in me in allowing me to measure, draw, photograph, and examine the spaces in which they live and work. Farid and Sajda Beg shared their substantial knowledge of Delhi, Persian and Urdu sources, and private collections of documents and photographs. I would also like to thank Jai Prakash Aggarwal, members of the Chunnamal family, Tejasna Dhari, Premchand Jain, Dwijendra Kalia, Atam Prakash Kaushik, the late Tarachand Khandelwal, Hemant Khandel- wal, members of the Khazanchi family, Atiya Habib Kidwai, Khurshida Kidwai, Lala Ram Lal, and Murlidhar Tiwari. My greatest debt in Delhi is to the late Saeed Khan in whose demise the old city lost an ardent advocate, a community leader, and a fund of knowledge. Saeed Khan *sahib* and Razia *baji* welcomed me into their home and their neighborhood and shared with me their private collections of documents, memories, and experiences. Shameem Jehan instructed me in Urdu and assisted me in reading maps, drawings, and numerous Urdu and Persian books and documents. Back in the U.S. it was reassuring to have the help of Huma Mody, and Shazia Zaidi to look over specific passages and my transla- tions.

I am grateful to the many officials in Delhi who made available their time, expertise, and resources for my research including those in the Delhi Administra- tion, Delhi Municipal Corporation, Delhi Development Authority, Institute of Social Work, the National Archives, the Archaeological Survey of India, the Min- istry for Urban Development, and the Town and Country Planning Organization. For their help in this regard my thanks are especially due to Arunachalam, Babu Ram, S. P. Bansal, B. K. Arora, Ambawani, R. K. Arora, Tara Chand Garg, J. C. Ghambir, Jagmohan, P. V. Jaikrishna, A. K. Jain, B. K. Jain, M. C. Joshi, M. L. Kachru, P. K. Khanna, Pradip Mehra, D. S. Meshram, Ravi Mallick, B. B. Nanda, Nazm, Sita Ram, Radhe Shyam Sharma, Rama Sharma, Manjeet Singh, Pradip Singh, and Krishnalekha Sood. I am also grateful to the archivists, librarians, and curators who have extended themselves beyond the call of duty. I must mention Veena Bhasin at the Delhi State Archives, Bhishamber Dutt of the record room at the Delhi Municipal Corporation, and Helen George at the Oriental and India Office Collections at the British Library in London. I am grateful also to Helen Ibbottson, Caroline Mallinder, Liza Mackenzie and their editorial staff at Rout- ledge in helping with the publication process.

Finally, I greatly appreciate the unwavering confidence that family and friends have shown me while enduring my neglect of them. Most remarkable in this regard have been my parents Vishalu and H. C. Visvesvaraya who have sup- ported the project throughout materially, intellectually, and emotionally. My parents-in-law, S. Shyam Sunder and the late Hira Shyam Sunder buoyed me with their enthusiasm. For their loving hospitality I would like to thank Sunil and Sarbajaya Kumar, Harish and Meera Rao, Raghunandan and Shyamala Rao,

Samir and Kavita Jain, Geetha Shanker, and Indira and S. Srikantiah. The individual who has collaborated in this work every step of the way is Shivsharan Someshwar. Without him, the book would not have been either conceived or completed. Nor would the journey have been so enjoyable. I can never thank him enough. Mere words are not sufficient to thank Amala and Himani who have accepted, lovingly and without rivalry, this book as their sibling.

Illustration Credits

Chapter 1: Introduction

Becoming 'Modern'

The nineteenth and early twentieth centuries witnessed dramatic cultural upheaval in many parts of the world. The period was significant for Western Europe's colonization of Asia and Africa. Europe's modernity was an outcome of both. Appropriating history and historiography, Europe constructed itself as the prototypical 'modern' subject. To be 'modern' was the prerogative of European rulers who claimed the right to define its meaning and assert its forms. The definition was based on difference: to be 'modern' was to be 'not traditional.' In this binary scheme of being 'modern' and 'traditional,' those that were not entirely one or the other were declared to be 'modernizing' towards a predetermined end. For those who regard the forms of Europe's modernity to be the only ones that are valid, all others were transitory, incomplete, inadequate, or 'traditional.' This fundamental opposition has been the premise of both scholarship and professional intervention in city planning and architecture. Questioning the binarism, this book relocates discussions of modernity to 'other' geographies outside its conventional locus of Western Europe and North America. Taking the position that the idea of 'modern' is a normative attribute culturally constructed in the extreme inequities of colonialism, and informed by the perspective that building, space, and society are (re)constitutively connected, I set out in this book to understand the anxieties of displacement and the fragmentation of experience in one city's engagement with extraordinary cultural change.

Investigating the circumstances in which mature architectural traditions and building cultures encountered modernity, and the forms that emerged from the cultural turmoil of the nineteenth and early twentieth centuries, this book aims to reclaim a history of a city that has been denied modernity. The arbiters of culture in Europe have asserted autonomy in the production of particular architectural and institutional arrangements that they have labeled as 'modern.' However, the fundamental connections of economic, political, and cultural interdependencies across the world made modernity an essentially global project. Dipesh Chakrabarty has persuasively argued that 'Europe's acquisition of the adjective *modern* for itself is a piece of global history of which an integral part is the story of European imperialism.'[1]

In the increasingly interconnected world of the nineteenth and early twentieth centuries with global flows of people, capital, ideas, and information, societies were thrown into cultural disarray. European rulers, imposed their versions of modernity as the only valid and universal ones. In unfamiliar terrain, however, and in moments of chaos, the built forms and institutions took on a life of their own. In places that the Europeans condemned as 'primitive' or 'traditional,' urban forms and institutions transplanted from the metropole contended with customary spatial practices as well as local responses to the cultural upheavals. My interest is in this process of indigenization. The emergent built forms, their use and meanings, though not identical to the ones idealized in Western Europe, were nevertheless modern. This work therefore seeks to acknowledge the plural forms of modernity and to legitimize its many interpretations. As Arjun Appadurai has reminded us, 'modernity is decisively at large, irregularly self-conscious, and unevenly experienced.'[2]

What then were the processes that transformed the urban landscapes of those societies that Europeans labeled as 'traditional,' that were already in flux, in their encounter with colonialism, and what governed the imposition of particular European structures and values? What forms emerged? Using the concept of *indigenous modernities* I explore the fragmented, complex, and paradoxical urbanism of a city's engagement, under the politics of colonialism, with the cultural turmoil of a rapidly globalizing world. An investigation of these 'other' modernities is also to observe the ways that dominant concepts from the metropole, proclaimed to be universal and liberating, translate into local spatial practices; and the ways that particular forms, places, and communities engage with a changing cultural milieu to adapt and also recreate themselves.

In this study I have elected to investigate the built form and culture of a single city, Delhi, over almost a century. Such an approach is critical to understand both cultural change and landscape transformation from the perspective of those intimately engaged in their production. I offer a reading of Delhi's landscape as a window onto the city's engagement with modernity and one informed by the particularities of its context. With detailed investigations I present insights into, and interpretations of, Delhi's urbanism to unsettle the calmness of an accepted categorization of architecture (and their societies) into 'modern' and 'traditional,' 'Western,' and 'non-Western.'

Delhi seems to fit the all-too-familiar tale of an ideal landscape, once picturesque and stable, that fell into decay. I look at a city rich in traditions of architecture and city building to study its complex and heterogenous built environment that some have seen as its 'failures:' its 'failure' to become 'modern' in European terms and a 'failure' to remain true to its inherited forms.[3] My study of Delhi begins with the dramatic political events of the First Indian War of Independence against British colonial rule in 1857 that brought into focus both the circumstances of Delhi's 'modern' milieu and the redefinition of space in the city.[4] The British East India Company conquered Delhi in 1803 but the

Mughal Emperor remained as titular head of the city until 1857. At this time Queen Victoria declared Crown rule in India. The year does less to mark the beginning of modernity in Delhi as it does to mark physical changes in the city due to social, economic, and political restructuring.[5] The accompanying decline of the nobility and the rise of the entrepreneurial classes brought about substantial changes in the use and perception of space. My period of study includes the building of the new imperial capital of New Delhi from 1911 to 1931, and ends just before India's independence in 1947.

Delhi is a city of many cities: imagined, lived, and controlled, the landscape has been re-created, rebuilt and made meaningful by the daily acts of inhabiting as well as planned interventions.[6] Since the early nineteenth century, Western Europeans had perceived and represented Delhi as the exotic antithesis of what was 'modern:' the quintessential oriental city of ornate minarets and bustling bazaars, a picturesque landscape dotted with the ruins of ancient cities.[7] During her travels through north India in 1823, Emily Eden wrote letters home to England describing her life and experiences in a strange and sublime land:

> . . . Delhi is one of the few sights, indeed the only one except Lucknow, that has quite equaled my expectations. Four miles round it there is nothing to be seen but gigantic ruins of mosques and palaces, and the actual living city has the finest mosque we have seen yet.[8]

Enthralled by the grandeur of the mosques and palaces, and the mystique of ancient ruins, harems, and dense city living, the Eden sisters were among the many nineteenth-century travelers who represented Delhi as the ultimate oriental city (Figure 1.1). As the *Illustrated London News* declared in 1857:

> Whoever has seen Grand Cairo may gain some idea of Delhi if he will but add to the picture gardens full of shading trees, brilliant flowers, lovely fountains of white marble, which cast up their bright waters among shining palaces, 'with sculptured mosques and

Figure 1.1
'Ruins of Old Delhi.'
Lithograph of the remains of one of the older cities of Delhi, 1845. A depiction of Delhi as an exotic and sublime landscape of ancient ruins.

minarets,' like obelisks of pearl, shooting into a sky whose color would shame the brightest turquoise that ever graced a Sultan's finger. Again, instead of camels, and horses, and mules, alone blocking up the narrow; shaded ways of the native city, as at El Misn, the reader must imagine strings of elephants, their large ears painted, their trunks decorated with gold rings; anklets of silver round their legs, and bearing large square curtained howdahs, in which recline possibly the favourites of the hareem. Luxury, even now, can go no further in the East than it is to be found at Delhi.[9]

Measured against such romanticized images, European observers, confronted with the realities of a tumultuous and changeful city, rejected all but the delightfully historic. Regardless of the representations, cultural upheavals due to technology, capitalist development, and colonization continued. On the one hand was a narrative of the civilizing and liberating qualities of science, reason, and the universals of modernism as conceived by those in positions of authority in Europe. On the other hand, the lived city, rooted in a place and a cultural context, was caught in chaos with familiar forms and meanings thrown into question. Their interaction in the particularities of Delhi created the many landscapes of indigenous modernities distinct from those idealized in the metropole.

RETHINKING MODERNITY AND ARCHITECTURE

Scholars differ on how and when to date the start of the 'modern' era even within the dominant European discourse around that theme. While the Renaissance set in motion new ways of considering human progress and historical development, Enlightenment thinkers brought into focus what Jurgen Habermas has called the 'project of modernity.'[10] The cornerstones of the modernist enterprise included the scientific domination of nature, rational modes of thinking, and the organization of society and space that together were to serve as vehicles for achieving liberation from myth, superstition, and religion. Architectural historians identify with the modern era a new way of thinking about history, antiquity, and the development of architecture.[11] However, fundamental to the emergence of modernity as a global project was Western Europe's colonization of Asia and Africa.

Having defined itself as 'modern' in relation to the Oriental 'other,' Europe's colonization also served to transplant elsewhere the ideals, agendas, and forms of a particular European notion of modernity. New forms of cultural, political, and economic interdependency articulated differently in various societies gave rise to a plurality of modernities. Their emergence, however, premised on a culture of extreme inequality, was intensely contentious.[12] What were taken as universally rational modes of thought and reason became the prerogative of European societies, attributing myth and superstition to the cultures of Asia and Africa.

Upon Europe's 'discovery' of lands and cultures in Asia and Africa, historiography essentialized and froze their architectural character, even as cultural upheavals transformed the landscapes. Histories of Western European architecture were accounts of social and moral progress, a narrative that was denied to those they conquered. Orientalism and colonialism worked together to produce what imperialist scholars claimed were objective histories of architecture of the unfamiliar built forms of distant lands. From Banister Fletcher to Viollet le Duc, early European historians cast the architecture of Asia and Africa as primitive, changeless, and irrational: an architecture without history.[13]

Once those in power had declared themselves the only legitimate moderns, those 'others' they labeled 'traditional' could only aspire, seek, adopt, or mimic modern forms in the dominant mould. However, they never complete the transition to become 'modern' like the original.[14] Alternative versions of modernity that unfolded in specific places and cultures must necessarily have different trajectories and outcomes in the built environment.[15] The particular circumstances of modernity in a place gave rise to new cultural, institutional, and spatial articulations that adapted the new and reconstituted the familiar. At the heart of my investigations, therefore, are these appropriations and localized interpretations of the 'modern.'

The cultural disarray under modernity in different circumstances took a variety of forms as a cycle of destruction and creation. Baudelaire refers to modernity as the transient and the fleeting; Octavio Paz to the 'dizzying manifestations of criticism.'[16] Marshall Berman has characterized the modern as the ephemeral, contingent, and discontinuous and declared that such environments promise adventure and transformation while at the same time threatening everything we have and know.[17] David Harvey notes that modernity has no respect even for its own past or any sense of historical continuity.[18]

The built environment of Delhi is a complex interplay between *modernization* as the deliberate reordering of space and of social, political, and economic forms of organization, and *modernism* as the subjective experience of the enterprise or as an expression of its transformative intent. I include both the un-self-conscious response to the modern milieu and projects of advancement, as well as the self-conscious engagement with, and expression of, an identifiable ideology that espouses a scientific doctrine in architecture and a specific aesthetic.[19] My study of modernity as the tumultuous cultural condition brought about by the rupture with history includes both the projects of modernization and the responses to them. The social and economic upheaval of breaking with the past creates dislocation while offering immense opportunities for building a future.[20]

Cities became the sites for the modernist enterprise, the most visible expression of the cultural upheaval in all its destructive and creative glory. They became the locus for both the disintegration of inherited traditions and for building anew. It is from this perspective that I study the landscape of a city in the throes of turmoil: imagined and lived, planned and perceived as a theater for the enactment of a modernity particular to its context.

In recent years, critical reading(s) of modernity have helped to enrich and expand our understanding of its experiences. Despite numerous studies in critical cultural theory, outside the conventional 'West' the city as the site of cultural transformations in the nineteenth and early twentieth centuries has remained largely neglected. A number of scholars have commented on complex and nuanced experiences of modernity and its relationship to colonialism, national-ism, transnationalism, gender, race, ethnicity, community, and identity. However, despite these illuminating studies of culture and society, most histories of archi-tecture and urbanism continue to assume 'traditional' and 'modern,' the 'West' and the 'non-West,' as irreconcilably separate and opposing categories. Accounts of architecture and modernity in the so-called 'non-West' have often been col-lapsed into narratives of particular forms or the architecture of the Modern Movement and its offshoots. The canonical histories of architecture and urban-ism have tended to exclude Asia and Africa even when their histories and archi-tecture are interconnected; the so-called 'traditional' societies continue to be placed outside the realm of the 'modern.' As an imperialist fantasy, the norm-ative models of modernism have excluded from the annals of 'modern' the ordinary, the irregular, and the changing vernacular, even within the coterie of 'modern' nations.[21]

My objective is not to treat built environments that have been typically referred to as 'traditional' and/or 'non-Western' as mirror images or extensions of the West. Rather than ignore the differences between what in dominant dis-course is referred to as 'traditional' and 'modern,' 'West' and 'non-West,' I examine critically the politics that have constructed the differences as opposing identities and categories. The project here is not merely to celebrate and give voice to minority discourses and knowledges in order to include them in their subordinate positions into existing privileged accounts of modernity, but to ques-tion the very master narrative. Recognition of modernity and colonialism as fundamentally connected accepts the global nature of modernity and 'tradi-tional' and 'modern' architecture as cultural constructs rather than inherent characteristics. A richer understanding of the values and agendas of modernism and its forms as specific to a culture, time, and place would give legitimacy to built forms and experiences generally excluded from the normative models of modernity, even in Western Europe and North America.

INDIGENIZED MODERNS

Indigenous modernities denotes the paradoxical features of modernities rooted in their particular conditions and located outside the dominant discourse of a universal paradigm centered on an imagined 'West.' As a seemingly coherent 'traditional' built environment ruptures, *indigenous modernities* are expressed in the irregular, the uneven, and the unexpected. In the actualization of universal agendas in a particular place, *indigenous modernities* negotiate the uniqueness of a region and its history with the 'universals' of science, reason, and liberation. In using the term 'indigenous' I emphasize context and locality, the regional interpretations and forms of modernity rather than engage in an exercise of dis-tinguishing endogenous and exogenous influences in architecture.

Although I focus on the development of modernity and its expressions in a particular place, my effort is not to identify essentialized attributes of a changeless geography and brand them as elements of a 'regional modern' character typical of India, or Delhi, or even the historic walled city. In the tumultuous experience of modernity, when all inherited categories are called into question, as the strange becomes familiar and the familiar becomes distant, the boundaries of 'place' and 'locale' become elusive and ephemeral. With the typical and the customary in flux, features labeled as such represent imagined characteristics: regions and their features have both become an imaginary terrain.[22]

Against the rigid opposition and monolithic identities of 'traditional' and 'modern,' the concept of indigenous modernities celebrates their simultaneity and engagement.[23] Rather than the typical dualities of 'traditional' and 'modern,' 'ruler' and 'subject,' 'Orient' and 'Occident,' *indigenous modernities* helps to recognize the polarization as politically derived and socially constructed.[24] Acknowledging simultaneity allows an examination of their interaction rather than expecting a simplistic and complete replacement of one well-defined form by another. Seeing *indigenous modernities* as negotiated forms implies that colonial designs and policies are not absolute and the subjects are not passive recipients. Homi Bhabha has observed:

> The borderline engagements of cultural difference may as often be consensual as conflictual; they may confound our definitions of tradition and modernity; realign the customary boundaries between the private and the public, high and low; and challenge normative expectations of development and progress.[25]

Global politics and the asymmetries of power relations influence a society's engagement with modernity.[26] Individuals and groups seek to annex the dislocating effects of globalization into their own practices. These appropriations and interpretations, however, remain tentative.

Indigenous modernities are expressed in built forms prompting ambivalent readings and reactions. As socially constructed identities, buildings and spaces cannot be labeled as inherently 'modern' or 'traditional' on the basis of their visual characteristics at a moment in time. Nor can the form, use, and significance of a space be understood in isolation of the cultural processes by which they are produced and consumed. In the tumult of cultural change, customary spatial practices and social institutions are in flux. The spatial experiences of *indigenous modernities* are marked by the presence of formal contradictions and the absence of coherence. For those who expect unity, and those who imagine 'modern' and 'traditional' to be complete, visually identifiable features of a built form, *indigenous modernities* are disturbing in their discontinuity and incompleteness. The irregular breaks and continuities in forms and meanings that appear place specific as well as the presence of overtly universal formations create a landscape of surprises that to some may appear as a kitsch version of European modernism or a sullied one of local traditionalism. Viewed in isolation, a form may appear to have persisted on the basis of local knowledge and timeless traditions, or it may mimic the recognizable forms that some have proclaimed as the original 'moderns.' In the altered context familiar forms acquire new uses and meanings and strange elements are incorporated into familiar arrangements.

Such a contextual view of 'modern' rejects a romanticization of an idealized 'traditional' architecture. Nostalgia for the past, even while breaking away from it, is a preoccupation of conventional modernism. The inhabitants of a place do not see themselves or their built forms as 'traditional' as they live their daily lives amidst buildings and streets that may be old or evolved from the accumulated knowledge of generations. In their interpretations of received forms, uses, and meanings, in the destructive/creative upheaval of modernity, the residents may see no reason for orthodoxy either in romanticized preservation, or in a complete rejection of existing forms.

DELHI: BUILDING, CITY, AND NATION IN INDIAN HISTORIOGRAPHY

During the nineteenth century, the British constructed a narrative of India as a land of ancient glory fallen into decay. The objective of reforming a culture in decline was used to justify British imperialism in India. European scholars framed their understanding of Indian architecture through a search for classical antiquity comparable to that of Greece and Rome.[27] Those interested in Indian architecture were most intrigued by ancient architectural remains. The interest of Alexander Cunningham and James Princep in antiquity resulted in the establishment of the Archaeological Survey of India in 1867.[28] The search for pure, authentic styles influenced James Fergusson and Alexander Cunningham to write architectural histories of India that gave primacy to isolated monuments of the ancient and medieval periods.[29] They characterized structures as based on religious differences, and perceived stylistic traits. These scholars imbued buildings with moral and religious characteristics reflective of their makers and categorized them as such. Their classification of structures into Hindu, Islamic, and Buddhist continues into the present. Such characterization obscured the complexities and conflicts in the building form, its uses and meanings.[30] Further, the categorization followed a loose chronology that was deceptive and over-simplified. A focus on permanent structures and elaborate monuments isolated them from the landscape of everyday dwellings and bazaars to which they belonged. Authenticity of styles rather than the social, economic, and political context of particular buildings were at the heart of Fergusson's monumental, *History of Indian and Eastern Architecture*. First published in 1876, the book became the most widely read and influential work of scholarship published on South Asian architecture for more than a century and continues to be used as the primary text in many schools of architecture in South Asia.[31]

Architectural histories of 'modern' India have largely focused either on buildings and city forms that European rulers authored to further the goals of colonial rule or on the architects and architecture of the post-independence period that have been self-conscious in their adoption of recognizable forms of European modernism. The grand public monuments, palaces, the bungalow, the

cantonment, and the buildings of the Public Works Division have all been subjects of study as also have Le Corbusier's design of Chandigarh and the work of
contemporary Indian architects.[32] In this piecemeal view, we have no explanation
of how the rich and evolving architectural traditions of South Asia responded to
the dramatic cultural transformations of the late nineteenth and early twentieth
centuries.

Many different streams of scholarship have influenced this study. First, the
recent cultural histories of nineteenth- and early twentieth-century cities in
Western Europe and North America have offered varied and nuanced readings of
their own distinctive experiences of modernity and architecture.[33] Second, recent
writings on architecture and modernity from locations that the dominant model
has regarded as subordinate have addressed key themes of colonialism, nationalism, and modernity and provided insightful readings of the relationship of power
and space.[34] Finally, other studies have explored the many interpretations of
modernity and the construction of history in South Asia. These recent studies of
modernity in South Asia have made enormous contributions to postcolonial
theory and thinking about other modernisms.[35] The works have broken new
ground in directing our attention to the fundamental relationship between
modernity and colonialism. They have alerted us to subordinate voices and the
complex experiences of women, the marginalized, and the transnational and
added significantly to our understanding of nationalism and historiography. This
book aims to advance the implications of these critical perspectives to the understanding of city, space, and the built environment.

The cultural landscape of Delhi presents an example of syncretism between
customary ways of building and inhabiting, imposed social and spatial forms
emerging from Europe's modernity, and the cultural chaos of modernity and
colonialism. After the conquest of the city in 1857, the British set about deliberately reshaping its space and redefining the relationships of people to their built
environment. However, the resulting transformations were not simply brought
about by any one force or policy but reflected the conflicts and tensions of cultural dislocation. The discontinuities and disjunctures express dynamic landscapes
that were the consequences of tireless mediations of changing power groups
and negotiations over conflicting interests. If British interventions in Delhi were
guided by a Victorian zeal for social and spatial differentiation, the visions of
European modernizers, and the ambitions of absolute imperial rule, in the lived
city, they had to contend with customary spatial practices, competing local interests, and the contestation of colonial authority.

In contrast to the grand architecture of imperial New Delhi as it had
developed by the 1930s, the historic walled city appeared to a visitor from
Europe as both exotic and dilapidated. Bazaars and narrow winding lanes, filled
with the clutter of everyday life, confronted boulevards and beaux-arts designs in
the new city. Tantalizing remains of skilled craftsmanship jarred with the workshops and shacks that crowded the once elaborate courtyards. Mansions became
decrepit communities of small apartments or warehouses. New technologies of

building and of mechanization, new and efficient forms of transportation, the centralized provision of infrastructure, new concerns of sanitation and public health, planned developments, new ideals of designed urban spaces, and the professionalization of municipal governance all came to India in the latter half of the nineteenth century as it did elsewhere in Western Europe and North America (although sometimes with a delay). However, the emergent built forms, meanings, and uses presented a different kind of the 'modern' than the ones assumed to be the universal ideal.

Received historical accounts in the nineteenth century have presented the architectural glories of the city both past and present: the great tower of Qutub Minar, the impressive Friday mosque of the Jami Masjid, the magnificent palace of the Mughal Emperor, the ruins of old forts, mosques, and tombs.[36] Travelogues and historical accounts in Urdu and Persian that describe Delhi's buildings and urban life have remained largely inaccessible to scholars in architecture, urban planning, and to historians of other cities.[37] Conservationists have identified and documented historic structures in and around the metropolis.[38] Recent scholarship posits Delhi either as an imperial city in the seventeenth and eighteenth centuries or as an exploding metropolis with a host of urban problems in the latter part of the twentieth century.[39] The notable exception here is Narayani Gupta's meticulous history chronicling Delhi's growth in the nineteenth and early twentieth centuries.[40] As a pioneering account of a South Asian city, Gupta's work was remarkable in making the city, its government, and politics a legitimate area of historical inquiry. Maheshwar Dayal's reminiscences of Delhi's urban life offered a personal view of Delhi's society and culture in Hindi and English (much of the literature on Delhi's culture is in Urdu).[41]

My study follows the city's transformation from a historic city over almost a century. The deliberate and self-conscious efforts of the colonial powers and some local inhabitants to impose particular forms of modernity combined with dislocation brought about by the destruction of an existing order and the creation of new ones. As a result, some forms and meanings changed dramatically, others seemingly very little. The liberating ideals of reason were thwarted by the oppressive realities of colonial domination. Where the inhabitants encountered disarray on the one hand, they were quick to recognize opportunities to build anew on the other. Out of the turmoil developed cultural forms built on the remains of partially dismantled traditions that were reconstituted and re-contextualized. This book focuses on the articulations of such emergent cultural landscapes.

In this book I have chosen to examine five aspects of the city that provide windows into the processes of transformation at different scales and at different times. Contrary to offering a linear tale of progress from one well-defined form to another, the thematic chapters offer different views of the many changing worlds within the city over almost a century. The narratives follow a loose chronological order from the beginnings of British imperial rule in 1857 to the time just before India's independence in 1947. The investigations begin with an account of the mansions and courtyard houses, and move on to explore public space, infrastructure, urban regulation and management, the expansion of commerce, and, finally, the development of 'new towns' or engineered extensions.

The next chapter, 'Fragmenting Domestic Landscapes: From mansions to margins,' examines the ways in which the private, domestic landscape of historic Delhi changed between 1857 and 1910. I explore the nuanced transformations in Delhi's ubiquitous mansions and courtyard houses, the *haveli*, during a time of dramatic social, political, and economic transformations. From sprawling princely mansion to modest dwelling and a cluster of small rental units, the *haveli* were fragmented, abandoned, rationalized, rebuilt, and variously interpreted. Changes in the social and political structure of Delhi, altered values of ideals, domestic environments, and technology, all contributed to new versions of a conventional house-form.

The new urban milieu influenced transformations in the *haveli* in the form of numerous individual responses in altering physical structures and spatial meanings. In contrast, the following chapter, 'Negotiating Streets and Squares: Spatial culture in the public realm,' addresses direct state efforts to construct public spaces that were self-consciously 'modern' according to the norms of the metropole. In a city where royalty and religion dominated public spaces, officials sought to construct a 'civic' realm. The new rulers undertook planned efforts to regulate, demolish, expand, and contain parts of the old city with the stated objective of sanitizing and improving it. Municipal officials sought to police, with legal codes, community spaces managed by unwritten social mores. The state's efforts to rebuild, regulate, and preserve resulted in contestation over the form and meaning of public space. The newly created 'civic' square provided a space for political meetings and public protests with the rise of Indian nationalism. The resident's responses to the official efforts created indigenized modernities. The redefined public spaces were distinct from existing patterns and yet entirely unlike the European ones either in form or meaning.

With progress in the sciences and medicine, and the growing ill effects of demographic growth and crowding, disquiet over public health dominated urban intervention in Western Europe. New perceptions of the body and space emerged. The imperial government and municipal officials together attempted to reorganize and regulate space in the city according to the values of Western science and technology, relegating indigenous knowledge to the realm of superstition. Urban interventions, guided by the tenets of a seemingly universal science, were deeply political as disease, health, slums, and gardens created a new social geography. In the chapter, 'Sanitizing Neighborhoods: Geographies of health,' I explore the visions of the ideal city implicit in the sanitary reforms as well as their contradictions. The intersection of official visions, hidden agendas, and the lived realities of customary local spatial practices influenced sanitary reform and the municipalization of infrastructure in Delhi. Measures to bring about sanitary reform were implicitly about the definition of disease and sickness, morality and improvement, covertly reinforcing new social hierarchies in the city and furthering colonial goals.

Where restructuring the physical environment of the existing fabric was not possible, the British proposed extensions to the walled city that idealized an urban experience dramatically different from the existing one. The fifth chapter, 'Beyond the Walls: Commerce of urban expansion,' examines some early municipal efforts at city improvement from 1880 to 1920 and the layout of the earliest planned extension outside the city walls. All properties in the city were surveyed, categorized, and assessed for future development. Improvement schemes defined new criteria for a healthy city. Progress meant planned and controlled growth, entrepreneurship, and maximizing the value of land. Disease was not the only measure of health in a city: the freedom of capital was as important. While official policies encouraged the privatization and commodification of community property what emerged was a new relationship of people to property and the organization of community itself. Municipal official, squatter, speculator, and merchant each fought for the right to construct the meanings of home, shop, city, and property.

In 1911, New Delhi was declared the new capital of British India. The layout of the capital complex and the politics of its making has been the subject of extensive scholarly attention.[42] In this book I focus more on the repercussions of its layout and development on the walled city and the city's development in general than on an analysis of New Delhi's design. The penultimate chapter, 'Imagining Modernity: Symbolic terrains of housing,' looks at the development of the residential landscape between 1935 and 1941 after the building of Lutyens' capital complex at New Delhi. The grand and imperial New Delhi was a visual representation of British sovereignty: an idealized world that had no room for the ordinary lives of ordinary people. Located between the old walled city and the new capital complex of New Delhi, official discourse and design constructed planned extensions as idealized dwelling environments whose functionalism echoed the imperatives of the Modern Movement. Based on 'rational' design and 'scientific' regulations, their identity of 'modern' was carefully constructed as different from the common buildings and neighborhoods of the walled city and resembling the recognizable forms of European modernity. However, paradoxes abound as the colonial state was torn between a desire to present itself as a social benefactor on the one hand, and a motivation to make profit through the development of real estate on the other. Nor were residents passive recipients of modernizing projects. Customary building practices contested the authority of the municipal codes, professional planners, and imperial institutions so that the seemingly recognizable European forms were, in fact, expressions of a different modernity: an 'informalized' landscape contrary to the imagined ideal of the blueprints.

The account of Delhi that emerges from the foregoing chapters is not by any means a comprehensive documentation of the city's development during the period of study. The built forms I choose to examine in each of the chapters are a few of the many similar expressions of indigenous modernities in Delhi. Addressing the development of nationalist thinking, popular agitations, and formal politics, the changing identities of women, and the architecture and urbanism of postcolonial Delhi would further enrich the perspective provided by this work.

Are indigenous modernities unique to Delhi? Or to India? Do they develop only in the presence of Western European colonization? As context and place-specific interpretations of a global condition, indigenous modernities are everywhere. Places with strong existing architectural and urban traditions reveal more clearly the dilemmas and politics of cultural transformation in their shifting landscapes and paradoxical forms. Lucknow, Lahore, Saigon, or Rabat all had a well-developed urban form before the advent of colonial rule and could have served equally well as the focus of this study. The indigenous modernities of Singapore, Hong Kong, Bombay, and Shanghai remind us that a 'difference' in spatial culture – form, function, social/economic, and symbolic/political meanings – created the juxtaposition of the recognizable and the unexpected. Global interdependencies and dramatic cultural upheaval did not need the direct presence of a Western European colonial power although authoritarianism played a significant role in the indigenous modernities of Tokyo after the Meiji revolution, Bangkok during the reign of King Chulalongkorn, and Istanbul under the rule of Kemal Ataturk. The question is whether, premised as it was on 'difference,' the indigenous modernities of Dublin, Prague, and New York were as disquieting as those of Delhi.

In Delhi, deliberate design came together with spontaneous responses, 'rational' modes of thinking with local knowledge, new spatial practices with existing customary ones, and oppressive colonial authority with subversive appropriations. The result was a multiplicity of competing orders. I write not only a history of the 'other' in the 'other's' terms but also reflect back on understandings of modernity and built form as defined by the dominant experiences of Western Europe and North America. Questioning the cultural authority of a particular narrative of modernity and its expressions in architecture that have generally been assumed to be universal and the only valid expressions, and exploring the political influences shaping the identities of 'modern' and 'not modern,' allows us to recognize that all modernisms emerged from the particularities of their context: the place, time, history, and society in which they were located. The conflicts, paradoxes, and compromises I highlight are not Delhi's alone. Far from it, indigenizations of the ideals of modernist ideals happened in different ways even in places that represent the standard for 'modern' built environments. In recovering a history of Delhi's modernity, this book hopes to nurture richer and more plural accounts of modern architecture and urbanism everywhere.

Chapter 2: Fragmented Domestic Landscapes

From Mansions to Margins

During the seventeenth and eighteenth centuries, Delhi, as Shahjahanabad, sovereign city of the Mughals, boasted of many distinguished *haveli*, grand establishments of the elite. The ubiquitous mansions and courtyard houses formed a primary unit of the urban fabric (Figure 2.1). By the early twentieth century, many of these elegant and sprawling mansions had suffered dilapidation and been converted into over-crowded multi-family 'tenement' houses, warehouses, and specialty markets. The transformation of the *haveli* from what European visitors saw as the picturesque to the decrepit occurred through a disarray of synchronous activities: demolishing and building, disclaiming and appropriating, redefining and abandoning. Like the city, the mansions – fragmented, commercialized, and rebuilt – remained vibrant even in their decrepitude.[1]

CITIES WITHIN THE CITY

Until the 1850s, the Mughal elite lived in extensive quarters that were almost self-contained neighborhoods. The seventeenth-century French traveler Francois Bernier observed the presence of many large, walled mansions in Delhi and noted:

> [Amid] . . . streets are dispersed the habitations of *Mansebdars*, or petty *Omrahs*, officers of justice, rich merchants, and others; . . . They consider that a house to be greatly admired ought to be situated in the middle of a large flower-garden, and should have four large divan-apartments raised the height of a man from the ground and exposed to the four winds, so that the coolness may be felt from any quarter . . . The interior of a good house has the whole floor covered with a cotton mattress four inches in thickness, over which a fine white cloth is spread during the summer, and a silk carpet in the winter. At the most conspicuous side of the chamber are one or two mattresses, with fine coverings quilted in the form of flowers and ornamented with delicate silk embroidery, interspersed with gold and silver . . . the sides of the room are full of niches, cut in a variety of shapes, tasteful and well proportioned, in which are seen porcelain vases and flower-pots. The ceiling is gilt and painted . . .[2]

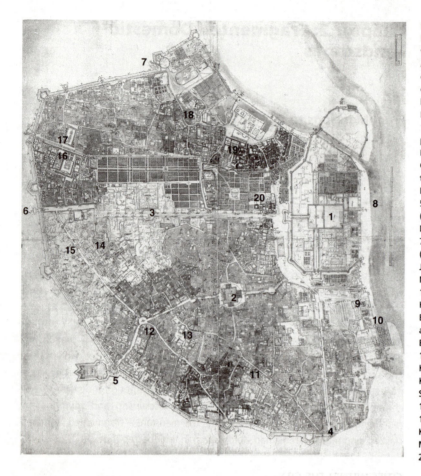

Figure 2.1
Delhi, *c.*1850 shows the walled compounds of the *haveli* complexes. A few of the numerous haveli on the original drawing have been highlighted. Key urban elements: 1. Qila Mubarak (King's palace); 2. Jami'ah Masjid; 3. Chandni Chowk (the square on the street); 4. Dihli Darvazah (Delhi Gate); 5. Ajmeri Darvazah (Ajmere Gate); 6. Lahori Darvazah (Lahore Gate); 7. Kashmiri Darvazah (Kashmere Gate); 8. River Jamuna; 9. *Haveli* of the Nawab of Jhajjar; 10. Kothi Shams ad-Din Khan; 11. Haveli Nawab Bangash; 12. Haveli Qamr ad-Din Khan; 13. Haveli Begum Shamru; 14. Haveli Hissam ad-Din Khan; 15. Haveli Sipahdar Khan; 16. Haveli Nawab Shahadat Khan; 17. Haveli Nawab Wazir; 18. Kothi Ahmad 'Ali Khan; 19. Haveli Nawab Mansur 'Ali Khan; 20. Kothi 'Ali Khan

Existing structures, descriptions, and drawings of the period suggest that the mansions consisted of interconnected apartments, courtyards, and pillared halls (Figure 2.2). Gardens, ponds, and water-courses were laid out for the pleasure of the *amīr* and his household.[3] In his diary for the period 1737 to 1741, the eighteenth-century traveler Dargah Quli Khan described the mansion of Mirza Abdul Khaliq, a wealthy noble, in a quatrain:

> This house is decorated like the blossoms of paradise,
> and shines like the pupils of the eyes,
> behold this fountain, *hauz* [pool], flowers as well as this
> quatrain [which illustrates the beauty of all these].

And again:

> Men of discernment name this [mansion] as a glass-house, decorated with colourful
> carpets and curtains of attractive colours and the niches filled with china wares. With a

Figure 2.2
Sketch of Haveli
Muzaffar Khan, 1847.
View of entrance from
street.

repertoire of euphuistic verses, the poets gather in this glass-house and indulge in lively conversation and enjoy themselves with the aid of the *qahwa* [coffee], *huqqa* [for smoking tobacco], confections, and perfumes.[4]

The mansion buildings were single- or double-storied, decorated with paint and stone carving. Walls and windows were richly embellished with *jharoka* and *jali*.[5] Elegant furnishings adorned the interior spaces; fine china and bejeweled boxes were on display. The grand mansions with multiple structures and courtyards were more like small communities that contained the private quarters of the *amīr* and also housed his treasure, harem, record offices, stables, and a vast retinue of service people.[6]

Qamr-al-Din Khan's *haveli*, for instance, was a walled area with several structures within and contiguous to it[7] (Figure 2.3). In addition to a public reception area for the patriarch, gardens, and separate quarters for the women of the household, the *haveli* included accommodation for an entourage of professionals, artisans, soldiers, and servants under the patronage of the nobleman. The women of the household lived in apartments in the buildings of the *mahal-sarāi*, where they were secluded from interaction with men outside the family (Figure 2.4). Included in the neighborhood-like complex were mansions for his daughters. In addition to the lavish quarters of the *amīr*, the *haveli* complex, contained apartments for various service personnel. Accountants, clerks, and personal servants lived in a few rooms or small houses within or around the main house. Merchants, traders, moneylenders, artisans, musicians, poets, calligraphers, physicians, and astrologers who owed their patronage to the *amīr* were all part of the community. The hierarchy and complexity of spaces, activities, and inhabitants within the *haveli* complex, as well as their sense of kinship and identity, made the mansions more like *mahallā*, or neighborhoods. The neighborhood-like *haveli* was also likely to have within it housing for laborers, soldiers, grooms, cart-drivers, tent-pitchers, torch-bearers, camel-drivers, elephant-grooms, blacksmiths, ironmongers, and others who worked under the protection of the *amīr*.[8]

Animals and storage facilities were once part of the *haveli* complex. Some, such as the mansion of Raja Sohan Lal, had stables in the vicinity of the *haveli*. These housed horses, elephants, camels, cows, and goats.[9] While provisions for the *amīr* and his retinue were stored in granaries, reserves were also necessary for perfumes, medicines, furniture, candles, palanquins, *rath* (ceremonial chariots), tents, and swords.[10] In addition, workshops for clothing, carpets, goldwork, and fine embroidery were included in each of the self-contained neighborhoods

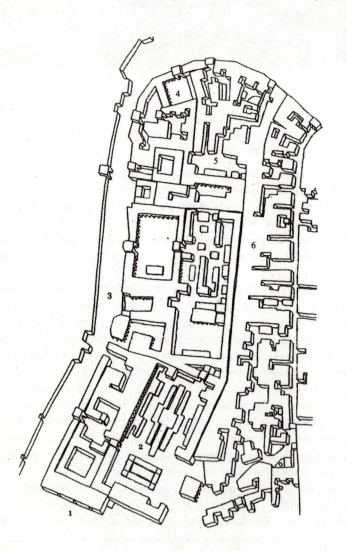

Figure 2.3
Haveli Qamr al-Din Khan
*c.*1850 showing pavilions
and units connected by
courtyards. The *haveli*
included a grand
gateway with guards and
musicians, an audience
hall to receive visitors,
women's quarters, a
library, a bath, and a
mosque. The street was
named after the great
personage as Kuchah
Qamr ad-Din Khan.
1. Kuchah Mir Khan;
2. Haveli Qamr ad-Din
Khan; 3. Kuchah Qamr
ad-Din Khan; 4. Mosque;
5. Women's quarters;
6. Staff quarters

Figure 2.4
Sketch of the interior of
the women's quarters,
1785. Entitled 'Inside of a
Mussalman's Zanannah,
with the various
amusements of the
oriental ladies.'

that formed the *haveli*. By the middle of the eighteenth century, however, many
of the craftsmen and artisans started to form guilds and live in enclaves in the
city that were not part of *haveli* neighborhoods.

Travelers of the time noted that the princely *haveli* were quite large. Qamr
al-Din Khan's *haveli* extended the length of an entire street and Safdar Jang's
contained room for 5,000 soldiers and 500 horses.[11] The architectural quality of
some of the structures of the eighteenth-century *haveli* such as Haveli Azam

Khan and Haveli Qutbuddin Khan were significant enough to be entered in a list of monuments in Delhi prepared by the Archaeological Survey of India in 1916.[12] Thus, both socially and architecturally, *haveli* were landmarks in the city and the symbolic centers of the neighborhoods as the King's palace was of Delhi (Figure 2.5).

At the head of the *haveli* and its neighborhood stood the *amīr*. The *umrah* constituted parent figures for the community they supported in much the same way that the emperor did for the empire and the city. The names of the thoroughfares themselves indicated the *amīr* 's protection and authority over the streets and their neighborhoods. The street in front of Qamr-al-Din Khan's *haveli* was named after the patriarch as were other streets named after the significant personages such as Raja Sohan Lal and Mir Khan. Descriptions of the period reinforce the idea that the identity of the mansion could not be distinguished from the neighborhood it ruled and that supported it.[13]

Limited and tangible as the grand mansions might have been, until the middle of the nineteenth century the powers of the *amīr* extended far beyond the immediate mansion buildings to the agricultural estates in the countryside and the labor that worked on it (Figure 2.6). Mughal rulers granted lands to royalty, significant members of the court, or those whom they favored. The grantees enjoyed taxes from the lands. The land grants, or *jagīr*, gave their holders rights over people and resources and by that enabled them to live in a style appropriate to a ruler. In return for the land grants or *jagīr*, the grantees were expected to pledge their service and allegiance to the Mughal Emperor and his empire.[14] Revenue from the *jagīr* served to maintain armies of men, horses, elephants, and weapons in readiness for wars they would fight on behalf of the empire. These small rulers – holders of land, rank, and title – were also patriarchs at the head of their *haveli*. The surplus beyond that necessary for maintaining the

Figure 2.5
Sketch of a *haveli* built shortly before the 1857 rebellion. Title reads 'House recently built near the Lahore Gate of Delhi.' The description reads '. . . one of the mansions lately erected in Delhi, which shows that the structures of the present day in richness vie with the older magnificence of the city.'

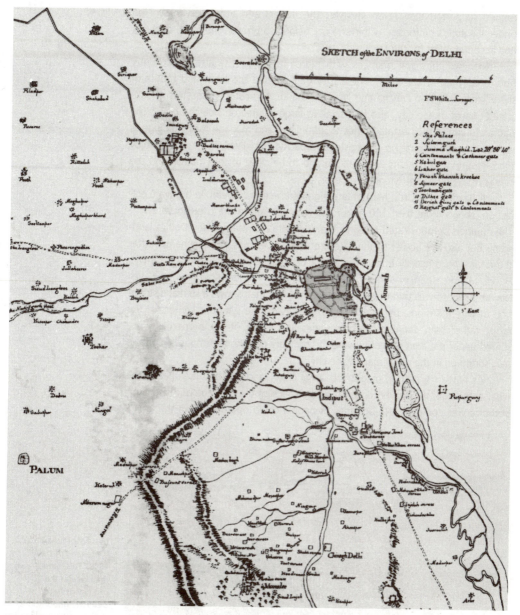

Figure 2.6
'Sketch of the Environs of Delhi,' hand-drawn map, 1807. At the turn of the nineteenth
century, Delhi was a dense urban center along a river and enclosed by walls. Orchards, gardens,
farms, and agricultural estates in the surrounding countryside supported the city.

retinue supported their lavish lifestyle. The traders and artisans who worked under the *amīr*'s patronage within the city helped to provide the food, clothing, and accoutrements for the troops.

Many of the royal grantees with mansions in the city also had country houses on their estates from where they commanded the labor and tribute of the villages.[15] Nawab Dojana and Nawab Pataudi, for instance, masters of substantial *haveli* in the city, also had titles to large estates outside the city.[16] The patriarchs visited their estate homes to administer and manage their holdings as well as to settle disputes in a magisterial capacity. They lived in the city to enjoy the pleasures and benefits of urban life and to be close to their patron and the center of all power, the Mughal emperor.

A hand-drawn Urdu map of late eighteenth-century Delhi, in a private collection, shows more than 100 *haveli* discreetly located in the city (Figure 2.7).[17] The numbers demonstrated not only the dominance of mansions in Delhi's landscape but also the power of the elite group. A *haveli* was typically named after the *amīr* who originally built it (or was a prominent personality in the family). Haveli Mandu Khan was the *haveli* of the *amīr*, Mandu Khan, while Haveli Nawab Bangash was that of Nawab Bangash.[18] The map shows a spatial distribution of elite mansions; by implication it focuses on the symbolic centers of the *haveli* rather than defining the boundaries and edges of the properties. Subsumed under the *amīr*'s identity were the ordinary people, their houses, and the neighborhood in the social map of the city.

As patriarch, patron, magistrate, army chief, landlord, and member of the royal entourage, the *amīr*'s control over the space of the mansion and its neighborhood was complete. No activities or people could operate within the *amīr*'s

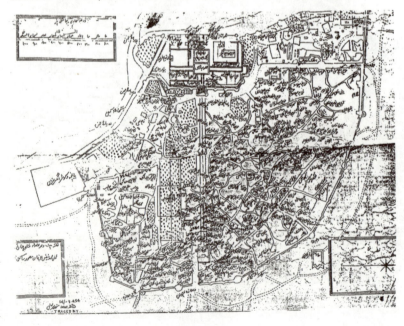

Figure 2.7
Musavvir Muhammad, 'Urdu map of Delhi, 1843.' This hand-drawn map locates the prominent *haveli* of Delhi. Neighborhoods, mansions, bazaars, and streets were named after their patrons. Even today, many neighborhoods and streets carry the names of the historical figures.

domain without his or her sanction (in some instances, the ruler of a *haveli* was a princess or other woman of high station). Like the Mughal emperor who ruled from the palace, the wealthy nobles reigned supreme over their city neighborhoods. In this sense, the *haveli* were miniature cities within the city and their patriarchs were rulers in their own right.

FRAGMENTATION OF THE *HAVELI*

After the middle of the nineteenth century the Mughal king had lost his crown and the city its royal patronage. Royal splendor became unsustainable in the city and the palace and princely grandeur in the elite mansions. As the old barons lost their wealth and power, the neighborhoods, the miniature cities, splintered to form more compact houses for the wealthy on the one hand, and cramped rental apartments for the poor on the other. The fragmentation and commodification of *haveli* paralleled the disintegration of the Mughal Empire and a loss of sovereign status for the city.

When the British laid siege to Delhi in 1857, the city was purged of all its inhabitants. When the residents returned to the city, they found that the British had seized much land and property. In the aftermath of the uprising, the British systematically appropriated properties all over the walled city of Delhi, restructured and sold them. The lands outside the walls of the city owned by the nobility and maintained as gardens, orchards, and farms became largely the property of the British to subdivide and redistribute.

As the new rulers of the city, the British punished the conspirators and mutineers by confiscating their properties. In keeping with their policy of rewards and punishments, the British honored with titles, land, and property those Indians who had been loyal to them. One example was the village of Ishakpur Panar within Delhi District which used to be the *jagīr* of the Nawab of Jhajjar. A leading patrician in Delhi under Mughal rule, the Nawab was hanged during the 1857 insurgency for his alleged involvement in the uprising. As retribution, British officials appropriated the Nawab's property, subdivided it and granted portions as rewards to those loyal to them, regardless of rank or status under the Mughals. Major H. C. Beadon, Revenue Secretary to the Punjab Government, noted of the village of Ishakpur Panar:

> It was confiscated along with the Jhajjar estate. Summary settlement was made with the zamindars of the village . . . an annuity of Rs.100/- from the village jama was granted to Khushhali Lambardar for life for his loyalty in the mutiny.[19]

In another instance, Raja Mohan Lal, one of the leading members of the Mughal Court, had title to the village of Madipur in the vicinity of Delhi. The British appropriated much of their lands in 1803 but the family retained their *haveli* in the city and continued to live there. During the siege of 1857, the family fled to a country house on their estates and forfeited most of their property in the city.[20] British appropriation of properties in the city during the siege left many from among the old nobility without their lands or the income from it. Some erstwhile patriarchs received small pensions from the British as compensation. Mirza Ghalib, the renowned Urdu poet and a member of Delhi's aristocracy, spent several years pleading unsuccessfully with the British to restore a pension that he had lost through these circumstances.[21]

The loss of income made it impossible for their owners to sustain either the patronage or the earlier opulence. This set in motion a decline of grand mansions

Figure 2.8
View of a decrepit entrance to a mansion. Many wealthy nobles lost their *haveli* or the agricultural estates that supported them in the aftermath of the 1857 rebellion. Without the wealth to maintain the substantial properties, the grand mansions fell into disrepair.

that continued over the following century (Figure 2.8). The impoverished *rais* (aristocrats) were caught between their old elite ways and the reduced incomes.[22] Having never worked, the gentry of yesteryear did not consider employment an option. Their sons were unskilled and quite often entirely uneducated. Incapable of selling their services, the new generation of the impoverished highborn became increasingly destitute. A few, who had obtained a Western education, received high posts in the British government. Others began to subdivide and sell their mansions, confining their own accommodations to a few rooms around a few courtyards. Between 1850 and 1910, Haveli Bangash Khan, for instance, lost its street fronts to shops and multiple owners subdivided the property.[23] As the city lost its orchards and gardens and shrank into the space within its walls, so did the *haveli* diminish in its grandeur (Figures 2.9 and 2.10).

The latter part of the nineteenth century saw the reduction of the grand *haveli* complexes to more ordinary dwellings. From extensive neighborhood-like quarters in the early nineteenth century, the *haveli* of the well-to-do were reduced a half century later to modest spaces around two or three small courtyards. Today, these mid-nineteenth-century *haveli* exist as barely recognizable skeletal remains.

We can, however, from vestiges of existing structures, oral histories, and interviews with old residents, as well as descriptions of *haveli*-life in scholarly and fictional work and travelogues, reconstruct a picture of how people lived in the introverted two-courtyard house. The patriarch of the Khazanchi family had served as the royal treasurer under the last Mughal Emperor, Bahadur Shah Zafar. He and members of his family earned high posts in the British service as accountants and treasurers. Their family home provides valuable information for the reconstruction of a typical two-courtyard *haveli* (Figure 2.11).[24]

The *haveli* included a separate public reception area that was primarily a male domain: a place where the older men of the household entertained their visitors and spent most of their time (Figure 2.12). An interior courtyard was the territory of the womenfolk. A carved gateway fronting the street led one through a vestibule into a courtyard with pavilions on three sides. In the center of the courtyard was a fountain with trees, shrubs, and a bower of creepers surrounding it. At one end stood an elaborate marble-tiled platform with more arched pavilions. The patriarch's office, his public chamber, overlooked the street with windows down to the floor. (Toward the latter part of the nineteenth century, the pavilions that had once been open were enclosed with panel doors and stained glass windows.) On one side of the courtyard a staircase led up to the men's quarters and down to the summer basement. Screened windows on the second floor allowed women of the household to conceal themselves from public view while they viewed the entertainment and festivities in the men's courtyard (Figure 2.13). Through a vestibule near the stairs one entered a modest courtyard that was the women's quarter, the *zenānkhānā*. Of course, only men of the household had permission to enter the women's quarters.[25] Two or three male servants and an equal number of maids may have served the *haveli* in

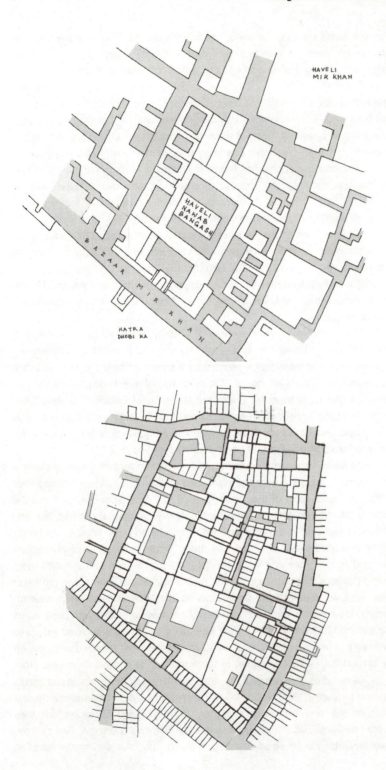

Figures 2.9 and 2.10
The British subdivided
and auctioned some
confiscated properties. In
many others, owners sold
or rented out portions of
their property. The
drawings reflect the
fragmentation that
occurred in the Haveli
Bangash Khan in a little
over a half century.
9. *c.*1850; 10. *c.*1910.

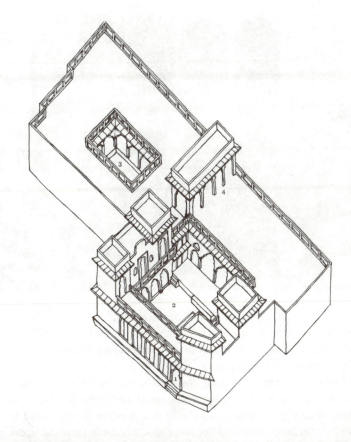

Figure 2.11
Haveli Khazanchi in the
late nineteenth century.
The ceremonial door
from the street 1. led
into the larger courtyard
2. that was the more
public men's courtyard.
Smaller courtyard 3.
supported the women's
quarters and had no
direct entry from the
main street. Pillared
spaces (*dhālān*)
surrounded the
courtyards. A large
terrace 4. included a
sleeping pavilion
(*bārsāti*).

Figure 2.12
Main courtyard of the
Haveli Khazanchi. Central
fountain, ornate, marble-
covered platform, and
surrounding pavilions are
still in evidence. Upper
floors to the left are
recent additions. Some of
the pavilions were
enclosed with doors early
in the twentieth century.

Figure 2.13
'Native Nautch at Delhi,'
1860s. Entertainers
performing in the main
courtyard of a *haveli*.
Women of the household
watch from upper level
secluded behind screens.

addition to cooks and cleaners. A male housekeeper-accountant was responsible for household accounts and the procuring of household provisions. A typical family living in a smaller *haveli* probably consisted of a patriarch, his wife, sons and their families, and his unmarried daughters.

The decline of the old nobility was accompanied by the rise of a mercantile class. As commerce and specialized trades proliferated in the city, the *haveli* was further reduced, since it now required only a handful of attendants. Maulvi Zafrur Rehman Dehlvi's four-volume encyclopedia of professions and trades prepared in the early twentieth century lists over two hundred occupations from basket-weaver to potter, tailor, and baker.[26] The reduced *haveli* signaled not only decreasing grandeur but also the increasing commodification of services. Cooks, barbers, tailors, all formed guilds and functioned in the bazaar independent of elite patronage. Even in the early part of the nineteenth century, Mrs. Mir Hasan Ali, an English woman married to an Indian, had been impressed by the professionalized services of cooks in the markets:

> Zenana [women's quarters] kitchen is not equipped to cook for large assemblies. Only the most choice dishes are cooked by the servants of the establishment for the highly favored guests. The needed abundance required on entertaining a large party is provided by a regular bazaar cook, several of whom establish themselves in Native cities . . . Orders being previously given, the morning and evening dinners are punctually forwarded at the appointed hours in covered trays.[27]

Artisan guilds and specialty markets enabled shops to gain citywide recognition as sources of certain items such as foods, saris, woolen shawls, and jewelry.[28] The phenomenon of specialized markets and professionalized services became even more powerful in the latter half of the nineteenth century.

28 □

Gradually, even the two- or three-courtyard *haveli* fragmented to yield shops, workshops, and rented rooms. Despite the loss of lands and revenue, the families of erstwhile barons continued to live lavishly for a while on inherited wealth. The *rais* were without professional skills or training since they had never considered the prospect of employment. Even under British rule, many who had lived sheltered lives of luxury without ever having worked for their living found life outside the limited confines of the *haveli* difficult to comprehend. As families grew and changed, sons married and brought wives and children to live with them, rooms were converted and added for their use. The property they lived on had already been impoverished by the sale of buildings adjacent to their living quarters. Financial crisis eventually forced the nobility to sell or rent even rooms within the structures that remained. In many cases, without buyers or mainte-nance, the *haveli* fell into a state of dilapidation (Figure 2.14).

Urdu literature represents a rich and complex view on the state of the *rais* of the late nineteenth century and the disintegration of their already diminished *haveli*.[29] The fictional accounts are rooted in the cultural context of Delhi and provide a valuable account of the decline of the *haveli* from the perspective of the residents. Mirza Mahmud Beg, a well-known Urdu literary figure of the early twentieth century, describes the twilight of a *ra'īs* family in the late nineteenth century in his short story 'Mumani Jan aur Badi *Haveli*' (My Aunt and the Large *Haveli*). Mumani Jan, a *ra'īs* woman and the central character of the tale, and her family had lived off the property of their forefathers. In the aftermath of the 1857 rebellion, they lost their *jagīr* and gradually sold off their properties until they were living in a small, two-courtyard *haveli*. Even in their destitution they continued to keep many servants and 'dress like *nawāb*.'[30] The author tells us that what became of the *haveli* was common among the older gentry of Delhi in

Figure 2.14
Dilapidated entrance of a
grand mansion.

the late nineteenth century. Naive and uneducated, the family sustained itself first by selling ancestral properties in the neighborhood of the *haveli* and in other parts of the city. Later, matters came to a head when the public reception hall (and spaces attached to it), the *dīwānkhānā*, symbol of status for the household, had to be sold:

> The ultimate humiliation [for Mumani Jan] was the auction and sale of the very house she had entered as a new bride. This was the house where she herself had matured from being a new bride to a mother-in-law and where she ruled over the domestic kingdom when her husband still had wealth, authority, and titles. [This was] the house where she saw children blossoming, . . . where every corner was bustling and life passed in comfort and leisure. Each fall of the auctioneer's hammer only made the pain and humiliation of the auction more acute . . . The eldest son paid the family's debts with the proceeds from the sale of the house. What money was left he invested in a hotel business in Bombay. The arrangements for Mumani Jan's care remained the same as what it had been earlier, that is, the middle and younger sons sent her a small sum they saved from their incomes. Some maids stayed on with Mumani Jan not for the money she paid them but out of a deep attachment to her . . . Badi Haveli stands even today. The gentleman who purchased the house in the auction passed away before he could occupy the structure. His sons honored their father's promise to allow Mumani Jan to continue living in the haveli. By the time Mumani Jan passed away, the financial circumstances of the new owners had changed hence, they could not fulfill the plans for which they had bought the house. At places the doorways caved in and the walls collapsed; the roofs sagged here and there and the projecting shades broke off. Now a community of water-sellers lived there. Each arched spaced in the pavilions is a home and each home is the residence of a bustling household with many children. Within the [small subdivided] space each family eats and cooks [and leads their life].[31]

The grand pillared pavilions became small cubicles that entire families made their home in. In contrast to the circumscribed hierarchy and segregation of spaces in Mumani Jan's *haveli*, each family cooked, ate, and slept within the confines of their cubicles. The courtyard was their shared open space. Abuzz with children and animals, the entire mansion became a squatter settlement for migrant labor from the countryside like many others in Delhi at the time. The dramatic changes in Mumani Jan's life and home are representative of the decline of the *ra'īs* families of Delhi.

With the emergence of a new class of merchants and traders in the nineteenth century, the grand mansions that had once signaled an aristocratic lineage and an elite status under the monarch became commodities that anyone could buy. C. A. Bayly, in his excellent study *Rulers, Townsmen, and Bazaars*, has observed that the rise of the trading classes had begun to take place in the eighteenth century but was greatly accelerated under British rule in the nineteenth century.[32] Previously, both the *haveli* and the city had been remarkable for the stark contrast between a small but opulent aristocracy served by a vast, impoverished populace. Bernier had declared almost two centuries earlier:

In Delhi there is no middle state. A man must either be of the highest rank or live miserably. My pay is considerable, nor am I sparing of money; yet does it often happen that I have not wherewithal to satisfy the cravings of hunger, the bazaars being so ill supplied, and frequently containing nothing but the refuse of the grandees . . . For two or three who wear decent apparel, there may always be reckoned seven or eight poor, ragged, and miserable beings, attracted to the capital by the army.[33]

But by the middle of the nineteenth century small traders and entrepreneurs established themselves as a new middle class.

Many from among this new class of merchants and traders acquired the *haveli* buildings. Some were actually used for residences but many were used to house workers or became sites for manufacturing activities (Figures 2.15). For

Figure 2.15
A view of the spice market in Sarai Bangash. The additions in the late nineteenth century show British influence in the use of architectural elements. Today, even the courtyard has been built up.

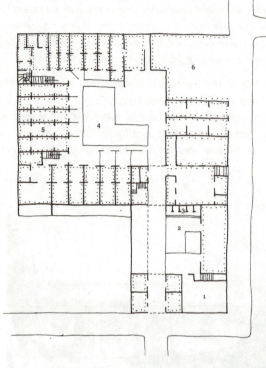

Figure 2.16
Structures that earlier served as stables for elephants and horses had become crowded multi-family houses by the end of the nineteenth century. Dotted lines indicate the areas of households that currently occupy the structure. Oral histories reveal that some families have lived in the tiny apartments for more than 3 generations. Separate areas include
1. manufacturing unit,
2. small courtyard,
3. toilets, 4. main courtyard, 5. dwelling units, and 6. house of wealthy jeweler.

entrepreneurs, the *haveli* buildings were investments to be converted to ware-houses and shops or rented as rooms for several families around a communal courtyard. Elaborate women's quarters in the grand mansions became multi-family 'tenement' houses.[34] For instance, Fath-al-Nisa Begum's house within the *haveli* of her father, Qamr-al-Din Khan, became a block of tiny rental units for workers.[35] Similarly, laborers filled Matiya Mahal near the Jami Masjid with their huts,[36] and a part of the sprawling residence of Nawab Sa'adat Khan became the communal house of oil sellers (Figure 2.16).[37]

REJECTION AND ABANDONMENT OF THE *HAVELI*

Before the 1857 insurgency British civilians resided within the walls in the north-ern and eastern parts of the city (Figure 2.17). Subsequently, they moved out of the walled city to establish a separate European quarter, the Civil Lines to the north. In staying outside the walled city the new rulers lived away from all that the local people perceived as urbane.[38] Yet, the locus of control had moved from the city and its *haveli* to the British quarters outside. Like the city, the *haveli* and their owners had become subservient to the Civil Lines.

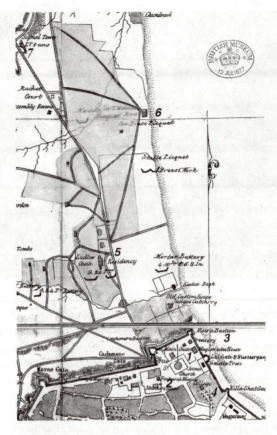

Figure 2.17
The northern part of the walled city and the area beyond, 1849.
1. St James Church;
2. Skinner's House;
3. Magistrate's House and Gazette Press just below; 4. Delhi College;
5. Ludlow Castle that served as the Residency;
6. Metcalfe House;
7. Military Cantonment

The green and airy landscape of the European enclave was in contrast to that of the walled city. Here, British military engineers laid out a settlement of broad regular streets and tidy lots amidst fields and orchards. The bungalows for Europeans were low, sprawling structures set in the midst of gardens on vast lots.[39] The Civil Lines had houses that were set back from the streets and isolated from each other by greenery. The layout was intended to recall English country life and represented to the Europeans the best principles of refined and healthful living in clean and airy surroundings (Figure 2.18).

In reality, the identities of the *haveli* landscape and that of the bungalow interpenetrated each other. Delhi was not alone in having a European quarter that suggested a suburban model that was the very antithesis of life in the indigenous city. Beneath the apparent opposition, however, was a charged inter-connection between the two spaces. The Indians did not passively accept the dualities. The residents of Delhi responded to the new model of urban life in a variety of ways: by disdaining and rejecting, mocking and mimicking, participating and conniving, and learning and accepting. The development of two seemingly antithetical house-forms was deeply inter-related.

Figure 2.18
Mid- to later nineteenth-century bungalow in the Civil Lines north of the walled city, set in a garden on a large lot amid shade trees. The structure uses jack arches, crenellations, concrete, and steel beams, all of which were new to the prevailing local building technology of Delhi.

The erstwhile elite found themselves dependent upon and yet disdainful of their new rulers. Having lived in *haveli* for generations, they simply dismissed the British landscape as an acceptable alternative, far from an inspiring one. The well-known Urdu writer, Vali Ashraf Sabuhi's fictional biography of an aristocrat in the late nineteenth century, *Khwaja Anis*, captures the bewilderment of the *ra'īs* at the growing power and presence of the new English *sāhibs*.[40] Khwaja Anis' forefathers had served the Mughal court and had held vast estates. In the aftermath of the 1857 revolt the Khwaja and his family had lost these lands as well their Mughal Emperor, Bahadur Shah Zafar, to seek favors from. Like his forefathers, the Khwaja had never worked for a living; nor did he have any skills to do so. The Khwaja had hardly ventured out of his *haveli* in years. He was particular to dress and speak like an aristocrat, his name carried the name of his forefathers and various titles, and rituals of etiquette structured his interactions with people. The Khwaja traveled about the city in a palanquin; he had never fought a war and barely acknowledged the presence of the new rulers. Like the women of *ra'īs* families secluded and veiled within the *zanānkhānā*, even the men knew little of the world outside their home.

Moved by the family's dwindling resources, the Khwaja decided to seek employment with the British, in itself a humiliation. In reality, his hope was that a British official would take pity on his impoverished condition and elite status and grant him some lands and the right to their revenues. Sabuhi then goes on to describe the Khwaja's struggles to understand and engage with a new terrain that had developed while he had remained reclusive. Despite his hereditary titles and rights, the Khwaja had to re-negotiate a position for himself in an altered social structure even as he faced rejection from the new order. He found that the shape and structure of the new spaces were as unacceptable to him as the rituals of inhabiting them. For him as well as for other residents of Delhi, the British bungalows to the north of the city were like houses in the midst of jungles, lacking all that the *ra'īs* valued so much in urban life. The new rulers lived outside the city walls, the walls that marked the outer-boundaries of refined urban culture. This blatant rejection of civilized life was incomprehensible to most residents of Delhi for whom the city remained unparalleled in its glory.

In contrast to the Khwaja's rejection of European ways of living, some among the declining old elite adopted Western habits out of admiration for the West or from opportunism. Social reformers, such as Sir Sayyid Ahmad Khan and Deputy Nazir Ahmad, served the British government as officials, and judges, or teachers. They founded schools, wrote textbooks, translated English works into Urdu, and edited journals.[41] Sir Sayyid Ahmad, for example, admired the British for their adherence to science and rationality. He urged Delhi's declining *rais* to resurrect themselves through education. The old nobility had neither the *jagir* lands to support them nor the training and acumen for business. The recourse Sir Sayyid advocated was for them to acquire an English education and earn the trust of the new masters by befriending them and coming close to them on their terms.[42]

By the late nineteenth century, Delhi acquired a new group of indigenous elite. Indians schooled in the British system of education joined the colonial bureaucracy. Members of the new cadre were English-educated, 'reformed,' and in the service of the Empire as magistrates, treasurers, accountants, and civil servants. Many Indians, especially during the early and mid-nineteenth century, adapted to British ways of working and to their spatial practices but continued customary ways of living and dressing (Figures 2.19 and 2.20). In the latter decades of the nineteenth century however, skilled and educated Indians sought to break away from tradition and reconstitute their identities as new professionals.

Figure 2.19
Early nineteenth-century painting from Delhi shows a wealthy accountant and his son in his *haveli*. He is seated on a carpet with a *gāv thakiyā* or cushion of honor behind him. The furnishings are sparse. The well-lit area in contrast to a dark interior suggests they might be in a pavilion around a courtyard. An attendant waits on them, a half-open door obscures a private interior space.

Figure 2.20
An Indian accountant or *munshi* in a bungalow with a British official. The accountant is seated on a chair at a table. They work with ledgers, quills, and inkwells. The British official had on his shoes, while the *munshi* was required to be barefoot. An attendant sits on the floor pulling a large ceiling fan. The space has a high ceiling and large glass windows. Framed paintings hang on the walls.

In their efforts to liberate themselves from convention, the modern elite repudiated the *haveli*. Like the British, they sought the 'clean, airy settings' of the civil station. Only by sharing the cultural landscape of the colonizer could the aspiring natives hope for a share in their authority.

Nazir Ahmad's 1888 novel *Ibnulvaqt* the (Opportunist), offers valuable insights on the dilemmas of becoming modern under these conditions. Nazir Ahmed was a prominent writer and celebrated intellectual of the time. Though highly educated in the Western system, and a senior bureaucrat in the British Imperial Government, he was critical of the manner in which some of the old elite quickly acquired a veneer of European ways and values.[43] He was a social reformer, a contemporary of Sir Sayyid, and a champion of education for women. In the novel the central character, Ibnulvaqt, comes from a family with some hereditary titles, property, and status. In the new circumstances, he quickly transforms himself into a 'gentleman' who talks, walks, dresses, eats, and thinks like the British. For having saved the life of an Englishman during the uprising, the British reward Ibnulvaqt with titles, a *jagīr* located outside the walls of Delhi that would bring him a good monthly income as well as a senior position in the British administration. Ibnulvaqt attributes his meteoric rise under the British to his own efforts to 'reform' himself.

In gratitude for having saved his life an English administrator, Noble *Sahib*, mentors and befriends Ibnulvaqt. He persuades him to abandon his residence in the city in favor of a new bungalow in the civil station, so as to make his home inviting for European visitors. Noble wishes to introduce him to his English friends but advises Ibnulvaqt to become more Westernized in order to make his company and his house more acceptable to them. A bungalow in an open and airy setting Noble tells Ibnulvaqt is the most basic requirement for entertaining Europeans:

> At the very least [you] should have a house that is built according to English tastes. You see that we [the English] always like to live in houses that are open and outside the city … First of all your house is situated in [in the interior of the city] amidst such lanes that one cannot even reach it. And then the lanes are narrow and unclean so that no [English] gentleman would like to go to a place that is so cramped and twisted.
> Although your house is not wanting you do not have the basic things necessary to make the English gentlemen comfortable such as tables and chairs. For these reasons, I have not made the effort to bring any [English] friends to visit you. Do you wish to befriend the English on these terms?[44]

For Ibnulvaqt, the rejection of the ancestral home in the city was symbolic of the liberation from the chains of history and tradition. He could define his identity anew as a modern man equal to any European. As it was for the British, Delhi within the walls was associated with filth, congestion, irrationality, and superstition in opposition to the bungalows and the civil station that epitomized reason, civilization, and science – qualities that exemplified progress.[45]

Ibnulvaqt was convinced that in order for the English *sahibs* to accept him, he needed to live in a bungalow outside the walled city in the European quarters amidst wide roads, trimmed lawns, and tidy paths and flowerbeds. Rather than continue as master of his ancestral home in the walled city, Ibnulvaqt preferred to rent a bungalow in the Civil Lines with the servants and paraphernalia necessary for a British colonial lifestyle. For the 'reformed' *rais* the bungalow symbolized a cultural space that demanded changes in lifestyle. The progressive-thinking *rais* accepted a redefinition of the boundaries between the inside and the outside, as street shoes entered the house and dogs became indoor pets.[46] Even the rhythms and the experience of time were different in the bungalow. The muezzin's calls for prayers five times a day were absent in the European neighborhood and Friday was a workday. The 'reformed' native acquired Western-styled dining tables, chairs, sofas, curtains, and carpets appropriate to entertain the English and learned to use and appreciate cutlery and fine china neither of which had been elements of fine dining in the *haveli*. A new wardrobe of Western clothes completed a transformation in the personality of *rais* such as Ibnulvaqt to match their new homes.

The story illustrates how a growing number of the new Indian professionals in the service of the British abandoned their ancestral homes in the walled city to move to bungalows in the European-dominated Civil Lines area. Whether prompted by ambition and opportunism, or a conviction in the value of European ways of living, they sought to identify themselves with the landscape of the rulers by disassociating themselves from the *haveli*. The 'reformed' native elite considered the *haveli* inadequate and inappropriate for those who wished to be identified with progress and upward mobility in society.

As owners moved to bungalows and adopted a new lifestyle, they largely neglected the fate of the *haveli*. The deserted *haveli* buildings often remained vacant or were subdivided and rented out as apartments to the growing numbers of migrants. Squatters and laborers took over structures that were falling into disrepair. The abandoned *haveli* also began to serve industrial and commercial uses. Rising trade, commerce and industries, and immigration of labor resulted in new demands on urban space. In a city that was already built up, subdivision and conversion of existing structures were the most obvious means of creating new spaces. By the turn of the nineteenth century some abandoned *haveli* began to function as transit warehouses for goods that arrived by train or road. The lofty entry gateways were equipped with metal doors. Large courtyards were roofed over by steel trusses and supporting corrugated iron sheeting. One *haveli* in the neighborhood of Chandni Chowk was divided to make dozens of small shops while many others became multifamily tenement houses with tens of families.

When the British chose to move out of the walled city in 1857 to establish the Civil Lines as the European quarter of Delhi, the indigenous city was redefined as the relic of a traditional society whose glory was past. Power and authority too, moved from the King's palace to the Chief Commissioner's office in the Civil Lines. The penetration of indigenous residents into the landscape of bungalows implied a dilution in the identity of the area as an exclusive European enclave. Servants, maids, and service people had always moved easily between the indigenous and European dominions. In so doing, they knitted together with their invisible landscape a more complex interdependency between the 'black' landscape of the indigenes and the 'white' world of the bungalows.[47] The presence of elite Indians as masters in their own right, however, threatened the purity of an idealized space of European rulers. In claiming space in the Civil Lines and appropriating the bungalow as another indigenous landscape, the residents of Delhi had implicitly scorned the distinction between the two that the British had sought to establish (Figure 2.21).

REBUILDING NEW FORMS FOR OLD

After 1857, extensive rebuilding accompanied the disintegration and abandonment of the *haveli*. The British planned interventions in the city that deliberately restructured urban space. They converted the King's palace into a military garrison and demolished many princely mansions, mosques, and familiar landmarks around the fort to create a *glacis* of 450 yards. With the establishment of the Delhi Municipal Committee in 1863, public construction proliferated. During the 1860s and 1870s the new government widened streets, built new broad vistas, and introduced the railroad.[48] This required more clearances to make room for

Figure 2.21
European furnishings in a formal room specifically assigned for receiving visitors in a 'modernized' *haveli, c.*1890.

the track and extensive areas in and around the city became its property. Orchards, gardens, and fields were unhesitatingly converted to accommodate railroad tracks and roads.[49] The newly inaugurated railroad and the Grand Trunk Road, an arterial road from Delhi to Calcutta, put Delhi on the commercial map in an unprecedented manner.

The new municipality of Delhi constructed a clock tower, a college, and a museum in addition to a railroad station. The city also acquired new roads, bridges, and several substantial public structures including schools, hotels, a library, fountains and gardens. Municipalization placed emphasis on city improvement and sanitation. The revamping of basic infrastructure reinforced the idea of the city as a machine. European designs and goods made their way into Delhi's market. New materials and technologies of construction brought changes to the *haveli* buildings. The engineering accomplishments of the British were awe-inspiring for Delhi's residents.

Based on my interviews with residents, oral histories, novels, and analysis of existing structures, I pieced together a picture of yet another transformation in the meaning and design of *haveli*. Toward the end of the nineteenth century, prospering entrepreneurs and traders rushed to rebuild residential structures, shops, and workshops from old abandoned or disused *haveli* buildings. Those who continued to live in the old city sometimes moved out of overcrowded houses to buy new ones or rebuild old, broken ones. On small lots carved from the old large *haveli*, merchants built new, redefined *haveli* consisting of a single central courtyard with rooms all around. Smaller and more modest in design, the redefined 'traditional' house was rational, efficient, and built with new materials and technology.

British rule had brought prosperity to the mercantile groups. Accepting and integrating technological innovations in building construction, new materials, and European architectural elements was a way of expressing their loyalty to the British and commitment to progress. In the redefined *haveli*, the pavilions that surrounded the courtyards were converted to rooms with wood-paneled doors and stained glass. Some were even furnished with sofas and chairs. Many *haveli* of this type still boast of English-tiled mantelpieces in the main reception room with mirrors and chandeliers to complete the 'modern' appearance. The *haveli* of prosperous business families displayed building materials imported from Europe: English porcelain tiles, Italian marble and stained glass. In keeping with industrial production and technological innovations the new *haveli* used steel girders and wrought iron. Many older *haveli* were renovated and converted to include Greek columns, wrought-iron balconies, cement lattice-screens, large framed mirrors, stained glass, and paneled doors. Together they reflected a European influence and distinguished the owners as successful and open-minded in contrast to those who continued to live in more traditional dwellings (Figure 2.22).

Figure 2.22
An upper-level balcony in a *haveli* rebuilt at the turn of the century. New materials such as wrought iron and cement were used prominently.

The Jain family's *haveli* in Katra Kushal Rai exemplifies this transformation from a sprawling *haveli* to a compact and relatively modest house. Katra Kushal Rai once housed the *haveli* and quarters of Raja Kushal Rai, an important administrative member in the court of the Mughal King, Shah Alam (Figure 2.23).[50] After the 1857 insurgency, the British confiscated all his property, subdivided and either sold them or gave them away as rewards. The entire neighborhood (the street and the properties on either side of it) was divided between eight families. Later, these properties were again subdivided and sold. One of the present owners, Premchand Jain, tells of how his grandfather, Lala Ranjeet Singhji, had been appointed to a high post in the colonial Punjab Government after he stood first in the Civil Services Examination in 1890.[51] The family had come from a long line of distinguished members of the royal court but had lost most of their property in the events following the 1857 uprising. Lala Ranjeet Singhji acquired a property in the Katra Kushal Rai in 1910. He demolished the dilapidated structures on the site and constructed anew the single-courtyard *haveli* that stands today.

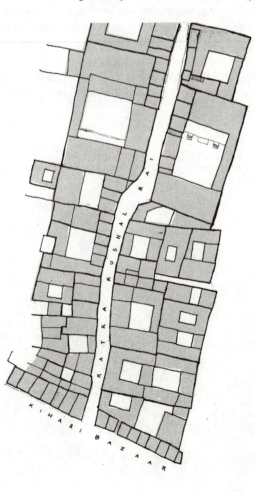

Figure 2.23
Katra Kushal Rai once housed the *haveli* and quarters of Raja Kushal Rai, an important administrator in the court of the Mughal king. After 1857, the British confiscated and subdivided his properties and auctioned or granted them to eight families. The new owners later further subdivided the lots and sold them.

The new *haveli* was far less elaborate than earlier ones (Figure 2.24). From the street one entered through a large doorway that was, nevertheless, small and simple compared to the monumental portals of the past. A vestibule led one into a compact courtyard with rooms all around it. The traditional pavilions became rooms with multiple doors. The ground floor consisted of a receiving room furnished in Western style where the men received their visitors, and offices from which to conduct business or seat clerks. The receiving room often indicated the status of the family and was decorated with mirrors, glass chandeliers, a mantelpiece (even though there was no fire place) and colorful tiles of English porcelain along high skirting lines (Figure 2.25). An additional public room was a *baithak* (reception room) furnished with floor cushions and spittoons customary to the local lifestyle. Visitors to the *haveli* entered the traditional reception room or the Western-styled living-room, depending on who they were and where they stood in Delhi's society. Those visiting the women of the household would go to the upper levels of the house. A staircase from the vestibule area led up to the living quarters so women folk never needed to enter the courtyard and the men's areas. Smaller terraces on the upper floors provided the open space necessary for them and for the children. Privacy for the living quarters and the women had been achieved by stratifying vertically.

The redefined *haveli*, such as that of the Jains, had only one opening to the street. The arches and pavilions, the raised platforms, water fountains and trees,

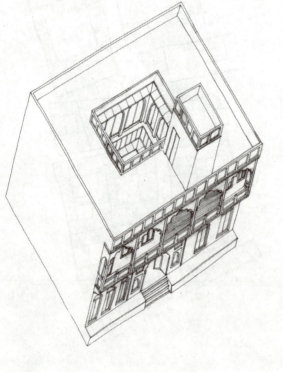

Figure 2.24
Haveli Jain c.1910. The compact *haveli* built around a single small courtyard had one entrance from the street; stairs next to the entrance led up to the women's quarters. Windows on the upper level opened on to a screened balcony that overlooked the street.

Figure 2.25
An interior space that
served as a receiving
room for work-related
visitors was decorated
with English porcelain
tiles, a faux fireplace,
Italian mirrors, and a
large glass chandelier.
Sofas, chairs, tables, and
curtains had once
furnished the room that
is currently a warehouse.

characteristic of the *haveli* of the old nobility, were markedly absent. Nor was there an entourage of servants. The redefined *haveli* of the early twentieth century could not accommodate the dancing, music, poetry, and parties that had captivated travelers to Delhi in the eighteenth century. Increasingly functions once performed within the house were now performed outside. Services of all types had become commodities that anyone could purchase in the bazaar. Professionals prospered independent of princely patronage. Smaller families and more compact houses needed fewer servants to clean and maintain. The reduced *haveli* was premised on decreased levels of wealth and power as well as greater fragmentation of families.

The *haveli* had been reinterpreted yet again in a way that continued customary ways of living and building as much as it departed from them. The compact modern version was a commodity that anyone with the means could aspire to. It embodied not only the current economic and social conditions but also its inhabitants' social aspirations. For the most part, the owners of the redefined *haveli* attempted to work their way up the new social order. The grandeur of the earlier mansions was irretrievable but a symbolic association with aristocratic life was possible. In building their homes the rising entrepreneurial classes adopted new materials, technology, and design as visible symbols of their

progressive outlook. Their mimicry of European architectural elements symbolized their willingness to shake the shackles of orthodoxy to accept the new. It
signified their acceptance of the English themselves. The entrepreneurs were
perhaps less preoccupied with characterizing themselves as modern than with
identifying with the new rulers and(thus representing themselves as progressive
and open-minded partners in commerce.) Implicitly, the eclecticism of the entrepreneurs served to obscure European efforts at constructing difference.

SHIFTING TERRAIN OF HYBRIDITY

In contemporary colloquial usage the word *haveli* has remained a signature of
traditional aristocratic living. However, in its many variations the *haveli* was not a
timeless or changeless house-form.(From princely mansion to a modest dwelling
and then into a dense multi-family house or a more rationally designed one, the
haveli was experienced and interpreted in many different ways.)

In large parts of Delhi, the form of the streets and the footprint of the
buildings remained substantially unchanged in the half century since the insurrection of 1857. Yet, even in these areas, subdivisions, extensions, and additions
diminished courtyards and made the streets narrower. Steel, glass, and concrete
redefined the forms of space, as did the vocabulary of pediments, pilasters, and
Grecian columns. Sprawling princely mansions became an assembly of smaller,
more modest *haveli*. With the physical transformations, the social significance of
the *haveli* altered as well. As the mercantile classes acquired new power in the
city, Western-educated professionals became the new elite. Spurned by the
'modern,' Westward-looking, indigenous elite, Delhi's *haveli* became home to a
petite bourgeois aspiring to greater status. The formal changes were perhaps less
dramatic than those in the meanings and significance of domestic spaces.
(Increasing commodification of property made *haveli* into functional dwellings or
anonymous structures to be used in the service of capital as warehouses, factories, or rental properties. Symbolically, the *haveli* went from representing the
feudal power of princes to signifying rationalism, efficiency, and technological
progress in its early twentieth-century incarnation.

We cannot continue to refer to the *haveli* as a 'traditional' domestic space
when it has reinvented itself in the maelstrom of modernity. Despite the ubiquity
of courtyard houses in Delhi and the seeming stasis in the built form, the
domestic landscape of the city during the late nineteenth and early twentieth
centuries was dynamic. As the great mansions fragmented, the very significance
of home and social identity underwent frequent changes. Indigenous notions of
what was 'modern' were different from European ones. And even among the
residents, a fragmented, smaller *haveli* was one idea of modern and another was
abandoning the old city altogether for a new life in a bungalow in the European
quarters. Both, however, carried some elements of indigenous living. Each house
was a unique resolution of particular tensions and conflicts.

Many of the changes in Delhi's *haveli* occurred synchronously and in

contradiction with one another. For instance, many *haveli* in Delhi suffered abandonment and dilapidation as their owners moved to the European-dominated
Civil Lines even as other *haveli* in the city were rebuilt along more simplified lines.
The consequences of the negotiations and the transformations were often tentative and incomplete. Every category and identity contained negations within it.

The processes of building and inhabiting the *haveli* reveal a multiplicity of
voices, identities, and interests that engage and negotiate to make and remake
space. Monolithic and oppositional categories masked the dynamism of identities
that were composite, nuanced, and at times contradictory. For instance, Delhi's
indigenous population included Western-educated 'natives,' speculators, and
Indian traders and merchants loyal to the British, as well as Indians serving in the
British administration. Together this diversity fractured and destabilized simple
categories. The values and identity of the old nobility became pedestrianized as
the small entrepreneurs appropriated them and as European beliefs influenced
indigenous ones. The ordinary citizens assumed the symbols of authority in order
to aspire to elite status. Hybrid forms of architecture in Delhi were elusive,
contradictory, tentative, negotiated, and fluid. The 'traditional' architecture of
the old city was a battleground for contesting and negotiating identities.

Chapter 3: Negotiating Streets and Squares

Spatial Culture in the Public Realm

Like other great cities, historic Delhi was rich with places for people to meet, mingle, display, observe, and command. When Dargah Quli Khan visited Delhi, the sovereign city of the Mughal kings in the eighteenth century, he was impressed by the prosperous bazaars, the grand mansions, the fine mosques, and the opulent soirees of the elites.[1] Within and outside the city walls, Khan visited the numerous tombs of Delhi's luminaries and saints, and the distinguished houses of music, dance, and prostitution. The bazaars, the *chowk* or intersections of major streets, the courtyards of mosques and temples, the entertainment houses of the *tavā'if (courtesans)*, the tombs of saints, the sites of ancient ruins, fairgrounds, water tanks, and the river bank and the many gardens were places of public gathering for the residents of Delhi (Figure 3.1). Although many were open to the public, admission to some was restricted by gender, caste, or religious sect. Wealthy sponsors controlled these spaces where unwritten codes and norms governed access and use. Women of rank rarely appeared in public and then, concealed in *purdāh* (veils and robes). Particular gardens and river banks were reserved for their pleasure. Both men and women of the lower castes were not expected to share the water sources and riverfront areas with their social superiors. The square in front of the *kotwālī*, the city magistrate's office, was an important landmark in the city and had also served for public hangings (Figure 3.2). The 'picturesque' quality of the bazaars and the 'noble architecture' of the Jami Masjid struck many travelers in the early nineteenth century including, Emily Eden and Bishop Heber (Figure 3.3).[2] After 1857, however, as city officials sought to redefine a public realm that was in their control, public spaces became contested terrain in their form, use, and symbolic significance.

Under the guise of security and sanitation, the new British rulers embarked on a massive program of urban restructuring. In the three decades following the 1857 rebellion almost a third of the city was demolished and rebuilt. The organic city, officials deemed, was unhealthy, unsafe, inefficient, and uncontrolled. The

Figure 3.1
'A Baolee near the Old City of Delhi,' *c.*1802. A large stepped well at the tomb of Nizam ud-Din Aulia. The wall on the right has a mechanism for drawing water.

Figure 3.2
The Kotwali Chabutra, 1842–44. The *kotwāli* that had functioned as an administrative and legal body to manage the city through the *thana*, *mahallā*, and *chowkidari* systems was replaced by the municipality and the police.

ideal city in their vision was one that was rationally ordered, commodious, beautiful, and salubrious. They were convinced that the perfect rational settlement was to have broad, tree-lined boulevards, orthogonal forms and streets, low densities, and distinct land uses. These elements were soon realized in the European enclave, the Civil Lines, that they established outside the city (Figure 3.4). But even within the city walls, officials proposed to displace existing symbols of authority with those that reaffirmed British supremacy, and controlled public life.

Figure 3.3
'Delhi. A Street at the Back of Jumma Musjid.' Delhi's bazaars impressed travelers from the east by its wares and Europeans for its picturesque quality.

Figure 3.4
Area to the north of the walled city in 1873. Europeans settled to the north of the walled city in the Civil Lines after 1857. Wide roads laid in rectilinear fashion or in sweeping curves connected bungalows set in the midst of gardens. Many new roads were constructed including ones that connected to the coronation durbar amphitheater to the far north. Walled city area has been darkened.

Caught between the rational agenda in the official notions of modernism and the coercive practices of the colonial state, conceptions of public space were fraught with contradictions. On the one hand it was to be a secular space distinct from the domestic and religious spaces that existed in Delhi: a space symbolizing a new libertarian government in contrast to that of the Mughal rulers, Public space was also intended to celebrate an idealized urban community that obscured the avarice of the marketplace even while it served to commodify and privatize properties. On the other hand, colonial urban policies assumed that all spaces in the city that were not under explicit private ownership were, in fact, public and therefore appropriate for policing as such. Although the idea of public space may have had its origins in the enlightenment idea of a sphere for public discourse, debate, and reasoning against the secret politics of monarchs, in Delhi, the idea of public space was overlaid with the local conditions of race, community, culture, and power. Contrary to what the colonial government had imagined in rebuilding a civic center, with the rise of Indian nationalism, Indians found that the newly developed civic spaces provided room for public debate, protests, and demonstrations. In this context, public space acquired a negotiated meaning. The disparity between indigenous conceptions of public space and those of city officials influenced by Western modernism was settled in different ways in different places and at different times in Delhi. In this chapter, I examine the changing landscape of public space during the late nineteenth century to reveal some of the mechanisms and processes by which officials attempted to construct it and citizens sought to contest the meanings and forms.

A CIVIC CENTER FOR DELHI

Until 1857, the King's palace and the main mosque, the Jami Masjid, were the key landmarks in the city.[4] They were outstanding both in their formal attributes as well as in their political and symbolic functions. The bazaar street of Chandni Chowk with its main square was the social and commercial hub of the city. Delhi existed mostly within its walls and consisted of a labyrinth of roads and lanes. In front of the palace, the two major streets crossed at the junction of Faiz Bazaar and Chandni Chowk. At the intersection stood the King's palace complex. The square in front of the palace was the site of a significant military display where, each week, the chief of a territory held guard and established camp.[5] The palaces of princes and the mansions of favored nobility lined the most prominent streets. Chandni Chowk (Street of the Silver Square) was a long, wide, and straight boulevard that stretched from the King's palace at the eastern end of the city to the Lahori Darvaza (the Lahore Gate of the City) at the western end (Figure 3.5). The Faiz canal (also known as the Nahr-i Bihist) ran down the center of its entire length, occasionally opening up into square and octagonal pools as at the main square (Figure 3.6). Prosperous shops with colorful displays specialized in the beautiful, the exotic, and the expensive. In 1739 the Mughal king Shahjahan's

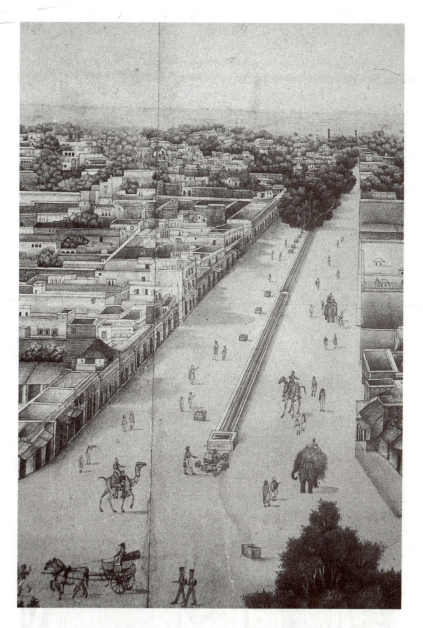

Figure 3.5
The main street of
Chandni Chowk, c.1846.

daughter, Jehanara Begum, had erected the finest and most extensive *sarā'i*
(shelter for travelers) at Chandni Chowk.[6] The *sarā'i* provided lodgings for a multitude of merchants who traveled to Delhi from distant lands. Adjacent to it,
Jehanara Begum had also set out gardens variously known as Chandni Bagh,
Bagh Sahibabad, Begum Bagh, and Jehanara Bagh, designed lavishly as paradise
gardens (Figure 3.7). On the street side of the *sarā'i*, an elaborate arcade and an
imposing gateway framed a large octagonal plaza. Jehanara Begum also had a

Figure 3.6
The main square of
Chandni Chowk and
entrance to Chandni
Sarai (also known as
Begum Sarai) to the
north, c.1843. The
octagonal square was
100 ft wide with double-
storied shops all around
that were narrow and
deep. The Nahar-i Bihist,
the canal that ran down
the length of the bazaar,
formed a pool at the
center of the square.

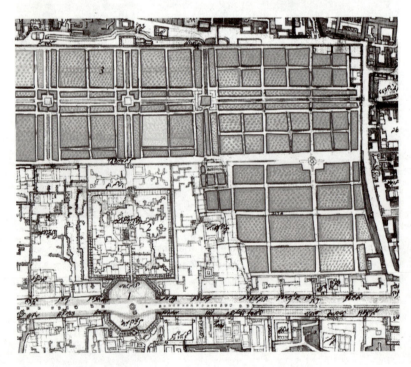

Figure 3.7
Plan of Chandni Chowk
and Chandni Sarai
c.1850. The square 1. and
the grand *sarai* (travelers'
lodge) 2. to the north
was built by Jehanara
Begum, a significant
political player and
daughter of the Mughal
Emperor Shahjahan. The
gardens of Begum Bagh
were designed on the
principles of the paradise
gardens. The gardens
formed the lungs of an
otherwise densely built-
up city.

hammām (bath) constructed on the south side of the square. Chandni Chowk was the route of parades and processions, while the square was the market center as well as home of the town crier. Royal patronage and benevolence was everywhere.

Chandni Chowk, with its legendary shops and wares, was once the most significant bazaar of Delhi, and had impressed travelers from Bernier to Emily Eden.[7] Arab, Afghan, and Persian traders among others had regularly come to Delhi. The main square of Chandni Chowk had served as a nerve center for trade and commerce, and fairs, mosques, the tombs of saints, temples, and *bā'oli* (large open wells or water tanks generally with steps down to the water) had once been the gathering places for people of different communities. In Delhi's society, divided as it was by race, caste, community, and religion, bazaars, primarily a male domain, were spaces of anonymity, identity, display, and interaction.[8] On conquering Delhi, the British chose the largest, most frequently traversed, and beautiful of squares on the Chandni Chowk as the site of a new civic center.

Four months after the start of the 1857 uprising against the colonial presence in India, the British gained control of Delhi city. Following the siege, substantial properties to the north of Chandni Chowk were destroyed, or confiscated.[9] Bombing and gunfire during the siege shattered many of the mansions and neighborhoods, especially in the northern parts of the city.[10] Lands belonging to the Mughal royalty such as the *sarā'i* at Chandni Chowk and the gardens came under British proprietorship.

The idea that 'a municipality represents the advance of mankind from primitive anarchy to civilized order' motivated colonial administrators to establish the Delhi Municipal Committee in 1863.[11] Headed by the Commissioner of Delhi and his deputy, the members of the Delhi Municipal Committee included three Europeans and seven Indians. In addition, nine of the top officials of Delhi were all European. The Indians appointed to the Municipality were those who had distinguished themselves in the service of the British.[12] Over and above providing urban infrastructure such as roads, water supply, and sewage disposal, the Municipality expected to build parks, a museum, and an imposing town hall, and undertake overall city improvement. By-laws helped to translate the idealized city into a tangible one. The impetus for such improvements was only partly aesthetic. An orderly city reflected a civilized society, and fine buildings a laudable 'civic spirit.'[13] One of the earliest building projects of the imperial government in Delhi was the construction of a civic square defined by public buildings and reflecting the new municipal resolve.

In the middle of Chandni Chowk, in the main square and on the site of the *serai*, municipal funds and subscriptions from wealthy citizens financed a civic monument: the Delhi Institute Building, later to become known as the Town Hall (Figure 3.8).[14] The edifice was intended to beautify the city; British architects, Messrs Mandreth and Cooper, prepared the design. At a time and a place when British military engineers were responsible for much building design in India, the hiring of professional architects of repute from the metropole itself indicated the

Figure 3.8
The Delhi Institute building or the Town Hall as it was later known. View from the main square. Built in place of Begum Sarai on Chandni Chowk, the building was set back from the square and the surrounding buildings. Rather than enclosing the public space, the building created a visual focus. The use of gabled roofs, cornices, porticos, and false pediments over the windows made references to Greek and Roman classicism and were unlike local architecture.

importance of the building. In addition to the offices of the recently established Delhi Municipal Committee, the Town Hall consisted of a college, a museum, a library and reading room, a hall of trade, a 'Darbar' room for senior British administrators to hold public audience, and a 'pleasant suite of rooms used for dances and other social reunions of the English residents.'[15] Mandreth and Cooper redesigned the paradise gardens of Jehanara Begum which were renamed Queen's Gardens.

The Town Hall was designed as a two-storied brick and plaster building (Figure 3.9). The rectilinear masses were simply proportioned with neoclassical symmetry to create a horizontal and substantial presence on the square, the design echoed, in some ways, town hall façades prevalent in England at this time. Rectangular windows punctured the walls and jack arches and pediments accentuated the openings; a classical portico adorned the entrance area. Ornamentation was limited to rustication in the plaster in the lower parts of the building, the articulation of arches in the windows, cornices, and a scalloped low-wall edging the top of the building. In the context of significant public buildings in Delhi, the structure was remarkable for its lack of stone and carving.

Until that time, more than a grand elevation, much of Delhi's indigenous architecture for local residents was designed as a sequence of experiences and views with much emphasis on shaping both the interior and exterior open spaces. In contrast, the Town Hall was intended to be viewed from a distance in the square and did not enclose an interior courtyard. Where the Begum Sarai had hugged the street, the Town Hall was set back from it. The formal, symmetrical entrance of the building framed a statue of Queen Victoria to the north,

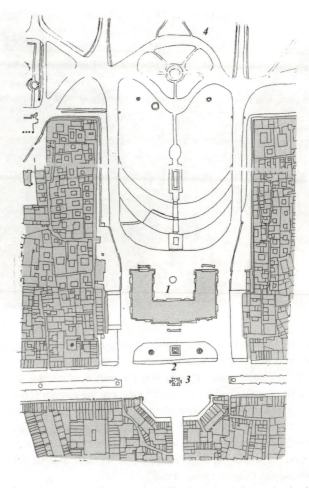

Figure 3.9
Plan of Chandni Chowk after rebuilding, 1910. Shops were cleared from the northern end of the square. The Town Hall building replaced the *sarā'i*, and the gardens were redesigned as Queen's Gardens. 1. Town Hall buildings, 2. a statue of Queen Victoria at the entrance to the building, 3. a clock-tower at the center of the square, 4. and a bandstand to the north of the building. A new street, Egerton Road, intersected the south side of the square. The complex also included a menagerie and a library.

symbolizing the political change of guard.[16] Located axially to the back was a bandstand. At the center of the square the Victoria Clock Tower superseded the bells and drums in the *naqqārkhānā* (the place where musicians with bells, drums, and instruments rang out the time) of the King's palace and the muezzin's call for prayers from the mosques in marking time.[17] The profile of the tall tower also vied with the minarets of the Jama Masjid in dominating the horizon. With the clock tower, the physical and symbolic reconstruction of the central urban space of the city was complete (Figure 3.10).

Intended to beautify, impress, and instruct, these buildings defined a new 'civic-ness' in opposition to the royal patronage that had once been prevalent and the parochial allegiances that persisted. The Town Hall honored the city government and was the first building to symbolize and venerate the new urban 'community.' The structures also exemplified a secular 'public-ness' that aimed to celebrate the libertarian ideals of a benevolent government. The dominant presence of the statue of Queen Victoria in the center of the square, however, was a

Figure 3.10
View of clock tower the
British built in the main
square of Chandni
Chowk. Early twentieth-
century view from
Egerton Road.

curious contradiction for a space that officials so idealized. Through the demolition and rebuilding, the reconstruction of the main square was evidence of the
power of the colonial state in controlling the built environment. In shifting the
spatial focus of authority from the King's palace at the eastern end of the city to
the Town Hall in the main square, the new rulers aimed to remind residents of
their new citizenship and loyalty to both a new ruler and a new regime. Re-inter-
preting a commercial center into a civic square also signified the government's
control over the anarchy of the market place, a hallmark of what the British officials believed was civilized administration.

While the Town Hall building was inspired by European governmental and
aesthetic ideals, the design itself was a unique hybrid. The stated intention was
to design the structure in what the British characterized as the prevailing
'mohammedan' style of architecture while still being distinctly modern in construction. In recommending Mandreth and Cooper's proposed design for
government approval the Deputy Commissioner of Delhi noted:

> The buildings are so arranged as to enclose a garden, the college being at one end, and
> the museum and public hall at the other, and the two ends being connected by cloisters.
> The style is intended to be very ornamental, and to accord with prevailing specimens of
> mohammedan architecture in the vicinity.[18]

The final design bore no resemblance to the surrounding buildings in form,
urban texture, use, or meaning. Although the siting of the building, its simple
forms, and its façade elements such as the balustrades, pediments, and pilasters
made references to European classicism, its design was not typical of town halls

in Europe. While the reference to 'mohammedan' architecture would imply an Islamic style typical of Muslims in Delhi, in fact, the neighborhood of the Town Hall contained buildings that were built and owned by both Hindus and Muslims. Hence, neither the architects' reading of the area nor the Deputy Commissioner's characterization of it were based on any study or analysis of existing structures in Delhi but rather on their own perceptions. Considering how little the building fitted into the existing fabric, it is remarkable that both the architects and key officials should have expressed an interest to design in sympathy with local spatial and building practices.

Further, the activities and uses of the building were unusual for both the typical European town hall and other public structures in Delhi. A Darbar room for British administrators to hold audiences with local people was a space ritual interaction peculiar to British colonials in India and inspired by the formal audiences held by the Mughal Emperors and lesser Kings on the subcontinent.[19] A room for 'dances and social reunions' was similarly a space unique to the context of European expatriates living in a distant colonial land.[20] While the building was meant to be both symbolic as a civic space and instructive to the public, much of the building did not welcome casual use by the ordinary Indian resident. Nor were band stands, curvilinear paths, or statues of human figures (even if they were royalty) culturally acceptable to the local people. New rules governed people's use and interpretation of the structures and open spaces and required residents to be schooled and acculturated into the norms of the unfamiliar spaces. In this sense, the vibrant square of Chandni Chowk was transformed into a moralizing and didactic space.

During the early twentieth century when Indian nationalism was on the rise as also were protests against British colonial rule, the transformed civic square of Chandni Chowk provided the political space for dissent and demonstrations. For some time, Company Bagh, as the redesigned gardens of Begum Bagh were now called, offered an outdoor area for various Indian professional groups to convene. Subsequently the nationalists used the area for political meetings. Until the declaration of independence in 1947, the square served as a site for political meetings, speeches, congresses, and silent marches. As a political 'hot spot' it was also the locus for British reprisals and arrests of demonstrators. This transformation of a place of legendary commerce and cosmopolitanism into a political space for ordinary people was a new one. The square that the colonial authorities had meant to be didactic and to appropriate the authority of the King's palace, ironically, was to serve against them as a public sphere in the development of democratic and Indian nationalist consciousness.[21]

NEW INSTITUTIONS AND NEW STREETS

The rebuilding of the Town Hall and a new civic center was possible because of extensive demolitions and a political structure that empowered such destruction and creation. Upon conquering Delhi, the first impulse of the British ascending to

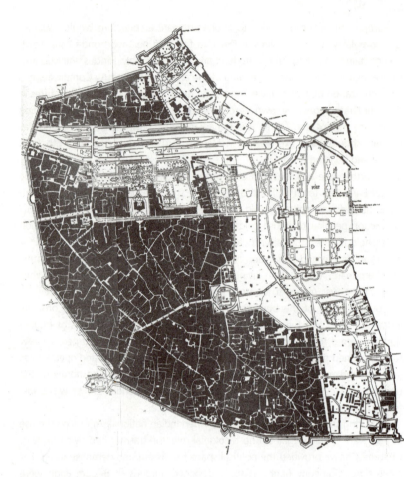

Figure 3.11
The walled city in 1873.
After the uprising of
1857, the colonial
government demolished
almost one third of the
city. During the 1860s
and 1870s, some streets
were widened, broad
new vistas were built,
and the railroad
introduced. Plan shows in
lighter tone the
clearance and rebuilding
areas.

rule had been to demolish the entire city including the King's Palace and the Jami Masjid. Eventually, they settled for a clearance of five hundred yards around the palace (Figure 3.11).[22] The area that was once heavily built up and thickly populated was cleared of all buildings and nicknamed 'Champs de Mars.'[23] The clearances in Delhi followed so soon after the large-scale demolition and rebuilding undertaken by Baron Haussmann in Paris that even the nickname signaled similar aspirations on the part of those now controlling the city.

Under the new rulers the palace-fortress of the Mughal Kings became a military garrison and was increasingly referred to as the 'Red Fort.' A majority of the buildings within the palace compounds were demolished to make room for military barracks and the movement of troops.[24] The government widened existing roads and constructed new ones that were wide, allowed easy vehicular access, and were connected to transportation arteries outside the city walls. A majority of the new roads were in the heavily demolished northern and eastern parts of the city including Hamilton Road, Elgin Road, Nicholson Road, Queen's

Road, Lothian Road, and Esplanade Roads, all names commemorating the new political, administrative, and military regime.[25]

New, sweeping boulevards transformed the landscape to the north of Chandni Chowk. From the perspective of Delhi's residents, streets were for the common folk. Women and elite men did not socialize in the bazaar and even concealed themselves from public view.[26] By contrast, wide boulevards such as the Esplanade Road became promenades for 'seeing and being seen' where Europeans, and Indians who had adopted their ways, went for leisurely rides and engaged in personal display.

The advent of the railways in 1867 changed the landscape of the city dramatically. A swathe of railway tracks cut through the city dividing and devouring neighborhoods. This introduction of the railroad into the heart of the historic walled city was unlike that in other cities in Western Europe. Much land to the north of Chandni Chowk was devoted to railroad tracks and the construction of a substantial railroad station (Figure 3.12). Residential quarters of those in service of the railroad, a gas house, power house, post office, rest houses, and police stations were further prominent additions to the northern part of the city. By 1877 large areas to the north and east had been cleared of buildings and railroad lines seared through the center of the city.

Along the new roads or in other rebuilt parts of the city buildings arose to house new institutions. Besides the Town Hall, new public institutions in Delhi included the railroad station, hospitals offering Western medical treatment on a racially segregated basis (Dufferin Hospital, Victoria Female Hospital, women's dispensaries, and veterinary hospitals), and schools (the Arabic School, Government High School, Normal School and the Industrial School). Bridges (Queen's Bridge and Dufferin Bridge), fountains (Lord Northbrook Fountain) and gardens

Figure 3.12
Railway Station in Delhi built in the 1870s to the north of the Town Hall. Wide paved roads for motor vehicles led to the station. Across from it in tidy rows were the railway-staff quarters. On the railway station note the pointed arches, circular columns, towers with crenellations, and the set back of building from street. The substantial building type had no precedent in Delhi.

(Nicholson Garden and Queen's Garden) were further additions.[27] New vehicular streets, buildings, and landmarks named after British administrators and royalty changed the scale and experience of urban space.[28] The area around Kashmiri Gate was most visibly transformed with a new post and telegraph office, clubs, and shops serving Europeans.

Historically, royalty, nobility, and wealthy citizens had sponsored public buildings in Delhi such as travelers' lodges (*musāfirkhānā*, *sarā'i*, and *dharamsālā*), temples, mosques, parochial schools (*madrasā*, *vidyāshālā*), *bā'oli* (tanks), and gardens (*bāgh*, and *baghīchā*) (Figures 3.13 and 3.14). The sponsored structures were named after the donor and benefactor and won them goodwill from the community for their philanthropy. In contrast, the modern institutional buildings of the British were projects led by the colonial state. Similarly, buildings sponsored by Indian philanthropists were, typically, for the use of a single caste, community, or religion. The new secular institutions, in contrast, included facilities like hospitals and clubs that were for Europeans only while some others were open to all Indians. These new institutional buildings represented novel ways of thinking in areas such as finance, education, health, and administration. They were intended to improve the physical and mental well-being of the people and acculturate them into British ways. As one official observed, 'a menagerie was constructed for the amusement and instruction of the public, from whom no charge was made.'[29] Whether to make Western institutions accessible to women or to gain acceptance from local residents, segregation of women continued for a while in the new spaces.

As hospitals and dispensaries displaced practitioners of indigenous systems of medicine such as *hakīm* and *vaid*, and banks took over from moneylenders,

Figure 3.13
Madrasa Ghaziuddin Khan. Established in 1710 by Nawab Ghaziuddin Khan Firuz Jung, the building had double-storied hallways with arches that ringed a large rectangular space that contained gardens. A mosque stood at one end. In 1825 the British housed the Delhi College in this building.

Figure 3.14
Dharamsala of
Chunnamal, Delhi, early
twentieth century. A
lodging house for
Hindus.

the wealthy and prominent citizens of the city participated in the financing and construction of schools, banks, hospitals, and hotels (Figures 3.15 and 3.16). Whether from political or cultural conviction or with an eye to commercial gain, from loyalty to or to curry favor with the new government, prosperous Indian residents supported and adopted the new institutions and aspects of architecture introduced by the British. While funds for many of the projects came from subscriptions by citizens of Delhi and municipal taxes, British administrators carefully screened the design proposals. British (or European-trained) architects drew up the designs, and government officials oversaw their construction and

Figure 3.15
'Chandni Chowk, Delhi,'
1860s. Note the Delhi
Exchange building in the
main bazaar on the right
as well as a sign for the
North Western Dak
Company. The new type
of financial institution
was marked by a pointed
arch with writing in
English around it.

management. Some buildings, such as the Dufferin Hospital, were constructed after holding a design competition (Figure 3.17).[30] Located on main thoroughfares, the structures created an imposing colonial presence, overshadowing the role of *haveli* as landmarks and as an organizing force in Delhi's society. The forms, architectural elements, and the large 'grain' of built and open spaces in the new structures were decidedly 'Western' in character and in contrast to the fine 'grain' and dense clustering of the surrounding fabric.[31]

Early European structures in Delhi, based on European cultural values and building styles, such as St James Church, Ludlow Castle, Skinner House, Metcalfe House, and the house built by William Frazer, had introduced new architectural elements into the northern part of Delhi by the early decades of the nineteenth century. One British traveler commented on the Chandni Chowk in the late 1830s:

> The Chandery Choke [sic], a principal street, is wide and handsome. One of the broadest avenues to be found in an Indian city. The houses are of various styles of architecture, partaking occasionally of the prevailing fashions of the west; Grecian piazas, porticos and pediments, are not unfrequently found fronting the dwellings of the Moslem or Hindoo; balconies are, of course, very common, and form the favorite resort of the gentlemen of the family, who, in a loose dishabille of white muslin, enjoy the pleasures of the hookah, while gazing on the passing crowd below, totally regardless of the dust which fills the air.[32]

However, during the latter part of the nineteenth century, the Town Hall and the new institutional buildings began to further transform the formal character of

Figure 3.16
A late nineteenth-century school building on Egerton Road shows European influences in the use of a columned entrance portico raised on wide steps and false pediments over symmetrically placed windows and scalloped cement railing around the flat roof.

the city in some areas. Soon, mansions on Chandni Chowk and Esplanade Road displayed features typical of the architecture of the British in Delhi. Neoclassical columns, pediments, and porticos became customary on these streets. As we saw in the previous chapter, motifs and materials gradually began to make inroads even on the interior streets (Figures 3.18 and 3.19).[33]

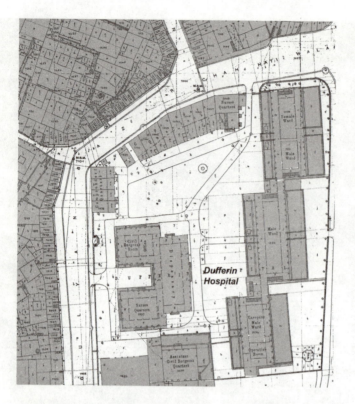

Figure 3.17
Plan of Dufferin Hospital,
1910. Shows rectilinear
forms with emphasis on
interior spaces and
sprawling layout in
contrast to compact and
irregular forms of the
surrounding
neighborhood. Also the
fine grain of existing
built forms and open
spaces were in contrast
to the new structure.

Figure 3.18
The sidewalk has been
covered over and built up
at upper levels. Shows
the extensive use of
wrought iron for grill
work and columns. Late
twentieth century view
of late nineteenth-
century structure.

Figure 3.19
Dormitory of St Stephen's College, *c.*1902, shows a new kind of institutional structure. The architectural form recalls the arched hallways around a courtyard typical of the local *madarsa*, but used new materials and European architectural elements like semicircular arches to make them a hybrid of European and Indian.

NEGOTIATING PUBLIC STREETS AND PRIVATE SPACES

In the southern part of the city, away from the main bazaars, the new rebuilt streets, and public buildings, the story was very different. In a densely inhabited walled city and a flourishing center of commerce, state policies focused on regulating design, development, and the use of space in the public realm. Officials attempted to rationalize the form of neighborhood pathways to conform to a universal 'public' character. With the stated intention of improving security and sanitation, they tried to coax irregular structures, narrow winding lanes and introverted courtyard houses into a semblance of reasoned order. All that was 'public' in the city was to be open and visible for the municipality to police. Further, building regulations aimed to govern the public face of private property. However, as will be seen, efforts to impose a preconceived vision of orthogonal order and predictable regularity proved extremely contentious.

For the British, Delhi's houses, with their introverted courtyards located in a maze of narrow winding lanes, were, by their mysterious and unpredictable character, threatening and inaccessible. At a time when architects and reformers in the Western world visualized architecture as embodying moral character, the apparent disorderliness of Delhi's inner streets was symptomatic of social degeneracy. From this perspective, irrational, superstitious, and traditional, the identity of the native landscape was in obvious opposition to ideas of discipline, civilization, and science, qualities the colonizers liked to see in themselves. Influenced by Victorian urban reformers in England who sought to overcome the social and environmental ills of industrial cities, colonial planners in Delhi disdained what they saw as the disorderly and dense living conditions of the old city.

Municipal regulations were legal instruments to make colonial visions of an idealized native city a manifest reality. The municipality in Delhi did not control European habitation in the Civil Lines nor were the by-laws the same. The by-laws included regulations such as the width of sidewalks, the height and width of overhead projections on to streets, location of benches and stairs on shop fronts, locations of stairwells, the proximity of animals to human habitation, the location, timing, and nature of vending and hawking, and so on. Within the walled area, however, the municipality intended the regulations to be implemented universally, and for constant policing to punish and rectify irregularities. In fact, so great was community control that much of the dense urban fabric of the city was difficult for inspectors and outsiders to penetrate, even less to be in command of.[34]

While the apparent purpose of the regulations was to achieve visual order and improved health, in fact they attempted to curb 'private' encroachments of 'public' space.[35] Building by-laws, for instance, laid out rules governing the street fronts of buildings. From those owners who proposed to rebuild or modify their properties, the municipality required extremely detailed plans showing the dimensions of the plinth, location of outer doors, access from street, height of buildings, number of stories, and size of overhead projections on to public streets. Deviations from the ideal were to be rectified and new proposals re-submitted for officials to consider. To make the smallest of changes to their building exteriors, property owners had to make a formal application to the municipality. Constructions not sanctioned were liable to be demolished.

Simple and obvious as the rules may sound today, their significance in Delhi at the time went far beyond a celebration of rationality and scientific progress. For local people, the regulations intruded on the space of community and family while seeking to normalize and re-categorize the city's streets according to the structures of what officials believed was 'modern' urban society as it was ideal-ized in the metropole. In a city where, historically, master-masons had designed and built houses, where the residents, despite their differences, shared a common spatial vocabulary, and where property lines and construction was negotiated between neighbors on an everyday basis, the municipality appointed itself the final authority to ensure order in the public street.[36]

The regulations were uniformly applicable to all areas under the Delhi Municipal Committee. The government supervised parks, squares, and streets as public spaces in contrast to the intimacies of domestic space. For the residents, seclusion and the public-ness of streets had not been absolute and opposing characteristics inherent in the spaces (Figure 3.20). Parks, squares, and streets had often been privately owned. Customary use and meaning reinforced and expressed complicated social and spatial structures of public-ness and privacy (Figure 3.21). The existing hierarchy of areas was to be replaced by universal space, a space that conformed to a normative vision that gave preference to effi-ciency, access, servicing, policing, and sanitation. In this, the municipality attempted to wrest control of neighborhoods, buildings, and streets from the

Figure 3.20
Plan of a neighborhood
in the interior of the
southern part of the city,
c.1910. Shows the texture
of built-up space to open
space. Also evident is the
gradation of
privacy/publicness in
moving from main
bazaar to the interior
courtyard of the
dwelling.

Figure 3.21
View from one entryway
through another across a
narrow street. In moving
from the main bazaar to
the very interior recesses
of the private quarters,
custom demanded that
individuals seek and be
granted permission.

residents. The apparent standardization also concealed revised categories of spatial differentiation, public from private, civic from commercial, clean from polluted, and safe from unsafe.

Customary spatial practices in Delhi did not conform to the simple polarity of private and public that the British officials sought to construct. Not only was the city highly privatized, and not only did the many shades of gray complicate the simplistic black and white of private and public spaces, but complex overlapping maps structured the city. As the grand *haveli*, the miniature cities of yesterday, fragmented to form smaller units, many of the pathways and open spaces within the elaborate maze of the neighborhoods continued to be owned by the erstwhile landlords. Pathways that cut through private properties created ambiguous ownership. The bazaars such as Chandni Chowk, Faiz Bazaar, Meena Bazaar, and Chawri Bazaar were the most public of spaces where anyone could pass, and where traders from Persia and Arabia rubbed shoulders with those from China.[37] Yet, women, except for prostitutes, were largely excluded from these spaces. As one moved inwards from the bazaar the streets got increasingly narrow and more private. In the old world of face-to-face interaction the gradation from public to private were one of decreasing anonymity and increasing control. In the intricate web of streets, squares, platforms and courtyards of the inner city, turf and territory was important and negotiated locally. Here, by disobedience, open protests, legal appeals, subversive construction, delays, feigned ignorance, and other such methods, residents contested municipal rules and regulations that endeavored to normalize streets and engender equal access. The *haveli* were shrinking and between the colonial administration and the merchants' associations, the *rais* controlled less and less space within the city. At such a time, of rapid property subdivision and land conversion, the new regulations sought to construct visual order in public space.

The municipality expended much effort in surveying and identifying the boundaries of individual holdings in order to mark the limits of public space. From improving urban services, the colonial Municipal authorities had appointed themselves the final arbiters of civic morality. Munshi Jamaluddin, for instance, requested permission to erect a *chattā* (over bridge) over the entrance of his house (Figure 3.22).[38] This raised problems for the Municipal Committee because his lane had been declared a public lane.[39] The municipality was categorical in rejecting his request, '(1) because the height [of the proposed *chattā*] is less than 15 feet, (2) the land below has already been declared public, and (3) the supports of the *chattā* will apparently rest on or against another man's property.'[40]

The anarchy the officials perceived in the city was, for residents, the triumph of local control. Historically, in Delhi construction and property lines were socially negotiated and disputes settled by community leaders and custom.[41] Aside from royal grants, no written rules or a reasoned vision had governed the city's development. Although scholars have proposed different theories for the layout of the city and its key elements at the time Shahjahanabad was established, over the centuries the neighborhood clusters developed accord-

Figure 3.22
A recently rebuilt *chattā*,
upper-story structure
spanning across a narrow
street.

ing to changing custom and local control and in the absence of written rules or a centralized vision for the whole city.[42] From the wealthy patron to the neighborhood elder, a community's interests were often the responsibility of a benevolent individual. Residents negotiated their claims over space and property. Intertwined as the buildings were, owners added to and extended their properties as they saw fit and as they could agree with their neighbors (Figure 3.23). As families enlarged and household sizes changed they added a room here, a floor there, sold off an entire wing or converted street front rooms to shops. For long-term residents and property owners, community respect as much as community

Figure 3.23
View of a typical narrow
residential *galī* or street
in the southern part of
the walled city. The
privacy or public-ness of
a street was related to its
width and spatial
volume, the type of
activities opening on to
it, and the position and
number of main
entrances off the street.

censure was of paramount importance. In the daily acts of living and building
what was right was determined by custom and by the relative social and political
status of the inhabitants involved.

During the nineteenth century, at a time of rapid socio-economic transformation, the land-owning nobility tussled with the rising entrepreneurial
classes for supremacy and conflicts had become customary. Debates over property and construction had become particularly significant and compromises
reflected and reinforced the shifting authority of the parties involved. In this
sense, the arbitration over the building of platforms on street edges, or re-building
houses and shops, were also ways of strengthening neighborhood power

structures. Under these circumstances, municipal visions and interventions were both threatening and unwelcome for the residents. Delhi's citizenry shared neither the ideals nor the values of their government. Even as the utilitarian colonial administrators attempted to make the city more rational and less arbitrary from their perspective, the citizens contested through confrontation and subversion not only the universalizing character of public space but the loss of local control over space and place.

A scrutiny of municipal and property records, correspondence, and oral histories reveal some of the mechanisms the residents adopted to negotiate official definitions of the form and meaning of public space. Rather than come together and protest against municipal governance, people bargained as they always had, sometimes collectively, at times individually. In a complex and unequal city, the normalizing regulations affected people in different ways. Accustomed to negotiating and adjusting claims, the inhabitants of Delhi found ways of skirting the rules and arriving at a compromise. While the interventions were indeed impositions, the final outcome of the efforts was not simply what the planners envisaged but one that the subjects negotiated even in their position of relative powerlessness.

The residents adopted various strategies to manipulate the definition of public streets from written petitions to quiet disobedience. For instance, when the municipality constructed a public facility on the street across from Azimuddin's shop, he took objection to such a profane activity being accommodated on the street space his shop occupied and petitioned the Municipal Committee for its removal.[43] Azimuddin's petition reveals that the central issue was the definition of the 'public' status of streets by the local community. For Azimuddin and his neighbors, the customary use of space ordained that the activities and use of the local street space be under their control. From the perspective of the Municipal Committee, however, the street was public space under municipal supervision.

Azimuddin's case was only one of several that the Municipality was faced with, and often forced to concede.[44] Most people went ahead and built what they wanted to without either seeking the Municipality's permission or following their regulations. Lala Sangam Lal, for instance, went through the formal application process only after he had built a new house. The Municipal Committee resolved that 'unless Lala Sangam Lal pays Rs.50 for the offense of building the house without permission under Section 92, the Secretary gives 15 days notice to remove the building.'[45] Given the expense and effort involved in constructing a house, Lala Sangam Lal would have found the payment of the fine an easy way to placate the officials.

Although the city government and its laws were apparently unrelenting in their control, much negotiation went on in practice. A decade after the promulgation of the by-laws, in one year alone there were close to 2,000 cases documented of breach of by-laws.[46] Although structures put up without the permission of the Municipal Committee were to be demolished, a provision was soon added that allowed fines to be paid in lieu of demolition. The very provision of payment of fines signaled a negotiated settlement of the original intent of the by-laws.

Increasingly, the collection of fines became extortionate in nature. Officials threatened those responsible for breach of by-laws with demolition unless a large sum of money was paid to the municipality. Depending on the offender's abilities to negotiate and pay, similar appropriations of public space had entirely different outcomes. While some individuals were able to arbitrate a payment, others found their structures demolished. For instance, Israrul Haq had built some enclosures on the *chattā* connecting two of his buildings across a street and fixed a *chowkhat* (entrance door frame) without permission from city officials. The Municipal Committee ruled that in fifteen days he was to remove all of the new construction. If he did not comply, then the Committee threatened to remove the offending structures itself.[47] In the case of Wali Mohammad Khansaman, the Committee had resolved that he was to remove a screen wall he had erected illegally. Khansaman petitioned the city officials that the wall be allowed to stand because its removal would not only put him to financial loss but that the seclusion of the women in his house (*purdāh*) would be interfered with. The municipality accepted his argument and the offer to 'pay' a penalty, and fined him the large sum of Rs.100. The notice reads,

> Resolved that if Wali Mohammad wishes the land encroached upon to remain in his possession he must pay Rs.95 to the Committee, and Rs.5. for building without permission. Total Rs.100/-. If he does not agree to these terms the building will be removed after 15 days notice, under section 147.[48]

The amount of the fine in this case is particularly significant since the original understanding had been that a maximum fine of Rs.5 would be charged for such minor offenses.[49]

Despite the by-laws, people continued to build without permission and waited to be found out. They would then agree on a compensation for the breach at an individual level with the local municipal inspector. The original intent of the by-laws was soon lost sight of. The negotiations made public space a commodity whose value was settled between individual officials and citizens. Those in a position to pay for the breach of by-laws obtained 'legal' sanction for encroaching the public space, to such an extent that officials began to view the regulations as instituted primarily to raise revenue for the Municipality.[50] The Commissioner of Delhi was forced to reprimand the Municipality for its practice of 'forcing people to pay large sums of money for technical breaches of the bye-laws under threat of demolishing expensive buildings.'[51]

Rent for the use of public space was another institutionalized mechanism for settling the privatization of streets and public lands. Vending and hawking along thoroughfares, extending shop displays on to streets, and temporarily occupying pedestrian paths for sales was typical of Delhi's bazaars. Under new laws, individuals extending shops on to the streets, or vending on the streets, were all required to pay sums of money, as rent, to the municipality. Merchants were expected to pay a rent even for *takhtas* (platforms or ledges) extending from their stores. According to the regulations, 'A charge of eight annas a month will be made for each takhta placed in front of each shop, provided that a takhta of 5 feet or less shall pay at half rate, and a double rate shall be charged for a takhta of greater length than 10 feet.'[52] Evidently, the rents specified were based on the extent of 'public' space taken up for private use. Over time, a sliding scale of prices was instituted for commercial use of public space (Figures 3.24 and 3.25).

The residents, for their part, adopted diverse tactics to get around regulations governing the payment of rent. Some, such as Tipper Chand Musaddi Lal, resident of Saddar Bazaar, petitioned for a decrease in the rent amount. Lal's petition for reduction in rent was discussed at a meeting of the Municipal Committee,

> Read application of Tipper Chand Musaddi Lal resident of Sudder Bazar begging the Committee to reduce the rent of their Saibans from Rs.6 to Rs.3 like the other shop keepers of Sudder Bazar with recommendation of Ward member . . .[53]

A few people organized signature campaigns to dismiss the rule, and many others refused to pay.[54] When Mahboob Baksh Mohammed Saddik and others declined to pay rent for the private appropriation of a public thoroughfare, some officials of the city confiscated their wares. A Municipal Committee official observed,

> Read Misl. regarding Rs.57 on account of arrears of Putri rent due from Mahboob Baksh Mohomed Saddik and others with report of Secretary that Rs.26-5-0 were realized by the public auction of the shoes etc., of these men and Rs.30-11-0 are still out standing against them and they refuse to pay and say that the price of their shoes was quite sufficient to cover the arrears.[55]

Figure 3.24
During special holidays, vendors appropriate almost the entire sidewalk for displaying their wares. Nineteenth-century historical accounts suggest that this contemporary view was typical in Delhi even at that time.

Figure 3.25
Private businesses
continue to appropriate
'public' space using
benches, platforms, and
ledges.

Non-conformity, the tactics of delay, foot dragging, or refusal to pay rent for the use of the public space, were not merely in defiance of authority but were also statements of the right of ordinary residents to privatize the public arena and make the city conform to their differing expectations. Far from the civic-centered urban community that the municipality hoped to symbolize and inspire, in their rent and fine-taking aspect, officials revealed an institutionalized interest in the control of public space. The strategies of contestation and negotiation the residents adopted in turn resulted in 'illegal' constructions. The municipality's efforts to rationalize and regulate the formal boundaries of public streets did not succeed. However, they did put in place a framework that forced residents to reason, question, and negotiate on the basis of a different logic. The efforts to protest and defy also reveal a greater awareness among ordinary residents of their rights and privileges in the public sphere. To that extent the regulations brought about a change in people's experience, perception, and development of public space.

CONTENTIOUS PROCESSIONS

Discipline and control, order and predictability were not just for the built form but for the rituals of interaction in public places as well. While officials sought to build a civic spirit, the competing claims of opposing groups of citizenry politicized community space. Under contention was the functional and social use of public streets as well as their symbolic significance. Both the colonial government and citizens employed traditions and rituals of spatial use as a strategy to claim their rights over public space. The contrary meanings of private and public were mediated in the symbolic appropriation of streets for processions.

Processions and public demonstrations were commonplace in Delhi. Royal processions, those by religious groups or sects marking particular holidays, and ones for weddings and funerals were some of the more frequent types (Figure 3.26). However, only the grandest of processions occupied the main streets. Most marriage and funeral processions tended to be small, along by-lanes, and limited to friends and relatives. Religious processions in contrast were often large and contentious. Grand processions on important holidays served to show the strength of a particular group, reinforce their identity, and gain potential followers.

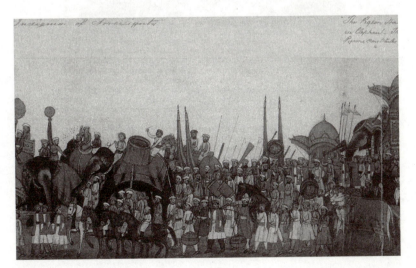

Figure 3.26
Detail of a state procession of the Mughal king on the festival of Eid, 1842–44. Caparisoned elephants, camels, horses, flag bearers, drummers, and general air of festivity is evident.

The processions were colorful and noisy events that often included caparisoned elephants and horses, tableaux, banners, chanting, singing, dancing, bells, cymbals, and horns, in addition to men, women, and children. Hindus and Jains carried decorated idols in their processions with much chanting, music, recitations, and fanfare. Ramlila and Moharrum, festivals of the Hindus and Muslims respectively, were occasions for Delhi's most significant demonstrations.[56] The Ramlila fanfare included much singing and chanting with some participants dressed as the central characters in the great Hindu epic, the *Ramayana* (Figure 3.27). The Moharrum parade to mark an important holiday of the Shia Muslims, was an emotionally charged event with public display of sorrow and lamentation; some participants whipped and flogged themselves. In most processions, a core group started out from a significant place and the numbers substantially swelled as they went along. People would cheer from balconies and shops along the route. However, members from one group that disagreed with the beliefs of another often tried to disrupt the festivities by stirring up trouble along the streets or even starting an alternate ceremonial show to interfere with the first.

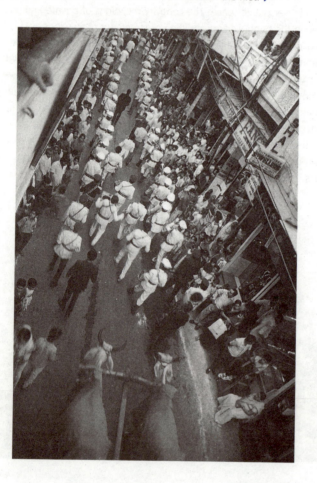

Figure 3.27
Ramlila procession. The religious procession of the Hindus now includes a marching band, an innovation introduced to India by the British.

The groups that led the processions showed their strength not only in their numbers and in the pomp but also in their ability to carry out impressive demonstrations. For each group, obstructing and overcoming impediments was integral to the claiming of public space and reaffirmation of identity. But grand processions by their appropriation of thoroughfares also restricted their use by other residents. Further, opposing religious sects sometimes viewed imposing pageants by one group, a show of strength in public, as threatening to their own identities and beliefs. Protests, if only token ones, by opposing sects during a religious demonstration was almost a ritualized necessity. With their accompanying disorder, the processions threatened the absolute authority of the city officials over public space and such symbolic debates over the meaning of communal space were entirely outside their purview. Hence, for stated reasons of security, the municipality required citizens to seek permission for all parades.

City officials expected to be notified in advance all details of a proposed event. For instance, when the Saraogis, a religious group, wished to carry out a procession in 1877, municipal officers asked them to submit a detailed proposal in advance. The list submitted by the Saraogis was as specific as it was extensive: an orchestra of fifty musicians, one elephant carrying a banner, seven female camels carrying flags, fifty palanquins, three chariots, and so on. Even the relative positions of the elephants to the camels and the palanquin to the chariot in the procession was furnished. In addition to the origin and destination of the procession, information on the route, the timing, the halts, the ceremonies, and the number of people participating all were provided.[57] In contrast to the spontaneity typical of such events, the city officials expected to review and approve complete information on each activity and every aspect of the procession.)

Clearly, the control of such fine points of the procession and complete ordering of communal events went beyond reasons of security. Implicit in the official position was an attempt to make activities in the public domain open to official scrutiny and regulation. While the interest of the Saraogis was in holding the procession and claiming their right to the streets, the officials sought singular command over the interpretation of public space. However, residents of the city did not passively submit to this appropriation of authority or the claiming of space. The Saraogis, who had to contend with state control of the streets, used their intimate knowledge of the city and its local history to manipulate the officials.

For the Saraogis, as for other religious groups in Delhi, processions signified more than the physical use of space: they were grand spectacles of group strength and conveyed the power of a particular social and political identity. The pomp and splendor of their pageants signaled their power in overcoming impediments put up not only by the state, but also by other, competing and opposing religious groups. Some processions more than others tended to stir up commotion and even lead to riots. The Mughal king had banned Saraogi parades some decades earlier since they had caused a great deal of disturbance. In presenting their request to hold a procession, the Saraogis avoided any mention of their turbulent history.[58] They also did not inform the officials about the celebration until just one day before. The event was not impromptu as it had been made out to be, since preparations had been afoot for months. Such tactics aimed at catching unawares opposing religious groups. Rather than carry their idol through the side streets, as the city officials suggested, the Saraogis persuaded them to allow a demonstration through the principal streets of the city. Significantly, the day chosen for the procession coincided with a major festival of another religious group, when the city was to be packed with people from all over the region. As a Saraogi leader declared, the parade was to be a grand demonstration of the power of the Saraogi religion and the strength of their following.[59]

As the inexperienced authors of a new kind of urban institution in Delhi, municipal officials, ignorant of the movement's history and its socio-political implications, granted permission. Expecting such manipulation of the authorities by the Saraogis, groups opposed to them were determined to prevent their grand celebration on the main streets. They spoke darkly of riots, looting, murder, and mayhem if the Saraogis were allowed along the primary thorough-fares.[60] They too used the city officials towards their own end. At the last minute, these parties pressured the police department to divert the procession on to secondary streets. Members of competing sects did their best to minimize the impact of the event, embarrass the Saraogis, and undermine their power. Tense as it was with police at hand to maintain order and prevent violent rioting, in the end the Saraogis succeeded in carrying out their demonstration. The rivalry between the groups, apparently over the physical use of the streets, was over the right of each to claim public space for its own use in defiance of official control.

Ceremonial presentations involving British royalty and senior officials of the colonial administration was a totally different matter. In this, officials contended, they had merely deferred to the tradition-bound indigenes who relished such displays of pomp and splendor. The appropriation of civic space for these shows of power was somehow acceptable. For visiting British Royalty, local officials arranged processions in the manner of the Mughals.[61] With tidy groups of liveried troops marching in rows, horses trotting to a beat, and a resplendent military band, British parades were as much a spectacle, an exhibition of discipline, as of the power and authority of the colonial government. Orderly lines of elephants, men, horses, and camels trooped down the streets in a rhythmic march and in stark contrast to the noisy crowds, music, dancing, fairs, and high emotions that accompanied the typical procession in Delhi.[62] While claiming to discredit myth and tradition, and aspiring to 'civilize' the 'natives' by helping them to break away from it, the British nonetheless invented new rituals in similar terms to reinforce their position and authority.[63]

BLURRED BOUNDARIES

By the turn of the century Delhi had acquired wide, straight roads, manicured gardens with curvilinear paths, an imposing town hall, a clock tower, a wide swathe of railroad tracks, a substantial railroad station, and new buildings with European influences in their design. More churches had also made their appearance in the northern part of the walled city. Municipalization had replaced local control of neighborhoods and a new civic center had superseded the focal position of the royal palace. In addition to official interventions, new materials and technologies of construction, spatial forms, and institutions altered the landscape to the north and east of Chandni Chowk to create an urbanism that was efficient, orderly, and, from the British perspective, decidedly 'modern.' Neoclassical and beaux-arts influences in architecture and urban design stood in sharp contrast to the existing practices. Yet, away from the carefully ordered public front, residential neighborhoods continued to thrive in seemingly rebellious disorder.

The spatial distribution of new roads and buildings reveal that many densely built-up neighborhoods to the south of Chandni Chowk were not rebuilt. Instead, building regulations called on residents to intervene as little as possible and preserve the footprints of the buildings and streets. On the part of the government, active rebuilding may have been impossible due to its inability to penetrate the interior areas; however, the implication of their policies was that the state had served to preserve some parts of Delhi while demolishing others. Although the British in Delhi had been tempted to raze the city in the aftermath of the rebellion and build anew, unlike the French in Morocco, the British were not driven by an overt desire to conserve the 'traditional' neighborhoods of the city. They demolished some areas and preserved others. Yet, the excluded spaces, backward, traditional, and entirely common, were the ones that supported the exalted new spaces of modernism. Symbolically, the best and the worst were bound together in the city, each dependent on the other: the past and the present, the magnificent and the apocalyptic. Local resistance, possibilities of further rebellion, financial interests of the colonial government, and complex politics determined the inconsistency of the decisions more than any ideology. The remaking of the streets and squares occurred primarily in the major public areas of the city. The transformations, since they could not occur consistently throughout the city, were, in that sense, symbolic gestures. In the interior streets, changes were small-scale, gradual, and everyday. The landscape of narrow winding ways with densely built-up neighborhoods created an apparent dualism with the newly created streets, open spaces, and grand monuments. The rebuilding efforts focused largely on creating a new center as if the experience of modernity would somehow emanate out from this center. Yet, much as the colonial officials wanted the new civic center to dominate the city, this 'modern' core could not exist in isolation of the neighborhoods around that sustained it. Co-opting the Raymond Williams analogy, one could say that official policies in Delhi created a dominant 'city' as the landscape inspired by European modernism, supported by a subordinate 'country' of indigenous neighborhoods.[64]

Implicit in the new urbanism was the discourse of an exalted way of building and inhabiting space that identified itself as self-consciously progressive and 'modern' in the conventional sense. This identity was constructed in opposition to one that was disdained as 'traditional'. Peter Stallybrass and Allon White tell us that differentiation is dependent on disgust.[65] The redesigned public parts projected an image of the city for Western visitors that was familiar. The partial redesign also obscured the interior parts and everyday lives and spaces of the residents that saw less dramatic changes. However, in both places, this new 'public sphere' was meant to exclude the popular, and the low and the dirty, the repulsive, the noisy, and the contaminating.

Despite official aspirations to differentiate, in reality, interplay between the two muted the stark dualism between the magnificently modern and trenchantly traditional. For their part, city officials conceded to, compromised, manipulated, and unwittingly included customary spatial practices. They did so for instance in the efforts to design a Town Hall that was sympathetic to the 'prevailing mohammedan style,' in the acceptance of fines as compromise for the privatization of public streets or building without permission, and in being party to the Saraogi's claim over public space in staging a grand spectacle. The residents contested, manipulated, and appropriated public spaces to interpret them as they saw fit. Even in a situation of extreme inequality, they played an active role in making Delhi modern on their own terms and in contradiction to recently formulated city regulations. Hawkers, vendors, pushcarts, and peddlers crowded the square in front of the town hall, and sullying its exalted civic-ness with mundane commerce and its imposing design with unceremonious squatting. Handcarts and piles of goods leaving and arriving by train created disorder in the newly established streets to the north. The remaining *haveli* were converted to warehouses to the north of Chandni Chowk while residents to the south found innovative ways of adding to, extending, and altering their buildings as families grew and business expanded. Faced with conflicts between reason and custom, coercion and subversion, authoritarian design and everyday use, between a new normalization and the accepted hierarchies of use and meaning, inhabitants adopted a variety of strategies for negotiating what they saw as their right to privatize the 'public' street, and to create a new awareness of 'public' in the nationalist move towards democratic self-government.

The motivations of the colonial state and the institutional self-interest of city officials also sullied their visions of an idealized urban community. Whether it was in demolishing neighborhoods that the British administration feared were harboring rebels, appropriating streets for processions to proclaim colonial supremacy, or charging fines and rents for the private encroachment of public space, the desire to reinforce their political and financial power compromised the government's stated intent of security, civic-ness, and orderliness.

The public space that emerged through the negotiations was not a single, universally defined space that was absolute in terms city officials had imagined nor did existing meanings continue unaffected. In the daily acts of building and inhabiting space, residents challenged the rational differentiation between private and public. Yet, they did so within the context of the new framework city officials had set in place. While citizens asserted their right to define the public face of their buildings in skirting and manipulating building by-laws, nevertheless they could not entirely disregard the regulations. As local professionals and Indian nationalists appropriated the square and the gardens of Chandni Chowk for their own political purposes, indigenous as they were, their interpretation of the spaces was altered from that of the early nineteenth century. In the new economic and political environment, a growing section of small entrepreneurs and small businessmen felt emboldened to test the limits of their power. The very engagement with new spatial forms and definitions meant that the old could not persist unquestioned. Rebuilt, redefined, reasoned, and reconstituted, public spaces in their many hues were indigenous modernities. Public space, however, persisted as male domain. Despite the transformations, women's spaces remained segregated and women largely excluded from both the public sphere and from public space. The growth of the Indian nationalist movement in the early twentieth century provided space for women to participate in public protests and demonstrations, if in a limited way.

The state efforts to rebuild, regulate, and preserve resulted in controversy over the form and meaning of public space in Delhi. A constantly shifting 'middle ground,' of hybrid space and less-than-ordered use, signaled the local people's subversion and contestation of the colonial state's vision. Equally, the ephemeral quality of the hybrid expressed the indigenous drive to innovate, problem solve, and engage with a rapidly changing urbanism. From that perspective municipal regulations were simply new boundaries to negotiate. People's response to the new circumstances was not based on custom alone but on reason and logic, albeit a different one. For instance, in their procession, the Saraogis did not openly confront officials, or challenge regulations, nor were the principal streets open claim for revelry and religious carnival. Yet they manipulated and pushed the boundaries to achieve their ends. The city's streets and squares were the collective expression of multiple and emergent settlements of these contradictions. In their plurality of forms and meanings, Delhi's public spaces and urban form were neither entirely planned and regulated, nor completely traditional and spontaneous, but the result of conflict, mediation, and negotiation.

Chapter 4: Sanitizing Neighborhoods

Geographies of Health

INTRODUCTION

From the mid-nineteenth century, public health was a growing concern in the cities of Western Europe and a new field of science was having an impact. 'Sanitary science' was premised on the idea that sanitary reform and hygiene could prevent the spread of infectious diseases and decrease mortality from them. In the industrial cities of Western Europe, the prevalence of dysentery, typhoid, and tuberculosis, as well as frequent and devastating epidemics of plague and cholera, brought public-health issues to the forefront.[1] Medical statistics also proved that these diseases were preventable. New concepts of sanitation and health redefined the functions and behavior of the body in space. After years of suffering the scourge of epidemics, the idea of applying scientific thought and reason to control sickness and even death was an undoubted progress for proponents of Western modernism.

Concerns about workers' housing, sanitation, and health were increasingly evident in British towns by the 1820s. With the cholera epidemic of 1831 demands for government intervention to improve the conditions affecting public health were widespread. In 1842, Edwin Chadwick's 'Report into the Sanitary Conditions of the Labouring Population of Great Britain' had an enormous impact.[2] In 1848, an act was passed to make public health the responsibility of local governments. However, several years passed before local authorities took significant action to improve the health condition of British towns. Among prevalent medical theories, the one linking disease to noxious gases or 'miasmas' arising from poor or contaminated soil or the exhalation of organic decomposition from the earth placed great emphasis on environmental conditions as central to health. Questions of drainage and slopes, disposal of human waste, stagnant pools of water, and dark, damp, unventilated quarters all became matters for government intervention.

For some, public-health concerns justified the large-scale eradication of overcrowded and poor quality housing. The ideal of a healthy industrial city had been used to justify Napoleon III's massive rebuilding of Paris in 1860.[3] For others, the persistent application of sanitary regulations and urban reforms was the route to improved health in the city. The idea of slums as spatial and social abominations took firm root in England, the U.S., and Australia during this time.[4] During the nineteenth century, slums were feared and denounced as health menaces, moral reproaches, and social dangers to society. They constituted an aesthetic affront and a functional liability to 'modern' cities. Experts on sanitary science and public health, 'sanitarians' as many at the time referred to them, proposed a variety of technological and architectural solutions to make the environment more salubrious; the emphasis was on scientific answers. As Banister Fletcher, the architectural historian, put it in the early twentieth century,

> Sanitary science is the bridge connecting the architectural and medical professions, and on it are found both architects and medical men . . . In sanitary science there is no lagging behind, no stopping on the forward march. In no other science have such strides been made during recent years.[5]

The latter decades of the nineteenth century saw experts and reformers propose improved layouts for cities and neighborhoods based on the principles of sanitation. In Britain, Benjamin Ward Richardson, a physician, scientist, and sanitary expert, proposed a model city of health that epitomized the idea of using sanitary science to transform urban life. As he described it:

> The acreage of our model city allows room for three wide main streets or boulevards, which run from east to west, and which are the main thoroughfares. Beneath each of these is a subway, a railway along which the heavy traffic of the city is carried on. The streets from north to south which cross the main thoroughfares at right angles, and the minor streets which run parallel, are all wide, and, owing to the lowness of the houses, are thoroughly ventilated, and in the day are filled with sunlight. They are planted on each side of the pathways with trees, and in many places with shrubs and evergreens. All the interspaces between the backs of houses are gardens. The churches, hospitals, theatres, banks, lecture-rooms, and other public buildings, as well as some private buildings such as warehouses and stables, stand alone, forming parts of streets, and occupying the position of several houses. They are surrounded with garden space, and add not only to the beauty but to the healthiness of the city. The large houses of the wealthy are situated in a similar manner.[6]

Based on scientific calculations and medical rationale, the imagined city promised health and progress for all citizens and all parts of the city. As he put it, 'Instead of the gutter, the poorest child has the garden; for the foul sight and smell of unwholesome garbage, he has flowers and green sward.'[7] Health was for all but the transformation was to be greatest for those most in need of it. As a city that was rationally laid out to maximize the health of its residents and lower mortality, his vision of Hygiea, the ideal city of health, was an important influence on the city planning movement in Britain in the late nineteenth century.

Modernity and progress were intimately related to science. Standing in opposition to religion, myth, superstition, and metaphysics, the British saw science, technology, and medicine as important aspects of their imperial mission to 'civilize' other cultures.[8] For the Europeans, India, like other societies in Asia and Africa, from this perspective was a land of dirt, disease, and sudden death. Unexplained illness had for long been impediments to European domination of India. Nineteenth-century Europeans particularly prided themselves on their scientific understanding of disease and mocked what they regarded as fatalism, superstition, and barbarity in indigenous responses. The emerging discipline of 'tropical medicine' gave scientific credence to the idea of the tropical world as one that was primitive and dangerous environmentally in contrast to that of the safe and sanitized temperate regions.[9]

In Delhi, public-health reform was to become a key concern after 1857. In the name of sanitation and security, almost a third of the city was demolished. Implicity, the new rulers saw the indigenous city as a diseased organism whose evil influence was to be contained and minimized.[10] Subsequently, with the advent of municipalization, officials began to view sanitary reform and the resolution of infrastructure such as drainage, water supply, and collection of sewage and garbage as steps towards transforming Delhi into a sanitary and modern city. The interventions were to construct a narrative where a filthy and disease-ridden city was transformed into a healthy landscape by enlightened and diligent officials. Any opposition from locals was ascribed to their ignorance and superstition.

Efforts at sanitation in Delhi drew much of its impetus and most of its principles from the experience of the public-health movement in Britain. Despite the near absence of industrialization in mid-nineteenth century Delhi, for the new rulers, the dense and irregular pattern of Delhi's streets and houses were reminiscent of the dire poverty and overcrowding of industrial slums in Britain. Several Victorian observers and reformers saw similarities between the physical (and social) environment of 'wretched slums' in Britain and 'the dark continents.'[11] In fact, the relative wealth of many neighborhoods, the city's narrow streets and large interior courtyards, as well as the existence of traditional systems of infrastructure and medicine, made the built form of Delhi quite unlike the slums of Britain. As sanitarians in Europe blamed high-density urban living (irrespective of society and culture), overcrowded tenements, and the lack of fresh air for the spread of diseases, so also did one British sanitation expert in India:

> Poverty is undoubtedly a great bar to sanitary improvement, and bad sanitary conditions beget poverty, so that poverty and sickness re-act upon each other and tend to diminish the vital power of a people and their capacity for improvement.[12]

The perception of mysterious illnesses and death in the tropics, the concern over the health of the troops, and the political agendas of 'civilizing' were all to be instrumental in shaping sanitary-reform policies in Delhi. However, it was only in the latter part of the nineteenth century, more than two decades after sanitary reformers such as Edwin Chadwick had been advocating sanitary reform in England, that the colonial administrators addressed the issue of urban sanitation in India, and another two decades before technological solutions could be effective, even in part.

In valorizing the achievements of Western science and technology in shaping the urban landscape, official colonial discourse discounted Indian scientific traditions. Having a variety of written and oral scientific and medical traditions, India was not simply a *tabula rasa* waiting to be shaped by gifts of progress from the West. Traditional systems of health care and infrastructure provision were still prevalent in Delhi when the British took over in 1857, as were the traditional processes of building and inhabiting space. Although some systems such as those provided by wells and the river may have become inadequate to meet the growing needs, or others such as the drains may have become overburdened, they still continued to serve a substantial population of the city. The new scientific methods and sanitary arrangements sought to replace existing techniques and, also, the people who provided the services.

The objective of this chapter is neither to romanticize local understanding of the body, health, and space, nor to reinforce the acknowledged superiority of sanitary reforms. Rather, my aim is to examine the reconstitution of the city both physically (by the introduction of new buildings and building types, and the removal of others) as well as culturally (by the altered meanings attached to these changes) under the guise of health. As the epitome of reason, followers of Western science celebrated it as neutral and universal. However, in its application as a transforming modernizing force, science and technology were also deeply political. Although official accounts claimed that the welfare of the citizens was at the heart of sanitary improvement projects, the rhetoric of liberalism and egalitarianism contradicted the ways in which sanitation measures themselves became instruments for reinforcing inequities and furthering colonial goals. At one level, British actions in Delhi were guided by the imperatives of safety, sanitation, and security, as Veena Oldenburg has identified in Lucknow.[13] However, indigenous views of health and urban life often conflicted with those of the officials. Municipalization and sanitation-improvement projects had to contend with existing physical and social infrastructure for the delivery of services. Residents objected to sanitary policing and did not always share the municipal ideals of progress. Local resistance to health-reform measures imposed from above was as responsible as the official interventions in shaping Delhi's urbanism. In this chapter I look at some of the ways in which sanitary and medical science as well as technologies of service provision redefined the shape form and working of the city.

REMOVAL AND PROTEST

One method of cleansing that colonial officials adopted in Delhi was the idea of eradicating what they saw as the diseased urban fabric or at least isolating it and spatially separating the healthy areas from those that were not. From the British perspective, tearing down buildings and opening up congested areas served to weed out some of the sources of disease. If the origin of the sickness could not be removed, what colonial officials saw as its evil influence upon 'civilized' society could at least, be contained. Yet, residents naturally protested about the injustice of the demolitions and the segregation, even in their position of relative powerlessness.

As stated in Chapter 3, when the British gained control of the city four months after the start of the 1857 rebellion, they expelled the native residents and appropriated properties within the walls and the lands outside. Day after day, the city was cleared of 'rebels' and eventually of all its native population (Figure 4.1). Those Indians suspected of participating in the rebellion or conspiring against the British were hanged and their properties confiscated or destroyed.[14] Many left to settle in other cities or on the outskirts of Delhi. High-ranking officials and the nobility under the Mughals and their houses were particular targets of suspicion. By contrast, those who had proved themselves loyal to the British were placed under protection.[15]

British officials attributed the rebellion to a conspiracy against them led by the King of Delhi along with his favored officers and nobles. The events of 1857 had seriously influenced colonial perceptions of disease, dirt, and disloyalty. During the period immediately following the rebellion, the inhabitants' houses, streets, and ways of living appeared to be even more unclean and diseased than before it. As a consequence, many of the buildings and neighborhoods demolished were those inhabited by prominent supporters of the Mughal kings. The very streets whose mansions and bazaars had earlier enchanted British travelers with their picturesque qualities were now denigrated as unsanitary and a danger

Figure 4.1
View of cleared area between Jama Masjid and the Red Fort, 1870s. The fort wall is in the distance.

Figure 4.2
A view of the city from
the top of the main gate
of the fort, *c.*1846.
Chandni Chowk is to the
far right and the Jami
Masjid to the far left.
Most of the buildings up
to the Jami Masjid were
cleared after 1857.

to public health. The clearance around the Fort was both a military strategy to provide a glacis, and also a punitive measure. Included in the demolitions were some of the city's most prestigious *mahallā*, the finest mosques and the grandest *haveli* (Figure 4.2).[16] In the wake of the unrest, distinctions made by official interventions between areas that were 'diseased' and those that were disloyal were ambiguous, to say the least. In 1858, the government also cleared five hundred yards around the city wall and moat (referred to as the 'ditch') and declared that no building activity was to be permitted in this area. Since the population of Delhi living outside the walls was scattered and small at the time, and since the few suburban settlements that did exist were distant from the wall, this clearance did not call for the mass-demolition that had been necessary around the Fort.

Delhi, the city of minarets and mansions that had impressed European travelers some decades earlier, was now reduced to a collection of 'native huts' as official accounts described it. Prevailing theories of sanitary and medical science were used to support such a view. A Public Works Department engineer observed of the clearances in the Chandni Chowk and Ellenborough Tank area, 'clearance is so strongly recommended by the Medical Officer and will besides be a public improvement adding to the general health and cleanliness of the neighborhood.'[17] Some clearances were also undertaken regardless of their proximity to European inhabitation. As one military officer noted:

Such clearances as appeared to the D.C. and myself advisable on general sanitary or other grounds independent of the question of the locality to be occupied by the troops – have been or are clearly completed. The principal clearance has been that of a broad street from the Chandnee Chowk and the Jumma Musjid by which a very thickly populated part of the city has been opened out through which there was no possibility of transit previously by wheeled conveyances. Through the other parts of the city the roads are generally I think sufficiently broad and open. This clearance together with one minor one that have also been effected appear to the D.C. and myself all that it is admirable and attempts under present circumstances.[18]

The British justified these aggressive, dramatic, and almost Napoleonic clearances as necessary for reasons of health, sanitation, and security – especially of the soldiers.[19] A British officer observed of the anxieties over the demolition expenses:

[I] have it always before my mind and I believe that it is a right way of regarding it that European soldiers in the country are very expensive and so thoroughly well worth lasting care of that any sums expended in providing for and increasing their comfort and general health, are well laid out as the loss of a well trained and thoroughly disciplined British soldier from causes which might have been prevented is in reality equivalent to far more than 1,000 Rupees that each man is generally supposed to cost to Government as not only money but time is required to replace them.[20]

Official documents of the period were dominated by such concerns over the health of the troops, particularly in the climate of Delhi. The heat, dust, and lashing monsoon rains had long been formidable climatic factors for Europeans in India. Unexplained diseases, sickness, and death had always been impediments to European domination of 'the tropics.'[21]

In Delhi, malaria, cholera, the 'Delhi fever,' poor water, heat, and damp all threatened the health of British soldiers. From the official perspective, Delhi, like other cities of the 'Orient,' was insanitary and disorderly. The *Report of the Royal Commission on the Sanitary State of the Army in India* in 1863 spoke of Delhi's 'bad air,' 'badly constructed and ill-ventilated habitations,' 'poor drainage,' 'unhealthy trades and depraved moral condition of vice and poverty,' and finally condemned the inhabitants of the city as 'irremediably vicious.'[22]

The clearances around the Fort and the relocation of European civilians to the north of the city distanced them from what were now seen as the threatening native areas. Following the uprising, British civilians moved out of the walled city to the newly established Civil Lines to the north. In addition to the cantonment area to the north, troops moved into strategic locations within the city and the Red Fort. The heavily policed area of the Civil Lines was also meant to exclude Indians. As the move was politically motivated, the spatial segregation of European dwellings from what the British now viewed as the unsanitary and unhealthy indigenous ones also required the articulation of boundaries.[23] In the aftermath of the rebellion, the principles guiding the earliest 'improvement' efforts of the British in Delhi were similar to convictions that led the French to formalize the *cordon sanitaire* in Algiers, and almost a century later, Rabat.[24] The spatial segregation of European troops and civilians was accomplished by massive clearances to the north and east of the city while Indian inhabitants crowded together in what remained of the southern and western portions.

Careful bureaucratic procedures in the execution of the clearances obscured the arbitrariness of official decisions.

In contrast to the peremptoriness of the demolitions, official correspondence shows a meticulous concern with their administration. An engineer was appointed to oversee the demolitions around the palace. Every aspect of the leveling was laboriously debated and meticulously documented. The exact line of clearance, the expense of razing, the value of the properties involved, the compensation to owners and the timing of the demolitions were all carefully considered.[25] Each wrecking operation was preceded by deliberations over the plan and expenses.[26] An appearance of fairness, objectivity, and formalized process was meant to contrast with the rule of Indian kings whom the British represented as despots. The bureaucratic structure of government also made what otherwise looked to be a brash action very systematic and helped to keep colonial officials accountable. This official process of decision-making was, however, exclusive to the colonial administrators and did not involve any of the native citizenry. Officials took it upon themselves to purge the city, a campaign that included both political cleansing through the eradication of disloyal factions and conspirators, and a physical cleansing through the demolition of neighborhoods perceived as congested and infested with disease.

Drastic and heavy-handed as the demolitions were, they were tempered by local resistance. After a four-month siege, residents were allowed into the evacuated city (Figure 4.3). First, the Hindus, paying ten percent of their wealth as tax, then the Muslims, paying twenty-five percent, and finally, free admission was granted to the remaining. However, all residents had to prove ownership before regaining their properties. Officials carefully surveyed and assessed houses that were confiscated and were to be torn down. Each house owner affected, and whose property had not been seized, received compensation. The reparation was in the form of a 'ticket' the value of which was equal to that of the property. In the auctions of confiscated land and houses, the tickets could be used in lieu of payment.[27] In this manner, the clearances not only altered the space of the city by removing houses and streets but also, through the auctions, reconstituted its social composition.

Some Indians, who had remained loyal to the British and aspired to share in the administrative authority of the new rulers, participated in the cleansing by supervising operations or disclosing the identities of rebels and conspirators. Most, however, were outraged, angered, and terrified by the bloody events. Many simply fled the city, never to return. Those who stayed reacted vociferously against the clearances. Property-owners registered their protests through petitions, pleas, and campaigns that brought together individuals, neighborhood groups, and communities.[28]

Merchants in Delhi came together to gain concessions from the new rulers. The British found the 'native gentlemen,' presumably men of property and wealth, a force to contend with. The initial line of demolition in the area around the Fort included the Dariba Kalan, a prosperous neighborhood with the promi-

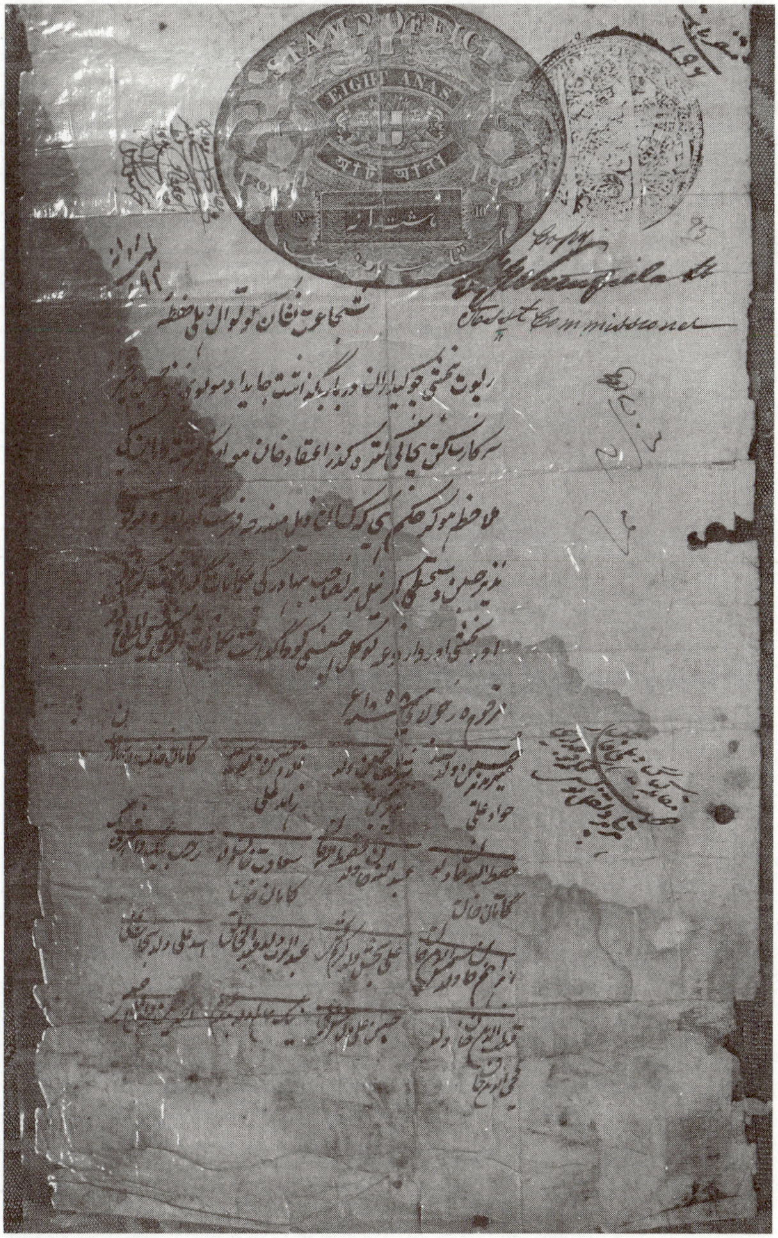

Figure 4.3
A sample *parvānāh* (order or pass) to re-enter the city after the British had cleared Delhi of all inhabitants in 1857. An instruction written to Kotwal, Delhi by Mr. J. B. Naverli, Officiating Commissioner of Delhi, to allow Mirza Nazir Hussain and other relatives along with Nawab Qutb-ud-Din Khan to enter Delhi city and that their property be restored to them. Dated August 30, 1859. Every family re-entering the city required permission to re-establish themselves.

nent bazaar of goldsmiths, silversmiths, jewelers, and dealers in precious stones. The Dariba bazaar remains today, as it was then, a stronghold of Delhi's *baniya* (trading) community and an important commercial center in the city.[29] A government order was issued for the clearance of the Dariba in 1860 (Figure 4.4).[30] Upon learning that their properties were to be demolished and fearing for the

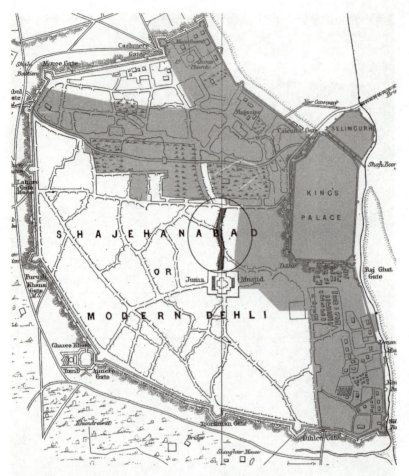

Figure 4.4
Plan of Delhi showing
the location of the
Dariba and the line of
clearances. Dariba leads
north from Jama Masjid
to Chandni Chowk.

loss of both their homes and businesses, the residents of the Dariba and of the city vehemently protested the clearances and wrote several petitions to the government.[31]

The Commissioner of Delhi, W. C. Plowden, received several of these pleas. The petitions represented the Dariba as the symbolic center of the entire Hindu population of Delhi. They argued that the route of the Ram Lila procession, one of the most significant for Hindus in the city, passed through the Dariba, demonstrating the importance of the street. From this perspective, the clearance of the Dariba would be a loss not only for the residents of that neighborhood but to the whole city. In addition, residents of the Dariba claimed that their properties were worth ten times the official estimate of a million Rupees.[32] By July 1860 the government conceded:

> His Excellency [the Lieut. Governor of the Punjab] has no hesitation in directing that the
> demolitions should *stop short of the Dureeba* and that *street*, for the preservation of

which a large part of the population are very desirous, should be spared. If the Governor General was not aware of the importance of what appears to be attached to this line of buildings by the Hindoo inhabitants, *and as it was contemplated by the Engineers* that the ground should eventually be *occupied* more or less *by new buildings* which can as well be placed . . . the demolition is certainly not necessary in a military view. The intention of *the street* in no way affects the security of the Palace and its Garrison.[33]

The merchants had clearly succeeded in persuading officials to alter the line of demolition to spare the main bazaar of the Dariba.

This concession on the part of the British was a major victory for the mercantile community. The propertied and politically organized group of merchants was a category of Indian society whose support was crucial to the success of British rule. While the idea of cleansing the city for reasons of sanitation had identified the Dariba as a diseased neighborhood, in fact the inhabitants of the area were among the most prosperous and powerful in Delhi. Despite the enormous emphasis on medical and sanitary science, it is obvious that the labeling of neighborhoods as either diseased or healthy, or as worthy of being preserved or demolished was clearly political. That the officials were forced to give in to the Dariba merchants, even in the midst of brash demolitions, is evidence of the power of local politics in shaping the outcome of colonial urban interventions.

MUNICIPALIZATION AND URBAN SANITATION

Once the dust had settled on the uprising and the demolitions that followed in its wake, official efforts at improving the sanitation of Delhi city focused on the development of a new infrastructure using the advanced industrial and engineering solutions of the West. In Western Europe and the United States, increasing attention to the scientific study of public health and technological innovations had imbued the idea of *city improvement* with the best progressive ideals. It implied collective energy towards the application of new technologies such as efficient systems for water supply and waste removal and transportation systems. By the turn of the century, electricity was also included. Solutions to a healthy urban life laid emphasis on the technological and administrative apparatus that would deliver them. A city that allowed the quick and effective movement of goods and services was the new urban ideal and, in the deteriorating environment of their industrialized cities, urban reformers in Western Europe increasingly held city governments responsible for the provision of clean, safe environments, often backed by national legislation. Scientific calculations for the provision of services assumed the space of the city to be a socially undifferentiated territory needing rationally provided facilities and for the residents to be undifferentiated beings. Emphasizing efficient and rationalized infrastructure, the municipalization of urban services in Delhi became at once a way of policing 'dangerous' disease as well as representing superior governance.[34]

Prior to British intervention, the provision of water had been taken as an aesthetic, symbolic, and functional element in Shahjahan's Delhi. In the seventeenth and eighteenth centuries, the Faiz *nahar* (canal) ran through the two main streets of Delhi, channeling water from the old Tughluq canals through the city.[35] Along Chandni Chowk the Faiz *nahar*, lined with stone, ran all the way from Lahore Gate at the western end of the city through the royal palace on the east, opening up to form square or octagonal pools at periodic intervals. To the south, a canal traveled down the center of Faiz Bazaar. Water from the Tughluq canals branched to bring a supply to the Faiz *nahar*, to the palaces, mosques and gardens of the city. Small pools in the courtyards of the larger *havelis* were connected to the Faiz *nahar* through underground *ganāts* (channels). In addition to the canals, a number of *bā'olī* (tanks) and wells supplied ground water to the city.[36] Over the years some of the canals had gone dry or become clogged. During the 1820s, the British cleaned, cleared, and reopened the Ali Mardan Canal (as the rebuilt Tughluq canals were called), providing a source of fresh water. In 1846, at the suggestion of Lord Ellenborough, the colonial government constructed a large pool (called Ellenborough Tank or Lal Diggi) in front of the palace as a reservoir for water.[37] In 1867, the canals were operative as were most

Figure 4.5
Map of southern part of Delhi showing *bā'olī* (open wells), canals, and other water bodies, 1873. The river Jumuna is to the right.

of the city wells (Figure 4.5). But the water had increasingly turned brackish and providing safe, potable water for the troops was of immediate military concern. Shahjahan's engineering accomplishments in the city also included a system of drains known as the Shahjahani drains.[38]

Rather than updating and improving existing systems, efforts to modernize the city rejected them in favor of advanced technical solutions under the guise of 'progress.' When W. H. Greathed, Deputy Superintendent of Delhi Canals, studied the engineering systems existing in the city in 1852, he had praised the Shahjahani systems and made a series of recommendations to improve the existing networks of water supply and drainage.[39] With the advent of the Delhi Municipal Committee in the aftermath of 1857, Greathed's recommendations were put aside in favor of new schemes based on recent accomplishments in engineering and technology. The city was a system that was to operate smoothly, effectively, and healthily. By 1902 Delhi had acquired new wide roads, vast open spaces around what was now known as the Red Fort, electric lights, water works, and new sewers all aimed at convincing the European observer that Delhi was now a 'healthy' city (Figure 4.6).

When the Delhi Municipal Committee was formed in 1863, the colonial government appointed Europeans to key positions.[40] Indians in the Committee were selected by the colonial government or elected by the subset of Delhi's residents, both European and Indian, who had voting rights.[41] The Indians chosen were those that were influential among the locals for their wealth and status as well being respected by the British for their loyal service and Westernized ways of living and working. Clearly, the policies of the Committee would be

Figure 4.6
A view of Chandni Chowk in the 1860s shows with a covered and paved Faiz canal that earlier ran down the length of the whole street.

informed by Western Europe's experience of 'progress' and the accomplishments of Western science.

Until the 1860s the city was under the authority of the *kotwāl* (city magistrate) and his 12 *thānedār* (head of a *thānā* or city ward) and their *mahallādār* (heads of *mahallā* or neighborhoods) who had administered, policed, collected taxes, and regulated the city. By 1906, in addition to direct control over the city police the Municipal Committee controlled the building, improving, maintaining, and administering of the city. The municipality provided for 'public safety' such as control over fire, lighting, police and rewards for the destruction of wild animals and snakes; 'public health and convenience' including water supply, drainage, cleaning of drains and sewers, garbage collection, night soil disposal, construction, repairing, and cleaning of streets, hospitals, dispensaries, plague charges, vaccination, the erection of slaughter houses and markets, the sale and vending of food, public bathing, cremations and burials, the prohibition of animals such as cows and pigs within the city, the collection of house tax and taxes on milk cattle, the provision of *dak-bungalows* and *sarā'ī*, arboriculture, public gardens and experimental cultivation, veterinary charges, regulation of building construction, setting up of health clinics, and the collection and maintenance of health statistics including the registration of births and deaths; and 'public instruction' including schools and colleges, libraries, museums, and menageries. They took exceptional interest in providing a purpose-built public

Figure 4.7
Plan of a new market.

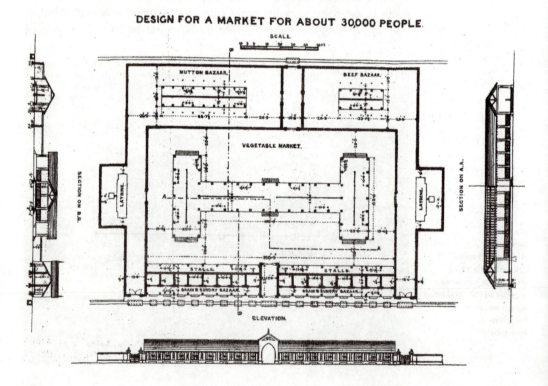

DESIGN FOR A MARKET FOR ABOUT 30,000 PEOPLE.

market (Figure 4.7).[42] While the municipality claimed as priorities the adequate supply of drinking water and sewage disposal, municipal engineers and officials also widened, repaired, and watered roads regularly to keep the dust down, introduced electricity, improved street lighting, built police stands and garbage dumps within each *mahallā*, constructed public latrines and urinals, cleared swampy vegetation, and filled ditches (Figure 4.8).[43] Although their primary responsibility was for maintaining a police force, municipalities in India were also expected to raise funds for sanitary upkeep. Taxes and fines were an important source of income for the municipality.

The Municipal Committee saw a new water-supply scheme as the first and most important scheme on their part and a significant step toward the sanitary improvement of the city, 'not only as one calculated to promote the welfare of the people at large, but also as ultimately connected with the health of the military cantonments at Delhi.'[44] Water was to be collected from the River Yamuna and purified before distribution so that filtered water would be supplied throughout the city in pipes under the ground. Officials assumed that well-to-do

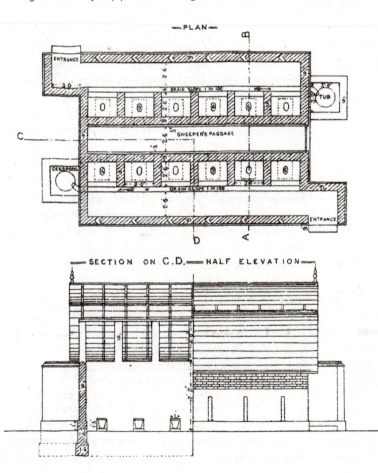

Figure 4.8
New designs for toilets for European-style sitting. The Western type of water closet was greatly encouraged. Intended for use by Indians, the design attempted to standardize optimum dimensions for efficient and effective functioning. Indian style ones for squatting were sometimes provided as a concession to local preferences.

gentlemen would be willing to pay extra rates to have pipes laid to bring water into their homes thus 'to save their women from parading themselves in public.'[45]

British engineers proposed advanced technical solutions to resolve the water supply and drainage problems in Delhi. In the 1880s, one scheme for the provision of water supply required the removal of Chandrawal village in the vicinity of the walled city as well as a substantial forested area, the Bela plantation. From the technical view, the human costs of the elimination and the impact of the loss were less important than the location of supply-wells and service reservoir, their capacity, and the yield that were all calculated by the latest principles of engineering. In contrast to the existing ground-water-supply system, the new distribution of water was based on an estimated daily demand. According to the calculations of the Chief Engineer of Punjab, Major General C. Pollard, in 1882,

> The various parts of the scheme have been designed to meet a demand of 3,200,000 gallons in 24 hours. The present population of Delhi is 167,000 souls, and as the daily provision is 16 gallons per head, the supply allows for an expansion of 20 per cent.[46]

Detailed regulations specified even the sizes of the pipes and ferules connecting houses to the supply and disposal systems.[47] Sanitary improvement depended on the introduction of scientific systems and the construction of new sanitary spaces as well as on the coercion and policing of the 'natives' to reform their use and management of the environment. The Municipal Committee divided the entire city into twelve administrative wards and appointed a *jamedar* for each ward to oversee garbage collection, street cleaning, and the collection of night soil.

For the officials caught up in their daily bureaucratic battles, technological achievements and regulation had become synonymous with urban improvement. Visible and quantifiable achievements convinced senior officials, distant European observers, and local inhabitants of the good work done by the Municipal Committee. The Delhi municipality measured its success in terms of technological innovations in infrastructure including telephones, electricity, water supply, sanitation, roads, and bridges (Figure 4.9).[48] Chronicling the achievements of the municipal administration, Madho Pershad, an ex-Municipal Commissioner of Delhi and an ex-magistrate, noted that between the years 1863 and 1921 much was done towards the improvement of the city.[49] His list included the specific number of roads repaired, drains cleared, and new ones constructed, and wells cleaned each year. Pleased at the achievements of the Delhi Municipal Committee in over three decades of its establishment, the Lieutenant Governor of Punjab congratulated the municipal staff during a visit to the city in 1902:

> I am pleased to notice your remarks regarding the development of the prosperity of your city and the scheme for its improvement which you have already carried out and now have under your consideration. I have to congratulate you on the progress made in your Water-Works and your drainage scheme, and I trust that the negotiation intended to

Figure 4.9
Sketch of an iron bridge
under construction in
Delhi. The large-span,
iron bridge carrying
railway tracks across the
river was an innovation
in Delhi as was the
industrial aesthetic.

provide the city with the advantages of electricity both for lighting and for traction, will
be successfully carried through.[50]

The officials certainly had no doubts that their actions were in the best interests
of the native citizens. Almost two decades later, Patrick Geddes, critical of the
approach of British sanitarians in India, remarked:

> The engineering and sanitary principles which the best conventional text-books, like
> Turner's 'Sanitation in India,' summarize, are simply those of in the first place performing
> the difficult task of collecting all these varieties of filth into gigantic accumulated
> quantities, and then of attempting, with more or less success, the even more
> extraordinary engineering feat of getting rid of these accumulations again.[51]

Despite an overwhelming concern for sanitation, the projects were only
partially successful in transforming the city. In 1869 the Municipal Committee
proposed installing an advanced network of wells, canals, and pipes to supply
piped drinking water to households. After funds had been arranged and the final
design approved, construction work on the water-works project began only in
1882. Residents protested against the additional taxation and the local government found it hard to convince the imperial authorities to give them loans.
Waterworks to bring water from the River Yamuna into people's homes, a
project that was conceived in 1869, took almost twenty years to be realized.[52] By
1894 a mere 146 private houses had water connections, however, with an overwhelming preference for the Civil Lines and Lothian Road areas inhabited by
Europeans. On a similar note, while the municipality saw road repair and construction as one of its charges, municipal documents indicate that by 1910 the
roads most regularly attended to and maintained included the Chandni Chowk,

Esplanade Road, Queen's Road, Lothian Road, and others in the northern part of the city most frequently used by the British officials, European tourists, and commercial vehicles. By 1912 the municipality had succeeded in building only twenty-five public latrines and three public urinals for a city with a population a little under 500,000.[53] After years of effort at improving hygiene, cleanliness, and sanitation in the city, the Sanitary Commissioner of the Government of India was appalled at the filth on a tour of the city in 1912:

> Most of the main thoroughfares outside the bazar were clean and well swept but immediately one left these and entered the bazar proper there was a general air of untidiness and neglect of sweeping and in the side lanes and back areas rubbish and litter were everywhere in evidence. Much of this it seems to me is due to the system of refuse collection in vogue whereby the sweepers are supposed to bring to places termed 'dalaos' all sweepings from the streets, silt from the drains and rubbish and garbage mixed with night-soil from the private houses and latrines. At most of these 'dalaos' no provision whatsoever is made for this filth which is merely dumped in a heap on the bare ground. With such a system one dumping place soon becomes as good as another and unauthorized 'dalaos' quickly increase in number till there is a heap of filth in every convenient corner.[54]

The partiality in the provision of municipal services was not limited to a focus on main streets to the exclusion of the smaller ones. The area of municipal jurisdiction omitted the European enclaves in the Civil Lines and the cantonment.[55] Yet, taxes and the income of the Delhi Municipal Committee paid for the provision of infrastructure and services for the cantonments and the civil station. The municipality annually contributed Rs.3,000 to the Cantonment Committee to pay for water supply to the cantonment area.[56]

For the British administrators, the welfare of the European troops and civilian population took precedence over the health of the local citizens in the provision of all infrastructure. As in the clearance of swampy vegetation, the early uses of electricity, too, were to benefit the health of the British troops:

> Sir Louis Dane personally inspected the defective drains in the Fort near the quarter guard and the hospital, and fully agrees that, in the interests of the troops, these are the most crying evils and should be treated at once as proposed by the committee. Electric power is being brought into the Fort for the gardens round the imperial buildings, and the cost of an extra pump for the drainage will be small. His Honour would again urge that, as proposed by the Commissioner, the power should be used for fans and lights in the barracks. A British garrison must always be retained in the Fort, and the present garrison there, unless it is constantly changed, is, owing to illness, liable to become a skeleton force and a source of grave political danger. If the improvements in the Fort are taken up at once, the place could be put into sanitary order before the malaria season sets in.[57]

Electric lighting came to Delhi only in 1902 to illuminate the camp of celebrations of visiting British Royalty. Tramlines were also introduced at that time connecting areas to the west and north to the heart of the walled city. In fact, improved infrastructure was more available to Europeans in the city (or rather, just outside of it) where it was also more visible to visitors from the Western world. Creating visible markers of improvement served to represent the government in a positive light: a well-managed city reflected the state's complete authority and superior rule.

During the visits of European dignitaries, the municipality and its provision of services was significantly to the fore. Grand Imperial assemblages in 1877, 1902, and 1911 celebrated the coronation of the British regent as Emperor of India (Figure 4.10).[58] The imperial assemblages in Delhi each gave impetus to new projects for the provision of water supply, electricity, garbage disposal, cleaning of drains and sewers, street cleaning, and even the electric tramway in the city.[59] For instance, an official report of the municipality noted:

Figure 4.10
The substantial arrangements for the Imperial Assemblage of 1877 when Queen Victoria was crowned Empress of India. Princes and kings from all over India came to pay homage at a grand *darbar* (Royal audience) held by Lord Lytton, Viceroy of India. Amphitheater for Europeans is on the left, Lord Lytton's canopy in the center, 'native' princes to the right, and spectators in the foreground.

> The great event of the year was the Visit of Their Royal Highnesses the Prince and Princess of Wales to Delhi in December 1905. In honour of the visit, the routes used by Their Royal Highnesses, were decorated by the Committee and citizens with triumphal arches, flags and banners, and on the night of the fireworks all the public and private principal buildings, street-gates and churches were illuminated; the Town Hall was specially illuminated and decorated.[60]

During the Coronation Durbar of 1902, Madho Pershad observed with pride that the municipality had paid special attention to water supply, 'conservancy,' lighting, road watering, and repairs.[61] He noted with satisfaction, 'Electric light

installation was ready before the Durbar events began and the lighting of main streets with lamps of 2,000 candle power each added much to the comfort of the enormous crowds.' This bias was in addition to a spatial prejudice in the provision of municipal services in the city whereby the municipality favored the northern and eastern parts of the city most frequented by European visitors.

The inherent favoritism towards Europeans was itself in conflict with the libertarian and apolitical sanitary utopia reflected in Benjamin Ward Richardson's vision of 'Hygiea.'[62] Ideally, the rationalized organization of health was meant to sanitize equally all areas of the city. The technical computations for the provision of infrastructure also calculated equally for the entire population of the city. However, the health of the European soldiers, officials, and settlers came before that of the indigenous populations. The political agendas of colonialism contradicted and undermined the rationalist ideals of modernity.

A lack of adequate funds inhibited the establishment of new schemes for the provision of services in the main city. The income of the Municipal Committee was based on taxes, including levies on goods coming in and out of the city, on rents from the confiscated properties that now belonged to the Municipal Committee, and on income tax. Delhi's residents vehemently opposed increased taxes to pay for sanitary improvements – especially when it benefited them marginally if at all.[63] Yet, municipal funds were scarce and largely dependent on taxation for many of the improvement efforts. The projects on which municipal funds were expended were most often those that were likely to bring returns to the municipality such as the facilitation of commerce through the improvement and reorganization of roads and transportation.

EQUITY AND OPPOSITION IN THE REGULATIONS

City officials did not apply sanitary reform uniformly even within the native sections of the city. Many among the educated elite of Delhi had become ardent followers of Western science and were convinced of its transformative powers. Some residents, for instance, especially those educated in the British system, believed in the virtues of municipal governance. Such citizens held the municipality accountable for delivering a clean and well-maintained city. Increasingly, professionals, the educated elite, and those employed in the colonial administration, moved out of the city to live in the healthier environment of the bungalows in the Civil Lines.[64] For them, the efforts of the Delhi Municipal Committee were too feeble and inadequate to achieve the sanitary environment they desired.

As early as the 1860s English-language newspapers in Delhi criticized the municipality and its individual members for falling short of European standards.[65] Those residents who were in agreement with the colonial ideals of sanitation and health not only resented the preferential treatment of the cantonment and civil station but also the unequal treatment of different areas within the city. Some residents of Kutcha Nawab Mirza, for example, felt that their neighborhood had been discriminated against in the improvement schemes. Three residents, Abbas

Hussain, Haider Hasan, and Hazi Abdul Samed, upset that the construction of new drains was causing them more nuisance than they had suffered previously, complained to the Commissioner of Delhi:

> The open drains just constructed in this quarter have been a source of general inconvenience, and a special causation of epidemics. They are always over-flooded with filthy and decaying matters, and produce so horrible and poisonous a smell to state.
>
> It seems obvious that the staff of the Municipality pays no heed to the sanitation as well as the protection of the poor native subjects. The cleanliness of this locality is totally overlooked, and whenever after four or five days the said drains are nominally washed off all the filth is too lavishly thrown along the ways which makes walking through extremely difficult, more especially in the darkness of the night.[66]

They alleged that the level of the drains had been twice rectified but the slopes were still incorrect. The residents accused the British government of negligence in regard to hygiene as well as poor engineering – the very issues they prided themselves as superior to the Mughal rulers. For all their professed commitment, they charged, the British had not accomplished sanitary reform:

> This fatal epidemic [the plague] was never dreamed of by the undersigned as long as the old underground drains were existing but thanks to the new scheme they did not remain unshared of the sufferings of their fellow sufferers. The winter season shall be expired anyhow, but this hot weather it is hoped shall be proved more unbearable when every body has to sleep in the small court yards of his . . . lodgings and the nasty drains flowing so closely over his head. If they remain the same as they are, the 'cholera' shall surely have its share of sweeping off the rest of the populace.[67]

Contrary to official statements that portrayed the citizens as ignorant and filthy and in need of British benevolence, the residents did not see themselves as the passive recipients of a sanitary environment. Clearly, some were quite well informed of the relationship between cholera, sanitation, and infection.

Yet, for many other citizens, the sanitary improvements were unnecessary, disruptive, and in conflict with their interests and customary ways. For instance, officials identified the lack of public utilities as one cause of disease and insanitation. They undertook the construction of neighborhood *dalao* (garbage-collection areas), public urinals, and latrines. The ideal locations of these facilities were based on 'scientific' calculations that included the precise distance between the facilities and the minimum number required per population. A Land Acquisition Act required residents to sell such properties as were necessary for municipal improvement efforts. If they refused to sell, the land was forcibly acquired under the Act and a minimum compensation granted to the owners. Municipal works undertaken also included the 'removal of nuisance.'[68]

Opposition from residents, however, prevented officials from achieving their sanitary objectives. The construction of public urinals was one improvement that residents frequently protested.[69] From the perspective of the Municipal Committee, the facilities were essential while the residents in the vicinity of their location were opposed to them.[70] As we saw in Chapter 3, Azimuddin, a shop-keeper in Pahargunj, opposed the construction of a public urinal across from his shop and petitioned the Municipal Committee for its removal. He saw the urinal as an intrusion onto his turf and expressed his displeasure by throwing *malba* (construction waste of stones and dirt) on it.[71] In some instances, officials appealed to the persuasive powers of prominent citizens to help enforce sanitary measures. The consistent opposition of the residents of Katra Tambakoo to the construction of urinals perplexed the authorities who felt that without them 'a great nuisance is caused.'[72] Eventually, the Municipal Committee elicited a promise from Lala Jawahar Lal, an elected representative of two Wards to the Municipal Committee and a part owner of the Katra Tambakoo, that he would have a urinal constructed within the month.[73] In the face of relentless opposition, officials chose locations inhabited by the disempowered and politically weak, such as the house of the prostitute Mussammmat Ghasiti Jan.[74] Officials passed orders to forcibly acquire her house, demolish and rebuild it as a *dalao* (garbage-collection area) in the neighborhood of Chatta Shahji.

Inequities in health reform were sometimes created by the very individuals in charge of implementing the measures. In practice, not all of the British were united in their commitment to sanitize. In the aftermath of the uprising, British troops were called upon to elect 'prize agents,' responsible for gathering movable property in the captured city. The items so confiscated were to con-tribute to a common fund, later distributed as rewards to those who fought valiantly. In his memoir, Charles Griffith gives a vivid account of the treasures obtained from the vacated houses.[75] Many merchants, eager to make peace and carry on their businesses, traded favors with the prize agents to reinstate them-selves. For instance, while most Indians were expelled from the city, the residents of Katra Neel, a prominent textile bazaar, gained re-admission three months before the other residents.[76] The merchants of this bazaar had negotiated their entry with local British officials. Prize agents sold out whole streets for sums ranging from Rs.5,000 to Rs.50,000.[77] While fighting for British interests and gathering assets for the common fund, a few prize agents used their power for personal gains, even though it was in direct contravention of procedures.

CONTENDING WITH EXISTING SYSTEMS

Many traditions of science and medicine were prevalent in India during the nine-teenth century. From complex astronomical calculations to predict the movement of planets and constellations to formulating the ideal sizes of rooms and build-ings and their orientation, Indians followed a variety of oral and textual systems. Masons and builders often followed Islamic or Hindu principles of building that guided drainage slopes, types of vegetation, and orientation as well as the rela-tive location of spaces within structures.[78]

In the provision of urban infrastructure, where engineering structures did not prove adequate, human-service organizations prevailed. Sweepers serviced

Figure 4.11
A sweeper (*mehtar*) with
basket and broom, and a
water-carrier (*bihishti*)
with a leather water
sack, *c*.1840.

the pit latrines of houses, carrying refuse to designated spots outside the city walls where they developed and sold manure.[79] The sweepers also swept neighborhood streets on local contract. While most houses had wells for water supply, *bhistis* were water carriers whose primary occupation was to collect and sell water from leather containers slung over their shoulders. From selling drinking water in the bazaars to supplying daily water to homes without wells, the *bhistis* formed a human water-supply system in the city. The task of watering streets to keep down the dust was also traditionally assigned to *bihistī* (Figure 4.11).

More significant among the indigenous systems of medicine in the city were the *ayurvedic* method of the *vaid*, and the *unānī* practiced by the *hakīm*. Until the introduction of Western medicine in the nineteenth century, the *vaid* and *hakīm* guarded the city's health by dispensing drugs based on herbs and advice on a variety of ailments (Figure 4.12). *Dā'i* or midwives cared for pregnant women in their homes and delivered babies. Where Western sanitary science emphasized disinfecting the physical environment and isolating the source of the disease, both the *aryurvedic* and *unānī* schools focused on correcting imbalances within the body and strengthening the body's resistance.[80] In Delhi, environmental hygiene was governed by rituals of cleanliness such as in the spatial separation of toilets, and the absence of outdoor footwear inside the precincts of the home.

Whatever the ideals of sanitation, it was those charged with their implementation that shaped the extent of regulation and reform in Delhi. Both the execution and the policing of the new measures of hygiene was the work of local sanitary workers. From the official perspective, policing of regulations was imperative to achieving sanitary reform amongst a reluctant population. Surveillance and policing, negotiation and coercion, punishment and penalty, all were

Figure 4.12
A *vaid* or druggist in his store, 1825. A ledge projecting on to the street was probably used to serve customers. While some customers might conduct business from the street, others might have come up to the store to sit on floor mats. A wooden bench next to the steps may also have been used by customers.

integral to the making of a 'healthy' city. In India, municipalities were formed by the extension of a Police Act.[81] In the year 1878–79 one third of Delhi municipality's total income was spent on maintaining a police force.[82] Yet officials lamented the lack of sanitary inspectors in the city.[83] In 1875–76 the wards were further subdivided and an additional level introduced in the hierarchy of supervision over sanitary work in the city, including the collection of garbage and night soil, and the cleaning of streets, drains, and sewers:

The conservancy of the city absorbed earnest attention of the Committee throughout the year. The city and suburbs were divided into ilakas, each being entrusted to a subcommittee of three members. The members regularly inspected their ilakas, and remedied every evil that was brought to light. This system was found to be satisfactory, as it made every member thoroughly acquainted with his ilaka and its requirements. The cleaning of streets, the removal of sweepings and the flushing of drains were carefully attended to during the year.[84]

Whatever the supervisory hierarchy, the actual work of cleaning and sweeping remained that of neighborhood sanitary workers called *mehtar* or *mahallā* sweepers. Like other occupational groups in the city, historically, sweepers were under the protection of the wealthy patrons. With the rise of the bazaar and the increasing specialization of services, sweepers too operated as an occupational group much like any other, albeit one with low income and status. In a city where caste and occupation were intricately knit together and where both were hereditary, the sweepers claimed their work as their birth-right and enjoyed complete monopoly over it. Sweepers lived in small enclaves of their own, amidst the mansions and houses of mid-nineteenth-century Delhi.[85] As a specialized occupational body, sweepers had a tacit agreement among their members over their responsibilities and duties.

The sweepers divided the city into territories according to their rules of operation independent of the municipal divisions.[86] Included in their agreement was a mutual respect for turf. In a society where women of 'respectable' households were secluded from public view, and where social hierarchies were spatially delineated in the interactions, sweepers enjoyed free entry to all households – through the back entrance. Both men and women worked as sweepers though the latter had greater access to the *zanānā* areas of households. They entered houses through a back or side entrance that led up to the privy pit. Accessibility of the privy from the outside was a major factor in its placement within the house.[87] Night soil from the privies was collected as head-load or, later, in carts.[88] The sweepers had entry to every house in their area and were knowledgeable about the daily affairs of the household through a network of servants and service people.[89] Although at the bottom rung of the city's social hierarchy, even elite households were beholden to the sweepers for their services.

Prior to the municipal take-over of sewage and garbage collection as well as the cleaning of drains and sewers, the sweepers had enjoyed a monopoly over the night-soil in the city. Their daily collections were carried to vacant lands outside the city as land fills of their own design. They sold the manure to farmers and gardeners for additional income. The sanitary reform and conservancy measures of the Municipal Committee came in direct conflict not only with their social positions, their professional agreement, and their turf but also with their economic interests since the municipality threatened to claim rights over the night-soil. While the ideal of municipalized urban services rendered the sweepers redundant, in reality the municipality was dependent on the sweepers for the cleaning of and collection from privy pits, streets, and drains. Organized as a professional body, the sweepers were able to press their demands as a group and to pressure the city into accepting their terms. While they worked for the municipality, they refused to be hired on to their rolls. Madho Pershad noted:

> The *mohalla* sweepers positively refused to enroll themselves as servants of the Municipality as they were clever enough to know that if they once did so, the Committee would exercise the right of dismissing and replacing those who neglected their work. These men were paid by a supply of food and clothes and by a varying rate from one anna to one rupee per dwelling. They neglected the privies and houses and the gallies [streets] under their charge and the house-owners were afraid of being still more neglected if they were to interfere.[90]

Curiously, municipal officials held the sweepers responsible for the sanitary condition of households rather than the owners themselves. Until 1912 waterborne latrines had yet to be introduced to the city (although they were the norm in the cantonments and civil lines). Sweepers were penalized for the unhygienic condition of the pit latrines. Rather than serving notices to the owner or occupier where the premises were dirty, the Municipal Committee prosecuted the sweepers.[91]

For their part, the sweepers did not hesitate to strike work to assert their demands. Madho Pershad noted the Municipal Committee's failure in implementing 'conservancy' measures one year:

> An attempt was made to get the whole of the Committee's carts into thorough repair with some success, and a number of smaller basket carts were introduced; but the mohalla sweepers threatened a strike, to be followed by legal proceedings if their monopoly of night-soil was interfered with or their birth-rights disturbed. These rights had all along been a very great stumbling block to improvement in the mohalla and house to house conservancy, and on one occasion, a few years back, a most inconvenient strike had occurred.[92]

While the municipality wrestled to control the sweepers, on other occasions they functioned as informal 'spies' for the municipal authorities, supplying household information on births and deaths.

During 1874–75 officials undertook the numbering of all houses within the city walls and outside it for census purposes.[93] Municipal regulations required people to register births and deaths in the family – an entirely new phenomenon in the city. Counting living members of the family was contrary to local custom, let alone making a public record of it. Although required by municipal regulation to do so, distrustful of city officials, people were reluctant to notify events in the family. Pershad observed that despite all efforts city officials were frustrated that 'the registration of births was not satisfactorily carried out as the people generally hid the same believing that the registers of births were kept with the intention of imposing some tax.'[94]

In order to overcome the problem, officials appointed the *mahallā* sweepers in charge of reporting births and deaths in the quarters of their beat. As social units, *mahallās* discouraged the presence of strangers and were even less amenable to surveillance and policing. Sweepers, by contrast, had access to the intimate confidences of every household through their daily visits to the houses and interactions with others in service of the households.

Shanno, an imaginary sweeper at the time, would have moved through the back alleys to enter the most elite *haveli* in her 'area.' While inside, she would exchange pleasantries with the maids and the cooks. She might even run into the barber who had been trying to win her favor. From all of them she would learn about the household. Her low social status would have rendered her 'invisible' to the members of the family leaving her free to observe them. As an experienced scavenger, Shanno was also an expert at interpreting household garbage for its own story. Had she not learnt otherwise, events such as birth, deaths, and marriages would have revealed themselves to Shanno in the household trash, with flowers and food indicating ceremonies of one kind or another.

The households themselves were likely innocent of the sweepers' mission. Even where they did know, families were forced to overlook their intrusion and win their favor since they depended on sweepers, and were threatened by the daunting task of finding replacements for them. At any event, silencing the entire network of service people associated with the household was an impossible task. Thus, through the sweepers, information about the household's domestic affairs was conveyed to the municipality. This policing by espionage was more insidious than any inspection by armed guards. By a curious inversion of power, the profane landscape of the sweepers – the privies and backdoors, the garbage bins and alleys – achieved police status as well as visibility and legitimacy in official eyes.

Indigenous medical systems, and concepts of hygiene too, confronted sanitary officials. In his study of sanitary professionals in India, Mark Harrison has observed that sanitary officers perceived themselves to be the vanguard not only of Western medicine but of Western culture in general and saw hygiene as a precondition for moral and material progress in India.[95] The *dawākhānā* and *vaidyashālā* (dispensaries) of well-known *hakīm* and *vaid* had been familiar landmarks in the busy bazaar streets. The birth of a child was an exciting event for the entire neighborhood as a *dai* would be brought to deliver the child at home. Municipal dispensaries and hospitals came to replace traditional medical services as well as their locales in people's mental maps of the city. By their celebration of Western medical and sanitary science, municipal improvements undermined the position of the customary guardians of health in the city who, in turn, were openly adversarial and particularly unhappy with the official endorsement of Western medical services, dispensaries, and hospitals.[96]

For the *vaid* and the *hakīm* the new Western science of sanitation meant not only a loss in business and clientele but also in their social status. Organized as a political group, they did what they could to discredit doctors of Western medicine and retain their own position in the city. At a time when Delhi was gripped by the fear of plague, for instance, widespread rumors of poison and earthquakes added to the panic in the city. The colonial government, having experienced opposition from the practitioners of indigenous medicine before, immediately held them responsible. They had been vocal in their protestations at the opening of new clinics and hospitals. Captain Davies, the Deputy Commissioner of Delhi observed:

> One of the chief rumours which have been consistently current is that people are to be poisoned by the Doctors. This at once diminished the attendance at the hospitals and was the cause of the women not going out to bathe, as it was rumoured that they would be seized and examined on the way and then given poisoned medicine. As showing to what extent such rumours spread, it was passed round that the Water Works tank was to be poisoned so that all those who drank the pipe water would die. The cause of the rumours cannot be stated with any certainty. I think however that they originated with the Hakims and Baids [vaids] as a simple way of discrediting European medicine and increasing their own practice.[97]

The officials' distrust of local health workers points to rivalry between two competing systems of medicine as much as it does to past experiences and inherent prejudices.

CONCLUSION

The overall statistics for child mortality and death rate as indicators of health showed that despite the greater incidence of disease in some years, health in the city's population had generally improved by the beginning of the twentieth century.[98] However, the records do not indicate that most of the city was in a 'dangerous,' 'diseased,' and 'slum'-like condition before the sanitary reforms. At the center of the foregoing discussion is not so much a quantitative analysis of colonial health achievements as a critical examination of the perceptions, interventions, and interpretations that reconstituted the physical form, social structure, and symbolic meaning of the urban landscape.

Numerous dispensaries and hospitals of Western medicine were in service by the early decades of the twentieth century as were new sewage and water-supply systems. Municipal regulations controlled every aspect of health in the city from building public facilities and garbage dumps to inspecting buildings and the sale of meat and vegetables. After more than a half century of sanitary improvements, new roads, railways, bridges, waterworks, electricity, tramways and telegraph lines, transformed the physical city – at least in some parts.

The clearances around the fort and the 'cleansing' of the city's most 'dangerous' neighborhoods effectively decimated Delhi's elite nobility; the confiscation of properties and the auctions that followed reconstituted the social geography of the communities. The discrediting of the vaid and hakīm and the informal upgrading of sweepers to census surveyors, also altered existing hierarchies. Sometimes purposefully and sometimes unwittingly, the location of public utilities and facilities interfered with or reinforced the social status of streets and places.

The most significant transformation in Delhi was the re-inscription of the meanings of disease, public health, good governance, and urban administration. The prominence given to environmental controls redefined the relationship of people to their surroundings. And the categorization of streets and neighborhoods as healthy and unhealthy assigned new values and created new hierarchies based on access to wellbeing. Biases in the provision of infrastructure too created new social and spatial ladders. In the supply of water (as also roads, sewage, and garbage disposal) the emphasis was on efficient distribution and functional availability rather than the significance of its presence or the rituals of interaction surrounding its use.

As remarkable as what the colonial officials accomplished was what they did not. With the application of sanitary science and rational planning, the physical, social, and symbolic transformation of the city was by no means complete. Despite the Haussmann-like clearances in Delhi, and grand re-naming of new places and roads such as, 'Champs Mars,' 'Esplanade,' and 'Boulevard,' the actual extent of rebuilding in Delhi was small in comparison to the comprehensive redesign of Paris. Sanitary science and municipalization sought at once to isolate the 'traditional' city and to transform it into a 'modern' one. The conflicts, paradoxes, and contradictions reveal the multiple perceptions of the city and the less visible alterations in the cultural landscape.

The simple application of scientific principles and absolute rationality to shape Delhi's landscape of health was complicated by many factors. The colonial administration felt a driving need to make urban life in India safe from the infectious diseases that threatened Europeans and demanded that the most recent advances in sanitary science be applied to control them. The British also needed to establish and maintain absolute authority and make the cities safe and secure for themselves. Perceptions of sanitary practices and slums in England made officials suspicious of Delhi's dense and irregular built form. Supporters of Western science and medicine were convinced of the transforming power of sanitation and technology. The deeply rooted beliefs and knowledge of indigenous scientific and medical systems were a force to contend with. Differences and self-interest among the officials allowed interpretations of policing and regulatory responsibilities that were at variance with the stated sanitary goals. Contrary to appearances and official representations, sanitary improvement was not simply a bureaucratic and scientific effort at urban management but was also a deeply political endeavor to construct a specific cultural vision of health.

Under the guise of sanitation, colonial officials undertook interventions that were sometimes dramatic and heavy-handed, as in the demolition of neighborhoods; at other times, they were less visible as in the by-laws, or even insidious as in the employment of sweepers to obtain demographic information. The various means were meant to achieve the common goal of a 'modern' sanitary utopia, one that conformed to what its proponents believed were objective scientific standards. The emphasis on clean air, water, and waste disposal was not only new to the locals but also in conflict with some indigenous practices and theories of health.[99]

Organized petitions, demonstrations, deliberate delay, non-cooperation, disobedience, vandalism, and non-compliance were all tactics the city people employed to negate the idealized vision of health of the officials. Those Indians who were convinced of the methods and ideals of Western science protested the inequity of municipal policies and regulations that served the European inhabited areas better than their own. Deep in the pockets of a seemingly 'traditional' city, some residents fought to be a part of the new sanitary utopia. These people were not only educated in the new medical theories and concepts of hygiene but were also equally well informed of both their rights and the government's responsibilities in what was purported to be a 'modern' administration in European terms.

The spatial separation of European and indigenous Indian populations was blurred by the large number of local service people who moved easily and constantly between the two spaces and also by the elite and educated Indians who moved out to inhabit the European enclaves outside the walled city. The isolation of the densely populated neighborhoods by the clearances around the fort and around the city walls only served to make the city more overcrowded and therefore an even greater threat to disease than before. The privileging of European enclaves in the provision of municipalized services meant that the modern sanitation and technology did not remedy the sources of disease in the old neighborhoods to an equal extent.

In Delhi notions of 'disease' and 'improvement' were themselves problematic. Whilst the purported objective of the official interventions was the amelioration of a deteriorating urban environment, the actions were guided, on the one hand, by changing notions of disease and disorder, and, on the other, by a desire of the colonial officials to represent themselves as a benevolent government able to reform what they saw as a backward society. As an instrument of modernization, municipalization in Delhi served to justify British rule in India. For the numerous visitors and travelers from Europe, Delhi was an example of the ultimate oriental city. The new wide roads and improved infrastructure signaled progress (to them, and to others in Europe), and the technological superiority of the colonial government. They helped to represent the British Empire in India as a benevolent state that used scientific knowledge and technological innovations to raise an ignorant and morally deficient population to a more healthy and civilized living. However, despite the statistics of improvements, Europeans continued to perceive the city in terms of Orientalist stereotypes. A British visitor at the turn of the twentieth century wrote:

> inside [the city walls] there is the well-remembered jostle and stench of every native quarter of the East, and so through eight-foot thoroughfares below jutting eaves and, rarely, dirty balconies, one reaches the one great street that cleaves the town in halves, the famous Chandni Chauk.

Meager, ramshackle houses – one-storeyed, and plastered with torn paper, their dirty blue paint smeared over decayed whitewash – lean one against the other, and expose on their vermin-haunted walls, and raised floors cheap European goods or trays of fly-blown native sweets, bowls of chilies or onions, framed oleographs of gods or English princes, American nickel clocks, or scrap-iron heaps.[100]

The British viewed insurgency itself as a sort of disease that grew and spread much like other infectious epidemics and indigenous areas as the source of disease and disaffection. In his *Hygiea*, Richardson envisioned the ideal city of health as also morally clean: no bars, no gaming houses, no saloons, and no alcohol to defile its purity. So also in Delhi, sanitation was as much about establishing cultural norms with respect to the behavior of people and activities in urban space and policing irregularities as it was about removing disease.[101] Not only did policing make sanitary reform coercive but it also blurred the boundaries between disease and deviance.

Even given the limited resources of the municipality, it could have undertaken incremental improvement of existing infrastructure. Instead, officials opted to replace inherited networks with new capital-intensive ones that celebrated technological and engineering accomplishments and needed materials and knowledge from outside the local area. The result was a partial and token provision of some services rather than any substantial improvement in sanitation for the general masses.

The grand plan of conquering myth, religion, and superstition with the power of science and universal reason did not come to pass in the way the British had imagined it might in Delhi. The political agendas of colonial domination, Orientalist perceptions of race and disease, existing systems of scientific and technological knowledge, the logic of individuals and groups struggling to survive the destruction of tradition – each undermined and distorted the idealized rational order of health in the city. However, local cultural and religious understandings did not continue unchanged either. Together they created a landscape that expressed a different modernity. Sanitary science itself became an instrument for reinforcing fundamental inequities and furthering the goals of colonialism in Delhi.

Chapter 5: Beyond the Walls

Commerce of Urban Expansion

URBAN EXPANSION

> . . . one thing is certain – whether we have come by our empire righteously or
> unrighteously – whether we have been forced into possessions we did not covet, or have
> sought quarrels that we might gain by issue – the natives at large have essentially
> benefited by the change of masters. It is true we do not erect temples to idolatory, nor
> huge tombs, nor lofty fortresses; but we have done far more: we have done our best,
> amidst enormous difficulties and obstructions, to give the people education, and a
> wholesome administration of Justice; we have constructed roads and canals, built
> bridges, introduced steam navigation, and improved agriculture; and much more has to
> be done.[1]

By the late 1880s, Delhi had become a significant railroad terminus with three lines in operation connecting it to major cities in the subcontinent in the east, north-west, and south, and a fourth line was under construction. Industrial expansion was also evident in the steam flour mill, two spinning and weaving mill companies, and a number of cotton presses and iron foundries.[2] Grain and textile piece goods were the staples of Delhi's trade. Colonial policies carefully facilitated and nurtured budding entrepreneurship. Newly developed roads and railways increased the connections of the city to the region and accompanied a growth in industries. Agricultural reforms and changes in the structure of land ownership and taxes further motivated people to migrate from the countryside to the city. Together, they resulted in rapid commercial expansion as well as substantial increase in population by 12.3 percent between 1868 and 1881. Most of the increase was attributed to the city's growing importance as a commercial center stimulated by the railroad (Figures 5.1 and 5.2).[3]

Since its establishment in the seventeenth century, the city had been contained largely in the area within its walls. With the establishment of British imperial rule, the indigenous city was further constrained within these limits because the military controlled a five-hundred yard building-free zone all around the city walls. The Civil Lines to the north and the Cantonment further north-west of the city also defined the edges of the walled city.⁴ Clearances around the King's Palace and the construction of the railroad had reduced the habitable areas within the city by about a third (Figure 5.3). Unlike cities in Western Europe where the railroad and industrial growth propelled expansion beyond the medieval walls, colonial military control in Delhi meant that haphazard growth and congestion accompanied rapid urban expansion.

Towards the end of the nineteenth century, the colonial state struggled with the paradoxical demands of simultaneously promoting commercial expansion and controlling urban development. On the one hand was the desire to

Figures 5.1 and 5.2 With the growth of industrial needs, elephant stables from an eighteenth-century *haveli* were converted to a factory for manufacturing railway tracks in the late nineteenth century. The factory including the machinery lies in disuse today.

Figure 5.2

order the city rationally for the most efficient flow of goods and services with the objective of improving trade; on the other was the aspiration to create a utopia that supported moral and physical health. Official policies and perceptions re-conceptualized land as a commodity. Disease was not the only measure of health in a city: the freedom of capital was as important. In earlier decades, cities in Western Europe such as Paris and Vienna, had been subject to massive renewal efforts. Where the restructuring of Paris had focused on large-scale demolition and the rebuilding of inner-city slum areas, after 1880 officials in Delhi began increasingly to consider expanding beyond the city walls to develop and build on 'new' lands.

Having found through bitter experience that restructuring the existing fabric of the walled city was costly, contentious, and in the end unsuccessful, it was the land beyond the walls that held most promise for the city's advance-ment. The colonial government had claimed the right to the deposed king's properties in and around Delhi, called Nazul lands. Officials saw the orchards, gardens, farms, and villages surrounding the walled city as a blank canvas on which to etch an idealized urban vision dramatically different from the existing one. Commodification of land meant that every piece of property had to be rationally evaluated, measured, and classified according to its physical attributes.

Figure 5.3
Plan of walled city and
surrounding areas in
1869 showing the
clearances within the city
(darker gray) and the
500-yard zone around
the city (lighter gray)
that was cleared and
maintained as glacis until
the 1890s.

Yet utopian urban ideals conflicted with the idea of maximizing the value of land. As the ones responsible for the vast *nazul* estates, city officials translated their lofty ideals of modernity to develop and manage the properties for the financial benefit of government institutions. In this chapter I examine some early municipal interventions between 1880 and 1920, including the creation of the Clarkegunj scheme, the earliest planned extension outside the city walls. With official policies encouraging the privatization of community land, what emerged was a new relationship of people to property and consequently the re-organization of the community itself. Even as the city expanded and the rate of entrepreneurship grew, municipal official, squatter, speculator, and merchant each fought for the right to re-construct the inherited meanings of land and property.

EXPANSION BEYOND THE CITY WALLS

In 1857 only a few settlements had existed to the west of the city walls (Figure 5.4). British maps showed Sabzimandi, Trevelyanganj, and Kishenganj, a suburb established a few decades earlier, as small cluster-like neighborhoods some distance west of the city walls (Figure 5.5).[5] The maps also showed other small, almost rural, settlements scattered to the west of the walled city, including Teliwara, Seedipur, and Paharipoor. Following the massive clearances around the Fort in 1858, the government granted land outside the city walls in the new Sadar Bazar area, west of the city, to some of the traders dislocated in the clearances. Others, whose properties had been confiscated or destroyed in the uprising and clearance, squatted in the areas near Sadar Bazar. Major Trevelyan formalized these *ad hoc* developments into a market for nearby troops and permitted other evicted residents to settle in the area.[6] With new migrants settling outside the city walls, by 1888, officials estimated that a third of the city's residents lived in improvised neighborhoods outside the walls (Figure 5.6).[7]

A first step in expanding beyond the city walls was to bring down the walls themselves or at least parts of them. The earliest such effort began with the demolition of the Lahori Darwaza, the western gate of the city (Figure 5.7). The main grain bazaar was located immediately inside this entrance and heavy traffic caused carts to block the path of movement, leading to much congestion. The question of removing the gate to allow traffic to flow unimpeded had been considered for several years. Robert Clarke, Deputy Commissioner of Delhi District, supported developing the city in an orderly fashion beyond the walls.[8] The Civil Surgeon of Delhi and the District Superintendent of Police, along with the European members of the municipality, all defended the removal of the gate. They argued that this would not only relieve traffic but also be 'desirable on sanitary grounds allowing greater ventilation of the inner streets.'[9] However, most Indian

Figure 5.4
An aerial view of Delhi looking south. Shows negligible development outside the city walls (except for the British military encampment to the north), 1857.

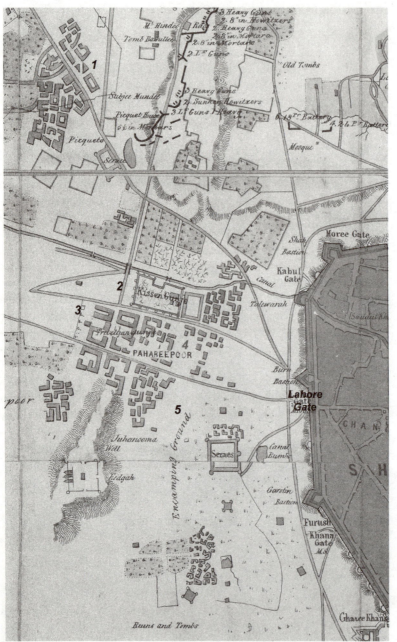

Figure 5.5
Settlements to the west
of the city in 1849.
1. Sabjee Mandee,
2. Kissengunj,
3. Trevelyangunj,
4. Pahareepur,
5. Encamping ground

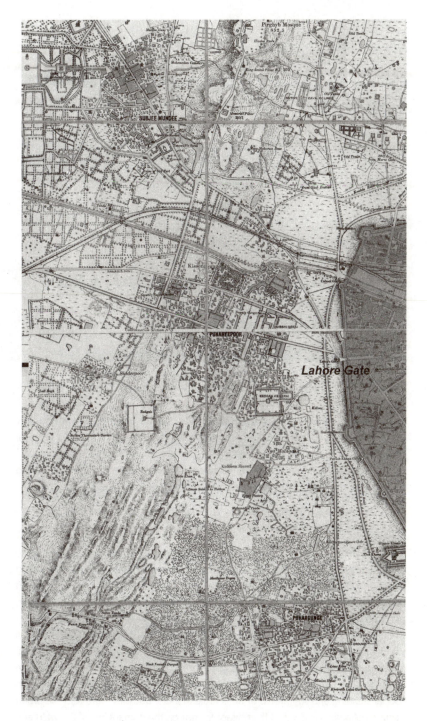

Figure 5.6
Settlements to the west
of the city in 1873.

Figure 5.7
View from West of the city's Lahori Darvaza (Lahore Gate), 1820–26.

members of the Delhi Municipal Committee were opposed to the demolition for reasons that Clarke interpreted as 'sentimental.'[10]

Similarly, Clarke and other senior officials sought to lower parts of the city wall adjacent to Lahori Darvaza. Again, the argument was that such a removal would help to improve 'the ventilation of the streets and lanes in the vicinity.'[11] Once more, local members of the municipality were opposed to the dismantling of the wall for what Clarke regarded as 'emotional reasons.' He declared,

> 'the only argument in favour of their retention is a sentimental one, and the Committee cannot indulge in sentiment when the material interests of the City are at stake.'[12]

While Clarke argued for the lowering of the wall as an improvement to the health of the city, there was also a monetary benefit for the government in doing so. Conscious of the material interests of 'the City,' he proposed re-using dressed stones from the dismantled wall for other building projects of the municipality in order to save 'public money.'[13]

Although interventions such as bringing down a single city gate, a small portion of the city walls, or declaring the glacis around the city available for building, appear unremarkable, they all became highly contentious in Delhi. The Indian members of the Municipal Committee were all respected residents with a high social standing and supportive of British rule in India. But they were also the proud citizens of a historic city and their disagreement on the dismantling of the walls and gate reflected their split loyalties. Eventually, the gate was demolished allowing for easier movement between the world within and that outside; the walls, however, remained.[14] Once the gate was removed, the 500-yard glacis outside the walls was the next impediment to urban expansion. The space had been considered a military necessity, but some officials argued that the glacis was now obsolete and an obstruction to the city opening out toward the west. For instance, Clarke argued:

> The trade and population of the city have however increased greatly since 1863. Large suburbs have sprung up especially outside the Lahore Gate. New Industries have been and are being started and finally a new line of railroad is under construction which will connect Delhi with Umballa and Simla. Building sites are not to be procured within the wall while the outer extremities of the suburbs are too far away for business purposes.[15]

For the reasons outlined above, Clarke insisted that keeping a five-hundred-yard ring free of construction made the city inefficient, uneconomic, and unsanitary. With permission to build in the area around the city walls, the way was clear for the development of an orderly and pre-planned extension to the walled city.

PLANNED SUBURBAN DEVELOPMENT

As the city government took on the task of constructing designed, predictable, and organized layouts, it assumed responsibility for the planning of new neighborhoods. The roles of promoter, developer, and builder were new for the state. In the past the colonial government had planned and built cantonments for the military, or enclaves for European settlers; grand monuments and public buildings or even bungalows were constructed to support and house the machinery of empire and its governance. But organizing undeveloped land into orderly settlements for private Indian residents was an entirely new phenomenon in Delhi.

As early as 1888, Robert Clarke was very much in favor of extension schemes for the city at the earliest instance and strongly argued for them. Planned arrangements would add new quarters to the city that were 'constructed systematically with due regard to ventilation, drainage and communications, instead of haphazard as in the case of the present suburbs.'[16] Clarke saw the existing settlements outside the walls as 'healthier than the City proper' but nevertheless lacking in supervision with regard to building operations as well as drainage and communications.[17] Some months later, he put forward the first proposal for a planned development called the Lahore Gate Improvement Scheme.

Clarke's idea for this scheme involved developing a bazaar to connect the Lahori Darvaza with the suburban settlement of Sadar Bazaar to the west of the city walls. At the heart of the proposal was a market square (gunj) with a mosque in the center and shops around the edges. Clarkgunj (as the project came to be popularly referred to) was to span the 800 feet between the city wall and the Circular Road. The Lahori Darvaza was to be located along one side of the square since properties fronting the Circular Road were likely to fetch a good price. Sites along that side were to extend as far as there was good demand for them. A row of 'good houses and shops' were to be on both sides of the road leading from the new square to the Sadar Bazaar and on another main thoroughfare perpendicular to it. Plots abutting the main roads were to have a frontage of fifteen feet and a depth of 85 feet. A service lane fifteen-feet wide was to run behind the row of plots. Clarke calculated that the proposal would make available 5,000 running feet of 'excellent frontage' on the main roads in the 'heart of the city's business center.'[18] Elsewhere, the land behind the neatly divided and marked rows was to be divided into 'convenient blocks suitable for *serai* [neighborhoods] and *katrā* [market squares].' Any existing small roads would also provide frontage for shops, albeit less valuable ones.[19] The total area estimated for the project was fifteen acres.

Clarke aimed to accomplish many things with this plan. His intention was that the Clarkgunj project should serve as a spill-over area for the city and so relieve congestion within the walls. As an example of regulated and pre-planned development, the project would also serve as a model for the future expansion of the city. Through the careful layout of shops, it would encourage and facilitate commercial expansion. From the official perspective much of the unoccupied land was simply 'waste' that was being put to good use.[20] And finally, with this design, he sought to establish continuity with the existing urban fabric by creating outside the city walls familiar landmarks, such as squares and streets, and a main thoroughfare similar to Chandni Chowk.[21] The idea of streets lined with shops and a 'row of good houses and shops' suggests that the architectural pattern typical of Delhi, shops on the first floor with residences above, was to continue in the new extension. As Clarke conceived of it, the scheme could only succeed:

> It would relieve congestion, furnish facilities for trade and add a handsome quarter to the city. The street that would then run continuously from the Fort end of the Chandni Chowk to the Pahari would be without an equal in any City of Northern India.[22]

Clarke's proposal was not a grand vision of elegant city form as in Haussmann's Paris nor a formal utopian ideal such as those of Charles Fourier, Benjamin Ward Richardson, or Ebenezer Howard.[23] Rather, it was what officials in India began to refer to as an 'improvement scheme.' Although it was formal and intended to serve as a model for future development in the area, the scheme was not based on principles of social reform or abstracted diagrams present in Howard's work in England. The mixed uses proposed were in contrast to the segregated commercial and residential districts put forward by the idealists. His approach was a pragmatic effort to develop real estate but it shared with the utopians the idea of an ordered pre-planned urban environment, planned by experts, organized into plots, and partly built.[24] Many cities in Western Europe rebuilt to make their development controlled and predictable, however, Clarke's scheme was remarkable in choosing to do this on the margins of the walled city.

In Clarke's design, streets were of identical width, shape, size, and character with orthogonal connections. Their land values were predicted based on their location. The land was to be divided into parcels with regular lots, available for purchase by anyone who paid the market price for it. The Lahore Gate Improvement Scheme was to be successful assuming the availability of open land, free of cost, assured commercial interests in the area, and a foreseeable demand for real estate. These, however, were major assumptions.

Clarke's proposal spelled out a settlement with class-based neighborhoods where properties of equivalent value were grouped together. This contrasted to the social and spatial organization of the city at that time, where inherited cultural identities and status including caste, occupation, religion, and community significantly determined location. Residential mobility within the city was minimal. Central to the scheme was a rationalized design, typical of Western practices, and based on the concept of private property as an exchangeable commodity whose market value was to be maximized.[25] Unlike in the city, people of different castes, occupational groups, or religious persuasion could be neighbors in the new suburban development. In creating multiple lots with identical (or similar) characteristics, the commodification of land meant that the new urban community was constituted by the highest bidder. In the old city, neighborhoods had evolved incrementally so that lofty mansions stood next to humble dwellings. In contrast, in Clarke's proposed subdivision economically and socially segregated neighborhoods would be erected where there were none before.

Clarke had proposed a 400-feet square on a site outside the Lahori Darvaza. The idea of a square surrounded by shops was reminiscent of small market towns in seventeenth- or eighteenth-century Europe rather than of the cities of northern India. The mosque at the center of the square reinforced the notion of a religious institution at the center of public life in a pre-industrial city. The symbolism of the form was unmistakable: in a civilized city, while trade and competition were to be encouraged, the unbridled greed of commerce would be held in check by public institutions of a superior moral order. The imagery also recast the position of the Muslim clergy. The prominent presence of the mosque was a concession to a 'superstitious' and 'traditional' people. James Mill, an influential philosopher, writer, and senior government official in early nineteenth-century, England had proclaimed that for progress, India must be freed from the tyranny of the priests. In the celebration of the mosque, the design compromised this simple dictum.[26]

The scheme's imagery and apparent connection to local tradition was, however, only a veneer. Customarily, shops around large mosques such as the Jama Masjid or the Fatehpuri Masjid paid rent to the mosque board and were directly under the religious authority. Since the improvement scheme was designed to encourage private enterprise and contribute to municipal income, Clarke's proposal gave the mosque visual prominence rather than economic power. In reinterpreting customary spatial and social relationships between shop, square, public space, and religious institution in Delhi, the scheme signaled a shift from religious power to a secular one – that of the market. The square as a public space was municipal property and the commercial enterprises surrounding the mosque were to be privately owned.[27] The imagery of Clarkegunj revealed at once the perceptions, ideals, and agendas of the officials involved. The rectilinear streets and squares defined land use and property values in a foreseeable manner. The residents of such environments were assumed to be controlled, obedient, and predictable. Growth was a sign of health, and an organized and knowable city assumed to be a sanitary one. Thus, organized environments symbolized economic, moral, and physical health.

As urban improvement, Clarke's design defined new criteria for a healthy city. Official efforts were no longer limited to removing disease and providing infrastructure. City officials increasingly saw the city as a commodity and urban chaos as moral decay. The Lahore Gate Scheme, planned, designed, and rational, promised both commercial and sanitary health. In its rhetoric, the proposal was critical of the walled city's disorderliness. Yet, in the layout that was implemented, the measures taken to achieve the idealized landscape were modest. While every building constructed was to meet the city's building codes, the regulations were no different than those within the walled city where unsanitary conditions were apparently rampant. Even the mixed-use shop–house structure, typical within the city, was proposed as the primary unit of development in the new suburb. While officials hoped to represent the improvement schemes as the very antithesis of the walled city, the formal vocabulary of mosques, shops, and houses were analogous to those in the existing urban fabric but in quite new relationships.

Despite the rhetoric of bettering living conditions, an implicit agenda of the improvement project was to facilitate commercial expansion. Disease was no longer the only measure of health in the city: the freedom of capital was as important. The design was limited to the laying out of arterial streets and a square. Plots were marked out in some areas, but in others only major lanes were set out. *Sarā'i* and *katrā* were expected to develop along them through private enterprise. Officials anticipated and encouraged land speculation in the development of neighborhoods. The proposal detailed the construction of shops and houses along the main street and square, leaving much else to chance development. Once again, this was a move to encourage commerce to develop along primary routes of transportation. As Clarke observed:

> Our Water Works are at length within measurable distance of being commenced. Our Drainage Scheme will it is hoped soon be revised so as to meet the objections of the Sanitary Authorities, our Conservancy Tramway is all but purchased, but there is still much for the municipality to do not only in the direction of sanitation, but in providing facilities for that trade of which Delhi has become a great center.[28]

Clarke worried that Delhi's great mercantile future would be endangered by barring it from 'reasonable expansion.'[29]

Clarke had also hoped for a sort of ripple effect: the Lahore Gate Scheme was to be a model that would inspire other, similarly systematic, developments. The assumption was that those living in the congested, hurly-burly within the walls of the city would be immediately drawn to the tidy, modern neighborhoods and, by their flight, leave the walled city less crowded than before (Figure 5.8).

Figure 5.8
The pressures of
commerce and the
changing spatial needs
meant that old buildings
were adapted to new
uses.

The improvement scheme was to serve as an impetus to private development. Moreover, the very orderliness of the project was to inspire the 'public spirit of individuals' who would be willing to undertake public works as philanthropy.[30] And all of this was to be achieved at no cost to the government but, rather, to its financial benefit.

Clarke carefully worked out the finances of the scheme so that the gains to the government were anticipated at three times the amount invested. From the perspective of the municipality, profit remained primary to all discussions of improvement schemes. The apparent justification for this emphasis was that the municipality could apply the money raised by the sale of the sites to carrying out 'great works of sanitary improvement.' If the city was able to fund improvement projects without the necessity of borrowing then the burden of taxation on the inhabitants could also be reduced. Clarke calculated,

> The sites, if judiciously sold, would bring in at least two lakhs of Rupees. The construction of necessary roads, drains and bridges would cost about Rs.50,000; leaving a lakh and a half for the reduction of debt or for investment as Government might decide.[31]

But the efforts the municipality expended on maximizing the returns from investments was disproportionately more than the investments on improvement schemes.

For the government, profit making from developing 'waste' lands had become an end in itself. While waiting for the government to approve the Lahore Gate scheme, for instance, municipal officials worried about the value of the properties, the popularity of the scheme among the local people, and the terms on which the plots were to be leased. In order to test the value of sites the municipality leased lots fronting the Sadar Bazar Road and part of the Canal Road. The sites were given out with the constraint that no brick or stone be used in the construction. The assumption was that such a stipulation would guarantee that the lessee would only construct temporary structures that could be easily dismantled on receiving notice.[32] Despite the severe restriction, the experiment proved successful. Officials noted with delight, 'Not withstanding these rather stringent conditions handsome rows of shops have been built upon the Sadar Bazar road and some on the road at right angles and the Committee receives over Rs.2400 a year in rent.'[33]

Having established that the sites would be popular and the scheme financially viable, officials worried about the terms upon which the lots would be given out, debating the merits of leasing the land as opposed to selling it outright. Selling the sites meant that the government would lose the rent as well as the possible gain from the predicted increase in land values. In order to maximize the financial gain from the improvement project, municipal officials carefully considered not only the implications of selling, leasing, and the terms of the leases but also the location and number of plots that would be let out over time. Contrary to the apparent benevolence of the government in planning extension projects on its land, the nitty-gritty of financial management absorbed much official attention. While the stated motive for the Clarkegunj project was the welfare of the citizens, the financial calculations aimed to make the project not merely pay for itself but also bring in substantial profit to the municipality.

Most of the scheme was a failure, however, one part of the Lahore Gate Scheme, the Grand Parade area, proved very popular. The first part of scheme to be developed was the road behind the canal (now called the Qutub Road) from

Pul Mithai to the Old Idgah. However, the Improvement Scheme was inhabited not by old-time residents of the walled city but by the large number of small traders and entrepreneurs who had migrated to Delhi drawn by its commercial possibilities. Rich merchants from the Punjab, eager to establish their businesses close to the city, built prosperous shops on the Grand Parade plots. With the introduction of the railroad Delhi experienced an increasing volume of wholesale trade. The value of these sites was so high for businesses that the holdings changed hands for large sums of money. In not drawing out residents from within the walled city, the new development had expanded the city without decongesting it. The immense amount of 'goodwill money' that was exchanged when the holdings changed hands was noted by Whitehead (Table 5.1).

For all the months of planning, however, the Clarkegunj scheme was only partially laid out and built. The project had been, as senior British officials admitted, a failure.[34] Owing to a projected railroad track passing through the proposed site, city officials were forced to set aside the layout of much of the scheme. (Figure 5.9).[35] Even when the Sadar Bazar road eventually developed into a thoroughfare with a double tram-line running through it, the Clarkegunj sites had still not been in demand. Nor did the expected decrease in congestion within the walled city happen. The intent of the project had been to induce the grain merchants of the overcrowded Khari Baoli grain-market area in the western part of the walled city to move their businesses to the new shops in Sadar Bazar and Clarkegunj. By this officials hoped to move 'an undoubted centre of plague contagion' outside the city as well as relieve the city's main arteries from congestion.[36] But the anticipated flight from Khari Baoli to outside Lahori Darwaza did not take place. Rather, grain merchants continued to expand their trade in the same location within the walled city.

Despite official intentions of sanitary and rationally ordered developments outside the city walls, by the turn of the century the extramural developments remained largely haphazard. As late as 1912, more than two decades after Clarke's improvement schemes, one British observer noted that Pahargunj was 'merely a collection of mean houses occupied as a rule by the lower castes.'[37] Annual reports of the Municipal Committee indicated that although water-supply and drainage schemes had absorbed much official attention, the neighborhoods outside the walls had been excluded from these services.[38]

Improvement schemes that had initially been motivated by the abominable housing conditions, increasingly focused on facilitating commerce. Municipal officials now put much emphasis on the improvement of roads and transportation routes. Clarke, as Commissioner of Delhi, proposed several improvement schemes, most of them involving the construction of new roads near the railroad station. Smaller-scale municipal improvement schemes, too, emphasized efficient transportation through new roadways, rationalized markets, and proposed new shops arranged tidily along new roads.

Even with all the regulations and improvements, Sadar Bazaar and Pahargunj continued to expand with new houses, shops, and factories. The growth in

Table 5.1 A sampling of the 'goodwill money' far in excess of rent that incoming tenants paid on obtaining a shop in the Grand parade. The government did not sell the sites but gave them on long term leases. Building rights were given in return for a fixed ground rent. The merchants proceeded to erect fine shops and as the land values rapidly increased made a tidy profit by subletting them unofficially.

Number	Name of tenant	Amount of monthly rent (Rs.)		Area (square yards)	Price when property last changed hands (Rs.)
1	Muhammad Husain, son of Muhammad Umar	125	7 0	1,543	18,000
2	Muhammad Ibrahim, son of Haji Allah Baksh	12	8 0	609	15,000
3	Abdul Hasan, son of Muhammad Husain	16	8 0	90	6,080
4	Abdul Samad, son of Abdullah	20	0 0	1,285	6,500

Source: Whitehead, *Report on the Administration of the Delhi Crown Lands*, 1933, p. 32.

Note
Prices include the value of the building materials and the holders' interests in the land.

Figure 5.9
Detail plan of Lahori
Darvaza (Lahore Gate)
area in 1912. Railroad
tracks dominated the
area west of the walls
and hindered
connections developing
between the walled city
and the settlements
outside of it.
1. Electrical Engine
House, 2. Electrical
Workshops, 3. Bastion,
4. Engine House, 5. Police
Bastion, 6. Office,
7. Grain Shops, 8. Shops

Figure 5.10
View of the Sadar Bazar
area.

commerce also pleased officials because it meant more revenues. Major H. S. P. Davies, Deputy Commissioner of Delhi, observed in 1898 that income from Octroi taxes in the previous four years had shown a steady increase, pointing to Delhi's rising importance as a trade center.[39] Among eight of the largest businesses operating in Delhi in 1902, an official named four in Sabzimandi.[40] Sadar Bazar was marked by a goods station, a power station for the Electric Tramway, a wood depot, and a horse market. While the growth of the market pleased colonial officials, the disorderliness of the suburbs of Pahargunj, Sadar Bazar, and Sabzimandi continued to be of mounting concern (Figure 5.10).

LANDOWNERSHIP AND LAND MANAGEMENT

Municipal enthusiasm to develop and promote lands gradually turned to rationalizing property ownership as its central objective. Phenomenal commercial growth complicated the question of acquiring land for building new markets, roads, or residential areas. Interventions within the city were limited because the municipality only owned the streets, the public gardens, and specific properties appropriated during the 1857 rebellion.

From an official perspective, the situation with regard to land in Delhi by the turn of the century was cause for alarm. The area immediately surrounding the walls was of great and increasing value and was being rapidly built over. Despite all official controls, unregulated construction and the illegal appropriation of vacant land proliferated. Informal settlements and irregular entitlements were commonplace. These appropriations were irksome to the officials both because of the disorderly arrangement of buildings as well as their ambiguous leases and property rights. Further, Delhi's growth in industry and trade, and the substantial expansion in population, had all contributed to an escalation in the cost of land making 'squatter'-occupied properties only dearer. One senior official estimated that property in Sadar Bazaar had increased by 700 percent in value during the six years between 1902 and 1908. The increase in Pahargunj was 400 percent and 300 percent in Sabzimandi.[41] Sadar Bazar Road was the headquarters of the wholesale trade in provisions. From 1890 to 1909, Delhi's trade-center had shifted from the Lahori Darvaza area within the walled city to Kishengunj in the west. Officials, like the speculators, safely predicted a further rise in real-estate values since the growth could only occur to the west of the city.[42] The question of realizing maximum returns became increasingly important for the colonial officials since the government claimed ownership of substantial properties whose value had quickly appreciated manifold (Figure 5.11).

At the time of the 1857 uprising, the British claimed an area of about fourteen square miles from the Mughal royalty and from those they believed disloyal to the new rulers. Of this land, known as Nazul, the railways acquired substantial tracts with the result that, out of the fourteen square miles, by 1912 the government fully owned about seven square miles.[43] Nazul properties in and around a three-mile radius of the walled city, once the property of the ex-king of Delhi, were entrusted to the care and management of the Municipal Committee. The municipality enjoyed the income from these properties and was responsible for their preservation and improvement.

Escalating land values and the rapid growth of the city outside the walls precipitated the issue of a record of rights over state land within the municipal limits. Over the years as the land became dearer, officials regretted not having established stricter regulations for the habitation of areas outside the city walls. If officials expected to exercise control over the areas according to a preconceived design, then mapping and aligning assets was a necessary and formidable task. However, regulation was difficult until they had been brought under the jurisdiction of the Municipal Committee. As one official articulated:

> During the last few years the extension of Delhi has been enormous and it is bound to go on, probably increasing in extent and rapidity. The directions in which extension must take place are well known and it is essential that it should be foreseen as far as possible and guided and regulated. The areas which will be absorbed into the city during the next twenty years ought now to be mapped and definite conclusions arrived at as to the alignment of the principal roads and streets. These areas might then be brought within Municipal limits when the erection of buildings could be regulated by the Municipal Act and roads constructed and sites for open spaces for gardens and recreation grounds protected and where necessary acquired.[44]

By 1908, British administrators openly conceded the difficulty they were having in maintaining absolute control over the Nazul lands. Disputes between the occupiers of the land and the British officials were frequent.[45] For the government,

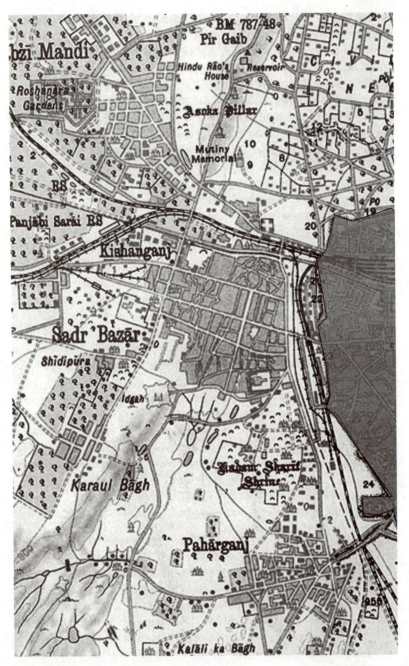

Figure 5.11
Settlements to the west
of city in 1912. The
walled city has been
darkened to emphasize
settlements outside of it.

the ground rent from building sites was the most significant source of Nazul income. Most of the vendors, hawkers, and shopkeepers extending on to government properties, paid *tehbazari* rents. Such rents derived from lands in the charge of the Municipal Committee included those from *patri* (footpaths and the central divide of wide roads), *takhtas* (platforms extending from shops), and *saibans* (overhangs). Private ownership of property in the Delhi region was historically complicated by the customs of patrilineal holding, *jagīr*, tenant farming, sharecropping, and *sardārakhtī* (titles). Aside from land privately owned as businesses, orchards, or residences, and Crown Lands (or Nazul), official bodies that held charge of land in Delhi in 1906 included the Rajputna, Malwa Railway, the East India Railway Company, Delhi Cantonment, the Police Department, the Municipal Committee, the Public Works Department, the Deputy Commissioner of Delhi, the District Board, Military Works, Irrigation Branch, and the Grand Trunk Road.

In the preceding half-century Nazul lands had been haphazardly settled. After the abandonment of the Old Cantonments in 1859, many members of the *banya* community (a trading community) and followers of the troops settled on the 'waste' lands. Previously, a group of people had obtained permission from Major Trevelyan to settle the lands. This quarter became known as Mandi Pan (near Sadar Bazar). After they took over the administration of Nazul lands in 1874, the municipality granted some dispossessed people permission to settle on the land on payment of a nominal rent. In addition, municipal officials had permitted those dislocated from other parts of the city to settle on the Nazul lands. During an outbreak of cholera in 1874, leather workers and tanners evicted from Pahari Dhiraj were settled upon government land at Qarol Bagh in Banskouli village.

In 1908, the government commissioned R. B. Whitehead to give an account of the conditions, extent, and management of the Crown Lands (i.e., Nazul lands) along with his recommendations. Whitehead noted with alarm that no leases had been drawn up for the original lessees but all paid a monthly rent to the Municipal Committee and could, technically, be evicted on a month's notice. Other Nazul lands were legally rented to *thelāwālā* (manual laborers who transported goods on hand carts), *gwālā* (dairymen), and sweepers. Critical of the administration Whitehead noted that in granting parcels of land, no provision had been made for setting out proper roads and streets. As a result, squatters and renters settled as they pleased in, what he considered, 'heterogeneous patches of dirty hovels.' These very properties had increased enormously in value and Sadar Bazar had become a prosperous business center. Hence the rents that the humble settlers paid were entirely disproportionate to the value of the land.[46]

Entrepreneurial spirit and resistance to an imposed regulation resulted in further irregularity. While the municipal leases had dictated that the tenants build nothing but a *kutccha* (temporary) structure and that they vacate land on request without compensation, the occupants had built structures that were anything but impermanent and the leases ran, for all practical purposes, in perpetuity:

Many of the sites let on Lease No. 3 are just behind the Sadar Bazar and their letting
value has probably increased ten times since they were first leased out by the
Committee. Valuable warehouses, anything but kutccha in character have been erected
on some of them and subletting to any extent has gone on, each tenant making a
handsome profit from the next.[47]

Subletting of properties had become so common that tenants made a profit
from the 'goodwill' money obtained from their successors. Since the lease deed
did not contain provisions against subletting, the removal of a tenant holding
such a lease was very difficult. Legal cases against such tenants were usually
carried to the Chief Court of the province, and lasted three to four years. From
the perspective of the municipality, the ambiguities of the contracts and the
expenses involved in the legal negotiations rendered the land as good as lost.
The commissioner was concerned:

As a matter of fact there are to my knowledge valuable properties irrespective of
innumerable patches and plots, cultivated and uncultivated, built upon and waste, and
of lands and roads, everywhere more or less the food of a hungry population eager for
spoliation, while on the other hand I do not see that any attempt is made by the
executive administration to check the action going on, and to protect the rights of the
Government and of the public.[48]

From his study of the Nazul properties in Delhi, Whitehead concluded that
the Nazul lands were 'properties which would be immensely prized in any European capital.' Developing these lands held the promise of both financial profit to
the municipality and 'improved health' for residents in the region. Improvements
could only serve to make the city more attractive to international travelers.[49]
Whitehead suggested some drastic measures to make Delhi conform to these
ideals. First of all, in the face of daily attempts at encroachment of government
lands, Whitehead declared war on the 'squatters':

No squatting should be allowed on land declared to be Nazul. Squatters should be at
once ejected, and no occupation on sufferance should be allowed, as it becomes very
troublesome to dispose of such rights when the land is really wanted. The Deputy
Commissioner or Committee should ascertain what is really Government property, and
protect its rights from trespass, right of way, and from injury by non-user . . . No kind of
tenure of house or shop property, other than on lease, which may have been presumed
to imply customary right of occupancy adverse to the absolute right of occupancy
adverse to the absolute right of Government to oust at the expiry of the year.[50]

As many paid a small rent, however, 'squatters,' were not easy to identify.
The prevalence of ambiguous and fluid identities of owner, tenant, sub-tenant,
and 'squatter' further complicated government control of land. Better policing
required a more rigorous system of classification. Rationalizing the management
of properties meant redefining the terms of land ownership and leasing (Figure
5.12). Whitehead recommended the adoption of standard forms of leasing and

Figure 5.12
Migrants created
communities with very
few resources and little
space. The colonial
government viewed
'squatters' and their
'congested' settlements
as an immense threat.

renting as well as the maintenance of detailed records of properties, their owner-ship, tenancy, and rents.[51] He suggested ways of defining and controlling the future expansion of the city so that the development of the Nazul lands could occur in an orderly and preconceived manner. In his report, Whitehead included a detailed analysis of properties in each village, categorizing them as Nazul, Government, Committee, and private lands. The report also made clear the historical basis on which the government would accept land titles of the occu-piers of existing holdings.

Whitehead's report was crucial to the making of Delhi's landscape since it outlined the terms on which the city was to develop. The report influenced land administration and policies towards urban development in Delhi in the following decades. As we see in the next chapter, Whitehead's report eventually led to the establishment of The Delhi Improvement Trust in 1936 to manage and develop the government's Nazul estates. Whitehead's report was significant also in the views it represented. He marked a clear departure from earlier official percep-tions of land, property, and Delhi society. Land and property in Whitehead's view were resources that needed to be efficiently administered to yield enhanced returns. If all property could be tidily classified then errant situations could be immediately identified and presumably rectified. Each owner could then go about developing their parcel to its fullest potential.

Whitehead's entire report was aimed at setting a new direction for making the Nazul lands more profitable to the colonial government. The implicit idea of improvement was one of investing towards a predictable, long-term gain. In his view, the goal was to achieve planned urban development comparable to that in 'European capitals.' Improvement was not about remedying environmental conditions but about enhancing the commercial value of land. For the colonial administrators, improving the productivity of land was coterminous with improving the quality of urban habitation. Land rather than the community had become the target of the up-gradation efforts.

POLICING, SURVEYING, AND CLASSIFICATION OF LAND

Following Whitehead's report, the efforts of the colonial administrators in Delhi focused on maximizing the productivity of land. On the 'vacant' Nazul lands outside the city walls officials set out to accomplish the European ideals of formal order and preconceived development in new, planned extensions. In fact, many of the areas around the city that the government considered 'waste land' were informal and spontaneous settlements of the poor and the powerless. Included in Whitehead's list of waste lands were those occupied by fuel-sellers and dairymen and others settled by weavers and sawyers. Even the growing settlement of Pahargunj was 'chiefly occupied by faqirs, sweepers, weavers, thelawalas and other low castes.'[52] Most of the inhabitants were legal tenants but of the humbler classes. Whitehead noted, for instance.

> Qadam Sharif is a series of graveyards, which are no longer in use. They became Government property in 1864 . . . The cells and homes in the graveyards are occupied by faqirs. They pay a nominal rent varying from 3 pies to one anna a month, and are tenants liable to ejectment on a month's notice.[53]

Not all tenants had leases, and most paid small amounts as rent. Whitehead counted over 1,500 'squatters' in the urban Nazul lands around Delhi from whom the government collected rent. This begs the definition of 'squatter' and 'squatting' and also reveals that rents from Nazul lands formed a substantial portion of the municipality's income.[54]

Regular and close scrutiny of land in the manner Whitehead suggested involved detailed records of income, expenditure, leases, tenants, and improvements.[55] Comprehensive planning and management of the lands was premised on complete and precise surveying. The classification of lands according to titles, uses, and market values was an enterprise based on the detailed study of land where accuracy was paramount. Arguing for the necessity of a detailed survey of all the government properties in and around the walled city, Deputy Commissioner Humphreys saw the scientific collection of accurate information as imperative:

> The essential object [of the Nazul land survey to be undertaken] to be immediately striven for is an accurate survey of all Nazul lands administered by the municipality coupled with an accurate and exhaustive record of rights of each plot and as a consequence the authoritative settlement of all outstanding disputes between the occupiers of Nazul land on the one hand and Government and the municipality on the other.[56]

Until this time the only record of rights was for agricultural lands maintained by village *patvārī* (accountants). Surveys of the city after municipalization had focused on identifying public areas – streets, parks, squares, and railroad lines – while the private properties appeared on maps as large, undifferentiated islands between the streets. Inadequate and outdated records of rights meant that officials were unable to detect and arbitrate on encroachments on state properties. Effective policing required a detailed and accurate map of all the properties and developments within the municipal limits. The question of revising an earlier map of Delhi had been under discussion since 1904.[57] In 1910, an official stressed the need for 'a new larger scale map of Delhi City and its suburbs.'[58] He argued that the suburbs to the west and north-west of the city were unrecognizable in their present state with respect to the out-of-date map in the city office.[59] The existing map of Delhi prepared in 1865–66 by the Public Works Department appeared in 1910 to be not only obsolete and inaccurate in places, but also heedless of systematic and scientific methods.

Officials argued that a careful record of rights showing the owner and occupier of each plot of land (both built and unbuilt) was a way of countering disputes and encroachments. An accurate survey would also facilitate the municipal provision of services:

> the Sanitary Engineer to the Punjab Government has recently impressed most strongly upon the Municipal Committee, the necessity of extending the Water Works with a view to giving a sufficient water supply to the suburbs of Subzi Mandi, Sadar Bazar and Paharganj. These three suburbs have never been properly surveyed; they have attained their present dimensions since the map of 1873 was prepared. And it would be a matter of great difficulty to formulate a scheme for the proper distribution of water supply in these areas, without a complete and accurate map.[60]

Towards this end, the Deputy Commissioner, C. A. Barron, appointed W. A. J. Wilson, a retired official of the Survey of India who had been largely responsible for the Lahore city survey, to prepare the maps of Delhi.

The Wilson Survey, a set of 250 plans and drawings, carefully documented the area within the municipal limits of Delhi. Every structure and street, however small, were surveyed and marked. The condition of the buildings were classified as 'pucca' (permanent), 'kutccha' (temporary), or 'broken.' Courtyards, staircases, wells, drains, standpipes, telegraph posts, letter boxes, wire fences, tramway posts and tracks were all denoted on the maps. Religious buildings were identified as temples or mosques. Dotted lines in the interior of each structure indicated the divisions used for area calculations. The lines generally corresponded with the layout of the rooms or pavilions.

Accompanying ledgers identified each building by its unique house tax number. A description of the house included a classification of every division (marked by dotted lines on the map) by its use such as house, shop, platform, courtyard, or steps. The condition of each space, the number of stories, its dimensions in inches and feet, and its total area were all carefully assessed and noted. The ownership information included the name and occupation of owner, name of employer, and the father's name. Similarly, details of tenancy were also documented. This was the first time that such an extensive survey and mapping of each structure had been undertaken in the city.

The implications of an extensive project, such as the Wilson Survey, were fourfold. First, the limited resources of the government were channeled towards accomplishing the most refined and accurate survey record rather than directly improving living conditions in the city.[61] Second, the records established and set a datum line for future development in the city. Future changes were expected to deviate minimally from that base or else the owners were to seek formal permission for change from the municipality. For a city that transformed incrementally, such a measure effectively captured and 'froze' the built form in a single moment in time. Third, while the maps clearly facilitated the resale of property and ownership disputes, the survey also served as a sophisticated instrument of policing construction and uses. The surveying and classification of land obviously led to disputes even as it settled some. Finally, through the survey the state insidiously gained access to the privacy of the homes. Activities in and uses of private property had gradually become a public concern.

Preoccupation with representing the technological superiority of the British impeded rather than assisted sanitary improvement since the application of technologies became ends in themselves.[62] Increasing refinement in techniques was both the cause and the consequence of extensive collection of census data, housing statistics, and figures on health. Surveys, maps, and the maintenance of records, meant as aids to the rationalized management of properties, became the objects of official attention in themselves.

CONCLUSION

The civilizing mission of the colonial government meant that enlightened officials would work to deliberately transform the city guided by the ideals of modernity. Although rational order, scientific classification, efficiency, and utilitarian principles were at the heart of the projects and interventions, other objectives and factors muddied the mission. The city government's (under the colonial regime) continued failure to completely control the walled city, its desire to promote commerce and free enterprise, its efforts to know and manage its territories, and its aspirations as a property owner to maximize financial returns and effectively police its properties, and the residents' differing interests in subverting, appropriating, and co-opting, were all at odds with the liberating intent of modernization and created instead eccentric and incomplete landscapes of indigenous modernity.

The same Benthamite principles that historians of India have observed underlying the late nineteenth and early twentieth-century judicial system and the administration of rural land influenced improvement schemes in urban Delhi of that period. Utilitarian doctrines saw good government, the development of private capital, and individual property rights as necessary conditions to civilization.[63] In his *Essay on Government*, James Mill argued that the only way that Indian society could be stirred out of its stagnation and put on to the path of

improvement was to free it from the despotism of custom, communal ownership, and the tyrannies of priests and nobles. These changes in turn would free
capital and labor and create the foundation for an individualistic, competitive
society, 'the acme of an advanced civilization,' as Mill called it. He urged that the
definition and protection of individual rights to land ownership was central to
dissolving traditional joint-ownership and communal control, which Mill considered to be 'the marks of a primitive state of society.'[64]

The colonial government of India, one of the wealthiest landlords, was consumed with maximizing returns from its land holdings. Far from its civilizing
mission, for the first time in Delhi, the state invited land speculation by developing new subdivisions for sale. The Clarkegunj proposal used a well-defined image
of a physical urban form to spell out the new relationship of the state to assets.
The Lahore Gate Improvement Scheme revealed the contradictions in improvement schemes. They depended on an imagined cohesive urban community while
celebrating individual capital; upheld established public institutions while encouraging free enterprise. Whitehead's recommendations aimed to enhance returns
from government lands and extract the greatest profit from them while promoting individual rights to property. In choosing this strategy Whitehead implicitly
put utilitarian doctrines into practice, intending to encourage individualism and
competition, advancing Delhi on the road to civilization.

Armed with the tidy categories of government land, private property,
owner, and tenant, officials proceeded with plans for the new extensions. After
the turn of the century, official attention was firmly focused on the developments outside the walled city. With the establishment after 1911 of the sprawling new imperial capital at New Delhi and the building of the magnificent capital
complex, the inversion was complete. The sovereign city of the Mughals had
become a relic, Old Delhi, with a 'diseased' and dense urban fabric needing to
be policed to prevent complete decay. It was on the vast 'waste land' of
orchards, gardens, fields, and iterant 'squatters' (outside the city walls) that officials set about constructing the idealized landscape of economic prosperity,
moral order, and public health. Underlying the municipality's rationalization of
property was the idea that the appropriation of public land by squatters was a
'blushing effrontery to peace and good government.'[65] No doubt, illegal settlers,
and poor records, were threatening to urban sanitation, but they also reflected
on the government. For the British in Delhi, the urban landscape was not about
building communities as much as it was about the controlled use of land and
maximizing its value.

The efforts to construct a competitive society in India yielded paradoxical
results. In the view of the utilitarians, Indian society was primitive and individual
enterprise 'modern.' In the application of official policies in Delhi, local enterprise
combined with European concepts of property ownership and rights.[66] Removing
a city gate opened the doors to expansion and allowing construction in the glacis
made way for further growth. The Clarkegunj scheme defined property as a
freely exchangeable commodity while placing a religious institution at the center

of the layout. The rise in commercial growth also led to an unbridled escalation in real-estate values. Yet the design, layout, and management of land was intended to yield the best returns rather than serve the best interests of the local population. State-sponsored improvement schemes had, in rhetoric, stemmed from a concern for the unsanitary environment of the 'native huts' and 'mean hovels.' By the turn of the century, however, improvement efforts focused on developing 'waste' lands for maximum profit. People from outside the city were able to purchase, own, and sell property as a commodity in a manner not known to the residents before. Even as officials defined more clearly the tidy categories of ownership and tenancy, all manner of squatting and subletting proliferated to muddy the order. In the end, with the mapping, policing, and regulation of ownership, officials had intervened to modify not just the layout and form of the houses and streets, but also the relationship of people to property and the organization of community itself.

The grand policies and visions of the government had to contend in practice with local residents. The unwillingness of old-time residents to uproot themselves from their community and their businesses from the traditional quarters meant that the city was not easily decongested. Contrary to the officials' expectations, the tidy new suburban development of Clarkgunj had failed and, also contrary to their calculations, did not inspire other similar settlements. Migrant labor continued to appropriate Nazul land and claim their rights despite all efforts to oust them. Local officials were often caught up in the more urgent and tangible tasks of making the municipality a profitable business. The conflict between the officials and the residents was, as much over classification and characterization as it was over rights. In their endeavors, officials attempted to impose their definitions of healthy and unsanitary, city and slum, private and public, and tenant and squatter, upon a reluctant population. Municipal official, squatter, speculator, and merchant each fought for the right to construct the meanings of home, shop, city, and property. The results of the ensuing battle were several partial statements and a landscape of multiple meanings.

In the early decades of the twentieth century, the increasingly impoverished colonial government reinforced its efforts to promote new commerce by building retail centers and developing residential neighborhoods. As owner-developer the government's profit-making motive dominated. With the completion of the grand imperial city and capital complex, the construction of the ideal modern subject became even more urgent. Torn between the demands of improving what officials viewed as 'abominable' living conditions, facilitating commerce, and improving its revenues, the colonial government found the role of a developer to be a fitting one. Whitehead's report led to the establishment of the Delhi Improvement Trust to manage the vast Nazul estates. In the next chapter I look at the undertakings of the Trust, its methods, and outcomes.

Chapter 6: Imagining Modernity

Symbolic Terrains of Housing

INTRODUCTION

By the 1930s signs of 'progress' were everywhere in Delhi for those who perceived them as such. Wide paved roads, tramlines, regional linkages by rail lines and roads, bridges, electricity, piped water supply, underground sewage lines and treatment plants, factories and mills, rationalized urban administration with clearly defined territories, by-laws, building codes, an organized police force, several large hospitals and a system of smaller dispensaries, colleges, schools, museums, and new retail – all were visible in the city. Above all was a shining new imperial city, New Delhi, three miles to the south of what increasingly became known as 'Old' Delhi. At the same time, the walled city had only become more congested, more haphazard, and more uncontrollable than ever. Beyond the walls, regardless of Whitehead's protestations over the mismanagement of government lands, and Clarke's enthusiasm to establish orderly extensions, spontaneous development continued. As the old city came to represent the limits of science and rationality, for the officials the planned development of the government's vast estates promised to celebrate the transformative powers of reason.

On the one hand was New Delhi, an impressive new testament to the power of British imperialism in the intensely symbolic and authoritarian capital complex, yet with no provision whatsoever for those occupied in manufacturing, laboring, or vending, or leading ordinary lives. On the other hand was the old walled city, by now showing changes to its forms, historic, incrementally developed and, to the British, chaotic. Blatant disregard of building regulations, illegal development, and defiant disorder in the spatial practices of the old city had frustrated the colonial officials in the preceding decades. Between these spaces developed the landscape of planned communities with tidy lots and identical units. Located on the outskirts of the old walled city of Delhi and the new imperial city of New Delhi, the new housing projects remained on the margins of both and for long, largely neglected in scholarship on Delhi.[1] From the perspective of European modernity, the new residential developments formed a 'modernizing' landscape: one that showed recognizable signs but that was as yet incompletely 'modern' in its progress towards a predetermined end.

For colonial officials, the walled city was overcrowded, irregular, uncontrollable, and lacking in basic facilities, increasingly resembling the industrial slums of cities in Western Europe such as Manchester, Paris, or Berlin. The establishment of the Delhi Improvement Trust in 1936 helped to administer and manage valuable government properties to keep them from following a similar fate but it was also an opportunity to demonstrate the power of considered urban development. 'Rationally' planned neighborhoods based on 'scientific' calculations regarding density with predictable lots, designs, and uses were not possible in the walled city or even in the spontaneous and rapidly growing enclaves just outside the walls. The quality of the housing environment was reduced to absolute and quantifiable determinants and the attributes were then applied to the new layouts.

A close examination, however, reveals complex and contradictory perceptions and realities. Implicit in the development of new housing for the local population was the idea of a regulated and 'modern' environment creating obedient and 'modern' citizens. In this chapter, I investigate the making of the new extensions in the context of the perceived differences in the society and spatial practices between the old and the new city. My study suggests that hidden agendas, political ambitions, and local customs of building and living countered British efforts and their stated intentions to deliberately reshape Delhi's landscape. The apparently recognizable forms that resembled familiar European ones were, in fact, expressions of a different modernity and its particular context.

VISUALIZING EMPIRE

Begun in 1911, the new imperial city was inaugurated in 1931. New Delhi emerged as the complete antithesis of the old city. The total area of the site was about ten square miles – more than five times that of the existing old city. On a site that included orchards, gardens, scattered villages, farmland, mosques, shrines, and *mazār* (tombs), Edwin Lutyens and Herbert Baker created a government center as a masterful and perfect whole (Figure 6.1). The design was intended to convey the idea of a 'peaceful domination and dignified rule over the traditions and life of India by the British Raj.'[2]

At the focus of the design were the Government House – the residence of the Viceroy – the Council Chamber and two symmetrical blocks of the Secretariats in which members of the Governor-General's Council administered the Imperial government (Figure 6.2). At the eastern end of the great main avenue that led from the government center was Indraprastha, the site of the oldest of all the former cities of Delhi preceding Shahjahanabad:

Figure 6.1
Layout of Imperial Delhi,
1939.
1. Viceroy's House;
2. Secretariat buildings;
3. War Memorial Arch;
4. Connaught Place

Figure 6.2
View of secretariat
buildings from King's
Way. The dome of the
Viceroy's House is in the
distance. Since
ˉndependence in 1947,
the Viceroy's House has
functioned as the
residence of the
President of India.

Right and left the roadways go and weld into one the empire of to-day with the empires of the past and unite Government with the business and lives of its people.[3]

Behind the Government House were gardens and parks flanked by the general buildings of the Viceregal estate. Another broad avenue, at right angles to the first connected the railway station, post office, and business quarters at its north-ern end to a Cathedral in the south. Scattered to the south-east were the tombs of Safdarjang and Lodi in an area designated for city expansion and public insti-tutions. An artery from the secretariat to the Jama Masjid was to be the principal business axis. A processional route due south from the railway station intersected the grand boulevard. The buildings of the Oriental Institute, the Museum, the Library, and the Imperial Record Office formed an intellectual center at this junc-tion (Figure 6.3).

Figure 6.3
War Memorial Arch or
India Gate at the end of
King's Way.

The spatial order of the new city had a carefully constructed hierarchy. Atop the hill was the Viceregal palace (or Government House) and the secretariat buildings. Fanning out from the core were the bungalows of those in service of the Empire. Members of Council, the Secretaries, European officials, 'Indian Princes and Chiefs,' members of the local administration, 'European clerks,' and 'Indian clerks,' all had a designated space in the scheme (Figure 6.4). Those in senior positions lived closest to the Government House, the center of power, and the petty clerks the farthest from the core. The size of the bungalow and the lot reflected the status of the official in the administration. The sprawling bungalows of senior European officials were set amidst vast gardens on a road with other sprawling bungalows in their vast gardens while lower-ranking workers and clerical staff crowded into two- and three-storied apartment buildings (Figure 6.5). Monuments, architectural splendors, gardens, banks, modern retail centers, administrative offices, postal and telegraph offices, halls of justice, a race course, golf course, clubs, hotels, and modern retail centers were all carefully located in this fastidiously orchestrated urban representation of the British Empire (Figure 6.6). The grand imperial city was about government and power, order and control, about an idealized 'modern' life as visualized by its British architects, drawing on 'garden city' ideals of 'light and air,' as well as notions of 'efficiency,' health, and moral uprightness prevalent at home (Figure 6.7). The city made no room for the humdrum daily life of ordinary people going about their mundane businesses. The common subjects of the empire crowded into the old walled city or spilled out into fast growing enclaves outside.

Figure 6.4
The residence of the Commander-in-Chief's of the British Army, 1930. This building became the residence of the first Prime Minister of India in 1948.

Figure 6.5
A European officer's
bungalow in New Delhi.

Figure 6.6
The commercial center of
Connaught Place, New
Delhi.

In a political environment of growing nationalism and antagonism to British rule in India, New Delhi presented a visual image of enduring stability that did not, in reality, exist. Making no room for industry, workshops or even a neighborhood grocer meant that ordinary people and small traders were excluded from the new city, forced to reside either in the old walled area or its already crowded extensions. In this manner, the spaces that were labeled 'backward,' 'traditional,' and 'un-modern,' in fact, serviced and supported the glorified 'modernism' of the new capital. Without these spaces, New Delhi could not have functioned.

Figure 6.7
Wide, tree-lined
boulevards of New Delhi.
Beyond the sidewalks on
either side are the low
red compound walls of
bungalows.

FROM PICTURESQUE CITY TO 'SLUM'

By the end of the First World War, industry and commerce had grown substantially in Delhi. Factories and mills had been established; roadways and railways
transported goods in and out of the city connecting Delhi to its immediate region
and to more distant cities around the country (Figure 6.8). Private enterprise and
economic prosperity were sprouting everywhere. Living conditions, however,
seemed only to deteriorate. With the completion of the new imperial city, the
walled city grew ever more congested and unplanned neighborhoods proliferated just beyond the walls. In less than a century after they had taken over, colonial officials declared Delhi, the home of Emperors and princes, the mystical and
exotic city of the Orient, an uncivilized 'slum.'

Despite municipal projects to provide piped water and sewage disposal, the
lack of water supply and sewage infrastructure combined with increasing overcrowding to create unsanitary conditions that seriously concerned the health officials. While the conditions in Delhi had long been a source of anxiety for the
British administrators, the Medical Officer of Health of Delhi published a report in
1934 that confirmed their worst fears.[4] The popular Bombay English-language
daily *The Times of India* was quick to sensationalize these concerns. Titled 'Delhi
the Death-Trap,' an article reported that although Delhi was comparatively small,
covering only six square miles, its population had increased enormously since the
Government of India had established their new capital.[5] The city, according to
the article, had become 'a hot bed of preventable disease.' In the Medical
Officer's representation, '. . . so great is the overcrowding in some parts of the
city that the houses are "nothing short of death traps." ' Further, 27 areas in
the city were without sewers and life was still worse in the unplanned

Figure 6.8
Plan of Delhi, 1930. This shows the walled city, the Civil Lines to the north and spontaneous developments to the West 1. Historic walled city, 2. Civil Lines, 3. Subzi Mandi, 4. Sadr Bazaar, 5. Paharganj, 6. New Delhi, 7. New military cantonment. Also shows gardens, orchards, and villages to the north and north-west and south-west.

neighborhoods that had sprung up to the west of the city walls. As the article noted,

> '... the population of 15,000 in the new area lives without drains or properly made roads and has to draw its water supply from wells sunk in the ground which receives the sullage from the houses.'[6]

Needless to say, such allegations from a Bombay-based daily caused much embarrassment to the administrative officials in Delhi. Readers were no doubt horrified to learn that in some new neighborhoods that had mushroomed outside the walls, sewage often found its way into sources of drinking water. But where officials blamed irresponsible citizens for Delhi's condition the public held the municipality guilty of neglect.

Representations of the indigenous city as overcrowded and unsanitary recall the language used in the late nineteenth-century portrayal of 'slums' in the industrial cities of Europe and North America: 'tortuous lanes,' 'densely packed quarters,' 'small dark rooms,' 'inadequate infrastructure,' and 'questionable morals.' As officials noted about the increasing density of building in the city,

> This cannot be viewed with any great equanimity . . . the apparent conclusion is that the congestion in the city is increasing, that buildings which were sufficient for one family are now housing more than one family, that as there is very little room for expanse outwards, extension is going upward notwithstanding the fact that the majority of the lanes and streets are narrow.[7]

Statistics and census data involving detailed, scientific counts of population were instrumental in declaring the city congested. After the capital of the British Empire in India had moved from Calcutta, the population of Delhi had increased manifold due to large-scale in-migration from the countryside. In one decade alone, from 1921 to 1931, the urban population of Delhi increased by 44 percent, from 304,420 to 439,180. In the neighborhoods just outside the city walls the population incease in the same decade was 63 percent. By contrast, the rural population increased only 7 percent, from 183,768 to 197,066.[8] Much of the increase was due to immigration. However, the new migrants did not spread across the city uniformly but had differential impacts on the old and new cities of Delhi. With most of the migrants moving into the old walled city and its extensions immediately outside the walls, population densities in these areas were 30 times greater than the population densities in New Delhi and 100 times greater than in the Cantonment (Table 6.1).

The wide variation in density only served to widen the disparities between the old city (Delhi Municipality) and those areas that the colonial authorities considered desirable for habitation such as New Delhi, the Civil Lines, and the Cantonment, all primarily occupied by Europeans and those in their service. Further,

Table 6.1 Population densities of municipalities and notified areas (1931)

Municipality or notified area	Area in acres	Population (census of 1931)	Population density (per acre)
Delhi municipality	3,840	347,539	90.5
New Delhi	20,308.5	64,855	3.16
Municipal civil lines (notified)	5,670	16,347	2.92
Fort (notified)	614.4	1,641	2.67
Delhi Cantonment	10,624	8,798	0.83

Source: *Health Report*, 1931, p. 25, (NAI).

as A. P. Hume pointed out in his report, the density of population in the Delhi Municipal area was far greater than that of any other city in India. The nearest to Delhi was Kanpur in northern India. An Indian daily observed that even in Calcutta, where the overcrowding in some areas was considered deplorable, the average was almost half that of Delhi.[9]

Unsanitary conditions in the old city were exacerbated by the absence of adequate infrastructure. Despite the stated intentions of the municipality, until 1931 very few houses in Delhi City had any water-borne latrines. Although the city projects provided some, the water-borne system served only about 20,000 people out of a total population of around 350,000.[10] And even this figure does not indicate how many had actually installed such equipment and gained connections.

Simultaneously with the visible deterioration of the walled city, new economic policies encouraged enterprise, set capital free, and made property a marketable commodity rather than a hereditary right. Petty entrepreneurs, landlords, and the emerging middle and lower-middle classes saw immense opportunities in the city. It was not only the government that was seeking to maximize returns from its land holdings, but also local property owners, developers, and small businesses. Subdividing property, adding a floor or extra rooms, converting courtyards into rooms, or appropriating communal open space adjacent to their properties became ways of expanding properties for rental or for sale, in this way accommodating the flood of immigrants. The creation of a land market combined with demographic changes to create an upsurge in the value of real estate in the city. The demand for housing as well as space for small businesses was far in excess of what was available. The result, as officials observed, was that landlords frequently added to existing buildings without due consideration to the health or safety of the inhabitants or the neighbors.[11] Despite all the efforts of the municipality, unregulated building persisted (Figures 6.9 and 6.10).

While Delhi's municipal building code had been revised and made more stringent over the years, with the city government's own team of representatives policing construction in the city, officials found it increasingly problematic to control and regulate building development.[12] Intertwined as the buildings were, owners added to and extended their properties as they saw fit, and as they could agree with their neighbors. The municipal vision of the city was frequently in conflict with customary spatial practices. The one was rigid and contrary to local logic where the other was flexible and responsive. The municipality set up a Building Committee expressly to review proposals for all construction work in order that they met the building codes and that plans could be reviewed and sanctioned. The typical small entrepreneur subdividing his property or adding a floor totally ignored these procedures and undertook his construction by stealth.

Inhabitants of the city found ingenious ways of getting around the most restrictive of regulations, frustrating administrators' attempts to 'safeguard' the health of the residents. Since building inspections typically occurred only once during construction, owners of properties would temporarily arrange for the

Figure 6.9
View of the unregulated
form of the walled city.
The dome and minarets
of the Jama Masjid are
on the horizon.

building to conform. For instance, when getting the second-floor structure approved, courtyards smaller than the minimum permissible were obscured from the inspector's view, being temporarily covered over as a floor.[13]

Residents learned that the legal instruments and institutional apparatus the British put in place to justify and implement colonial control could also be used to resist and counter it. Over the years, Delhi's residents became increasingly skilled at confronting the municipality through legal procedures. They brought restraining orders on demolitions and appealed through court injunctions. Municipal reports are replete with details of court proceedings regarding cases of irregularities in building. Property owners took advantage of loopholes in the regulations to legalize an illegal structure after construction. Renewing applications, filing appeals, and appealing to higher courts were all means that residents employed to work around a building code they likely considered restrictive and rigid.

Scant respect was shown for by-laws 'honored more in breach than in observance.'[14] Yet, construction did not take place with complete disregard for regulation either. Rather, residents sought to achieve their vision insidiously, with the least confrontation. The following commentary in the Delhi Municipal Authority annual report of 1938–39 is particularly revealing in this regard, and merits quoting at length:

> It is a distressingly common practice among a certain kind of citizen to start their building operations without waiting for the sanction of the Committee and in certain cases even without applying for any permission. Or, in the alternative, they attempt to circumvent the building bye-laws by ingenious devices, peculiar to each case, in order to have a building which will fetch them rent or afford personal satisfaction at the cost of human health. To defeat the object of 'set-back' the entire building is proposed to be

Figure 6.10
Buildings and spaces
adapted to accommodate
new uses. The entry
vestibule of a large
haveli has been
converted into a mini-
bazaar.

rebuilt excepting the wall abutting on the narrow lane on which the building is situated. The wall is then plastered and in some cases actually rebuilt at convenient hours when no member of the Municipal staff is expected to be there. This is one of the commonest devices. Every Bye-law is thus subjected to tests which were never contemplated and which obviously no law can normally withstand.

This state of affairs exists because the would-be law breaker is provided with so many loopholes at every stage. He feels that he can conveniently break the law and escape the consequences by simply bringing into play the influence of his well placed friends and supporters. Even if a notice is served for the removal of an unauthorised structure, the person concerned ignores it till the expiry of the first notice and when the final 6 hours notice is served upon him, he comes forward with an appeal which must take some time for disposal. When the demolition gang at last reaches the spot, he runs to his influential friends and makes them also run about in order to get the demolition postponed. He files amended plans and uses every other possible means of delaying the demolition. Then the amended plans reach the Committee stage, the applicant is found loitering and lobbying in the verandahs of the Town Hall and generally making a nuisance of himself to all concerned. The number of such persons is often so large that it is impossible to work in the adjoining office owing to the disturbance that goes on in the verandah. When even all such and other attempts to stop demolition fail the undaunted calmly goes to the civil court and obtains an injunction which affords him temporary relief and an opportunity for fresh attempts to prepare other amended plans and have them passed by the Committee.[15]

In 1939, more than half a century after municipal efforts at regulating the building form of the city had begun, officials documented 12,654 cases of offences under the Municipal Act.[16] In the circumstances, city authorities were grateful for what control they had. To them, the demolition of as many as 496 unauthorized constructions within the year appeared to be an achievement.

People's complex identities and multiple loyalties further complicated the city government's efforts to make the built form conform to the ideals underlying the by-law. Municipal inspectors and lower administrative members of the Committee were also local residents, members of extended families, neighborhoods, religious sects, and communities. The relationship of these individuals to their fellow citizens in their various capacities was significant. 'Goodwill money' or other political pressures were clearly not unknown.[17] So widespread were the subversive practices in building that officials in charge of reviewing building plans and sanctioning permission were forced to view the cases with leniency. Officials noted the practice of resubmitting building plans that had once been rejected for non-conformance with the by-laws. Since there was no rule to prohibit this, residents took advantage in resubmitting rejected plans and then applying pressure through political or financial means to have them passed. In this people used their social capital, the informal exchange of favors to accomplish their desired goals. In many instances even when the city's building committee had rejected a proposed plan outright, the owner simply resubmitted the same as a fresh application without any modification and obtained approval.[18] The inhabitants also fully exploited the rules for building a *barsāti* on the flat roof of a house. Customarily, a *barsāti* was a light structure or open pavilion on top of residential structures used for sleeping in the summer. However, *barsāti* structures were routinely converted or constructed as complete rooms for living.[19] Gradually, this expanded to become a whole additional floor. The consequence was that the semi-legal additional floor severely reduced the 'air and light planes' of adjacent buildings and public spaces.

Seemingly random acts of builders were not the only cause of disorder in the city. Over the decades, the conflicts over the definition of 'public space' discussed in Chapter 3, and the right to privatize it had only intensified. The more the authorities attempted to regulate the more people seemed to violate their rules. The state's efforts in controlling deviance began to extend into defining acceptable public behavior. Even as the municipal administrators proscribed stringent regulations against *takhtas* (platforms) and other projections from shops on to streets, the appropriation of public space by hawkers and vendors became more institutionalized.[20] Officials became increasingly frustrated in their efforts to keep the city free of the daily acts of appropriation:

Foot-paths were intended for pedestrians but at present they are infested with beggars and hawkers, especially Khari Baoli, Chandni Chowk Lal Kuan and Saddar Bazar . . . It has been a daily experience that a hawker would leave a place when asked to but would invariably return to it a few minutes after. He gives a false name and address and can not be traced when prosecuted. If we are able to find him out the Courts take their own time for the disposal of such petty cases. At the end the transgressor is fined a rupee or so.[21]

On the one hand was a government that identified itself as 'modern,' following the libertarian ideals, transparent laws, and equal justice that gave even ordinary residents a clear sense of their rights; on the other hand was the fundamentally unequal politics of colonialism. The rationale of the laws did not appeal to local logic. The colonial government had failed to gain the residents' confidence so that even the hawkers felt empowered to contest the laws. Many of the hawkers and beggars on footpaths saw it as their right to claim the use of public land and viewed the interference of the municipal authority as unjust harassment. When officials attempted to take vigorous action against such appropriation, they faced the possibility of attacks by the residents.[22]

For those who hoped that it would eventually resemble the 'modern' cities of Western Europe, Delhi proved disappointing. Clearly, officials had attempted without success for decades to re-shape the walled city to achieve at least some aspects of the idealized form of the 'modern' metropole. Yet even as officials struggled to control it, Delhi spilled out of the walls and rapidly developed into spontaneous arrangements in the Paharganj, Sadar Bazar, and Subzimandi areas to the West of the walls. Planned extensions on a small, piecemeal basis such as the one Robert Clarke proposed had failed to be effective. For the colonial government, with a glorious new imperial capital, and valuable properties at stake, the notion of creating ideal neighborhoods outside the walled city took root. The idea of the city as an organism firmly directed the imagination and policies of city officials. They were convinced that removing 'slums' was necessary to ameliorate what they were convinced were unsanitary conditions and excessive congestion.[23] For the city to be kept healthy 'slums' had to be removed like the gangrenous limbs that must be forgone to save the body. The ideal city, New Delhi's designers believed, was one that stood complete at its birth and yet still had the power to grow without losing its character.[24]

DIT'S VISIONS OF MODERNITY

The colonial government owned the vast *nazul* estates on all sides of the walled city. With the building of New Delhi, it had further acquired enormous properties to the West and South. In the face of rapid urban growth and rising land values, the administration of these assets was a matter of urgent concern. Following the study and recommendations of Whitehead, the Delhi Improvement Trust (DIT) was established in 1936 with the authority to administer large Government estates and deal with problems of slum clearance. Following A. P. Hume's study, the task of relieving congestion, improving living conditions, and providing new areas for extension were also the tasks of the new body.[25]

Extension schemes in previous decades had been premised on developing a relatively small area with shop-houses and a tightly knit, high-density neighborhood, similar to those in the walled city only more regular and less congested. The idea of comprehensive development providing for roads, streets, space for building, and services had not been previously undertaken. The DIT had the legal authority to acquire lands, relocate people, and undertake construction as well as the fiscal instruments and autonomy to raise funds to finance its projects.[26]

On government lands that still contained villages, orchards, and fields, the DIT set about developing new housing enclaves that exemplified everything the old city was not: straight wide roads, tidy lots, and units of predictable and equivalent character and value that were classified and grouped as such. The removal of 'slums' (including portions of the walled city) was central to DIT's responsibilities and, from an official perspective, necessary to achieve 'improvements' in the health of Delhi city:

> If the city is to be brought on lines more compatible with public health it is evident that a major portion of the city will have to be pulled down which is not a practicable proposition. All that would perhaps be possible to do is to clear out slums from highly congested areas or to drive one or two roads through the city and thus force a section of the public to move out of the city to settle down in new bastis [enclave or settlement] to be built outside the city wall.[27]

DIT's work in the city was wide-ranging: in addition to housing and 'slum clearance,' they included the grassing of the barren areas to the south and west of the Fort that were cleared soon after the 1857 uprising (known as the Champ-de-Mars Irrigation Scheme); the layout of housing for the well-to-do (Daryaganj South), the middle class (the Western Extension Scheme), and the poorer sections (the Ahata Kidara Scheme); numerous 'slum clearance' and relocation projects; the redevelopment of commercial streets (the Faiz Bazar scheme); the construction of markets (the Sabzimandi Fruit and Vegetable Market); and the relocation and construction of a new slaughter house. The efforts to reorganize and improve the city also included a proposal for developing an Industrial Area (Figure 6.11). This attempt at zoning was motivated by the proliferation of factories, large and small, in different parts of the city and a pressing demand for land to set up more industrial units for which neither New Delhi nor the historic walled city had any room. Creating a separate industrial area removed such uses from valuable land in the heart of the city to less expensive land on the outskirts.[28]

One of the earliest schemes that the DIT took up in 1936 was the development of Daryaganj South into a residential enclave for affluent Indians. An area of 21 acres just south of the palace had once been an elite neighborhood of princely mansions that the British had leveled, appropriated, and kept vacant

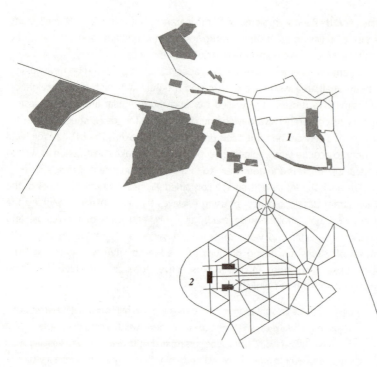

Figure 6.11
Map of Delhi showing
the location and layout
of the DIT schemes, 1939.
A comparison with the
map of 1930 shows that
many of the gardens and
orchards were developed
into residential areas.
1. Walled City, 2. New
Delhi. DIT project areas
in gray.

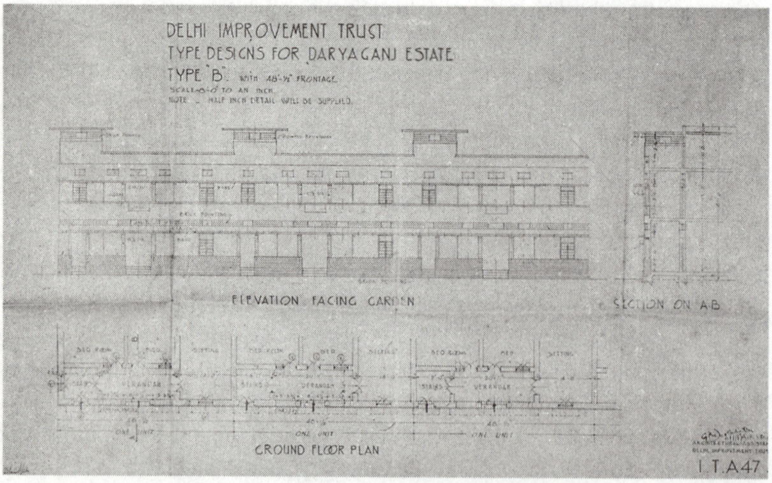

DELHI IMPROVEMENT TRUST
TYPE DESIGNS FOR DARYAGANJ ESTATE
TYPE "B" WITH 48'-0" FRONTAGE.
SCALE 1/0 TO AN INCH.
NOTE — HALF INCH DETAIL WILL BE SUPPLIED.

ELEVATION FACING GARDEN

SECTION ON AB

GROUND FLOOR PLAN

I.T.A.47

Figure 6.12
DIT designs for housing
for the well-to-do. The
DIT provided detailed
½-inch construction
drawings to the owners.
The units were grouped
around a park. The
buildings were narrow
and set back from the
streets with front lawns.
The front elevations
were regulated as was
the plan of the front
portion. Interior spaces
were functionally
separated and no
internal courtyard was
indicated.

after the 1857 clearances. The layout consisted of townhouses that were three stories high and occupied small lots that ranged in size from 300 to 550 square yards and bungalow sites that were a quarter of an acre each. The entire area was divided into tidy blocks with orthogonal streets. The design of the town houses where the DIT built them was identical (Figure 6.12). In the remainder areas, the building footprint, volume, entrances, openings, and relative arrangement of rooms were constrained by legal restrictions. Another feature of this project was a central park of about two and a half acres that was grassed and surrounded by a neat hedge.

More profitable than the residential developments was the reorganization of the main commercial spine running through Daryaganj, the once prosperous Faiz Bazaar (Figure 6.13). Property on both sides of the street were arranged into shop sites fronting on to the main street with small narrow lots of 200–350 square yards each. Strict design controls by the DIT enforced a standard frontage on the shops along Faiz Bazaar Road while a service access was made possible from the rear. The intention was to achieve a rhythmic and controlled façade with a predictable and high value for the property (Figure 6.14).

The DIT's design of Daryaganj South was an attempt to establish urban dwelling patterns modeled on European forms that most DIT officials believed were universally 'modern.' Both townhouses and bungalows were dwelling forms that were new to the walled city. The buildings were set back from the street edge with front lawns defining a different relationship to the street than was customary. The equivalent size and similar design of adjacent buildings assumed the absence of social hierarchy within a group of structures. Rooms with specific and separate uses such as 'sitting room' and 'bed room' were configured on European models of a small nuclear family, and modes of familial interaction and privacy different from those prevalent in the walled city. No internal courtyards or private open spaces were indicated in the proposals and the transition from public street to private interior space was abrupt by local

Figure 6.13
DIT Elevations and part plans for shops and 'flats' on Faiz Bazaar Road, Daryaganj. The ground floor had shop entries and the shops were narrow. The upper floors were intended for residential use with verandahs and balconies fronting the street.

Figure 6.14
View of DIT rebuilding
along Faiz Bazaar Road,
Daryaganj. Note the
regulation heights and
elevation types. Over the
years, these have been
modified by the owners
to suit their individual
needs.

standards. The expectation was that in adapting to their new dwelling, people would 'modernize' their way of living to fall in line with the normative model.

In marked contrast to schemes such as those for Daryaganj, housing for the poorer sections of the population were sited in less desirable locations on the outskirts of the city with higher densities and smaller units. The Andha Moghul colony, for instance, was established as a new area for the 'poor class' and as a way of relocating 'undesirable' people – those categorized as 'gypsies' and 'criminal tribes' as well as tanners, and pig-keepers from within the heart of another DIT project, the Western Extension scheme, an enormous and highly prized venture aimed at a 'middle-class' population.[29] The evicted tenants were relocated to Andha Mughal, on less desirable and hence, less valuable land near a sewage pumping station.

Lands were developed in relation to their estimated values after 'improvements.' Iterant gypsies and some communities of leatherworkers had long created for themselves enclaves on the outskirts of the walled city. When such settlements came in the heart of areas marked for redevelopment, the DIT chose to simply uproot and relocate them. Officials worried that the presence of such settlements in the midst of their perfectly ordered housing enclave would lower property values and jeopardize the success of the scheme. Meanwhile, poor-class housing such as Andha Moghul mixed in along with the gypsies and 'criminal tribes,' poor families dispossessed in other 'slum-clearance' schemes. Official efforts at 'improvement' thus actively involved restructuring the social landscape of the city by creating ghettos and affluent enclaves. The poor, the dispossessed, and the socially marginal were relegated to new 'slums' in less desirable locations and less visible to the well-to-do.[30] Homogeneity in architectural form and current economic status presumed homogeneity in social status and spatial practices that did not exist – or hoped to create it.

The layout of the 'poor-class' housing enclaves such as Basti Rehghar and Hathi Khana also proposed very small units closely packed together served by narrow but straight roads (Figure 6.15). Unlike the affluent housing, these now included multipurpose rooms, and shared blocks of toilets. Private open spaces were generally absent in these. By implication, the 'poor class' were further behind the affluent and Western-educated Indians on the road to achieving the European model of modernity.

Perhaps the most ambitious of all of DIT's projects was the Delhi Ajmeri Gate Slum Clearance Scheme. More than a decade before the project, the Municipality had identified the area adjacent to the city wall between Delhi Gate and Ajmeri Gate, including some of the most dense neighborhoods within the walled city, to be in urgent need of sanitary improvement in the interests of the city's public health. The project was impressive because the properties were not Nazul or government owned but instead were part of the city's dense fabric with its knotty system of titles, tenure, and ownership. Although the owners of the existing properties were prosperous, a vast majority of the inhabitants were poor tenants: sweepers, barbers, *mochis* (shoe-smiths), *tongawalas* (horse-carriage drivers), and *ghosis* (dairymen). Large-scale acquisition, demolition, and relocation was anticipated with an estimated 3,422 families involved.[31] The proposal involved bringing down the city wall between the two gates, acquiring outright all areas classified as 'slum' together with other 'congested, insanitary and ill-arranged buildings.' The acquired land would then be cleared and redeveloped according to a preconceived layout that would provide new wide roads and expansive open spaces, and community facilities such as children's playgrounds, schools, welfare centers, and health centers. The initial scheme required wholesale

Figure 6.15
DIT Layout plans for 'poor class' housing in Basti Rehghar, Karol Bagh. Note the very small size of the lots and the dense but regular layout of lots. The smaller plots to the right are about 15 ft × 30 ft and the larger ones about 42 ft × 42 ft. Small parks were provided between the rows of lots. Ironically, the parks were more frequent in the areas with larger lots than those with smaller lots.

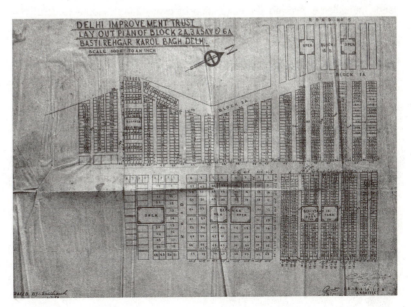

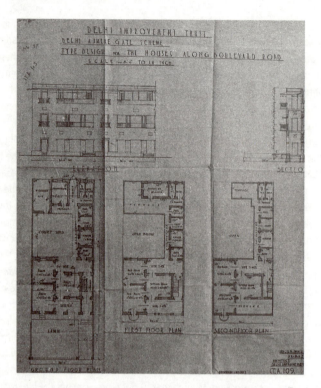

Figure 6.16
DIT-type designs for houses for the well-to-do, Delhi Ajmere Gate Scheme. The buildings were only 36 ft wide and set back from the street by a 25 ft lawn. The internal layout of these dwellings were more adapted to local spatial uses with each dwelling having a small private courtyard, a kitchen at one end of it, a servant's room at the back, a toilet to the rear that was set apart from the rest of the living spaces.

clearance of the neighborhood to a general depth of 150 feet from the city wall that bounded the area and the re-housing of over 2,300 families living in what officials classified as 'slum conditions.'[32] In addition to large plots of government land, the scheme involved the acquisition of over 42,000 square yards of privately owned land. The intention was to make around 65,000 square yards of plots available for residential construction.

So extensive was the scheme and so powerful the proposal that a good portion of the project was eventually implemented in the 1950s. Although the stated intention of the project was to alleviate the 'slum conditions,' the particular portion of the walled city selected for redevelopment was the southern part fronting on to the new capital of New Delhi. Creating wide roads, playgrounds, and expansive open spaces in the walled city meant that some areas were to be redesigned to include multistory blocks. Eighteen blocks of 'modern' buildings, shops, flats, and residential houses were to line the frontage of the development area overlooking New Delhi along the mile-long green area from Ajmeri Gate to Delhi Gate (Figure 6.16). This frontage was eventually built as five- and three-storied buildings with the first floor as large shops and showrooms and the upper floors as offices or residential flats. In order that DIT maintain control over the type and use of the buildings erected, the lots were let out on perpetual leases rather than as freehold.[33] Strict design controls were enforced on the façade to achieve a controlled modular pattern of level lines and rectilinear

Figure 6.17
View of a street adjacent
to the demolished wall.
The DIT developed this
area as part of the Delhi
Ajmere Gate Scheme.

volumes along a straight street. The buildings, while maintaining the line of the
city wall, presented a recognizably 'modern' front to New Delhi (Figure 6.17).

A 'SCIENTIFIC' APPROACH TO ARCHITECTURE

Two fundamental notions provided the underpinnings of the DITs work. First, it
was assumed that environments shaped societies and people and that people
who lived in similar environments shared a similar culture. Second, architecture
derived from 'scientific reason' and the principles of 'rational design' must be
universally valid regardless of culture and politics. The presumed supremacy and
universality of a science that was, in fact, rooted in a particular European context

justified the denigration of the walled city and its architecture as what the officials called a 'slum' and the replacement by a new kind of built form as a superior alternative.

From statistical analyses to land surveys, accurate measurement and documentation of properties to the mathematical estimation of their market values, the DIT projects celebrated the triumph of 'science' and the 'scientific' method. In contrast to what DIT officials perceived as irrational, disorderly, and accidental development within the walled city, in the new layouts land, roads, lots, buildings, house sizes, densities of units, family sizes, house plans, property values, and income levels, were all classified and arranged in what they believed was a rational order. The assumed neutrality of scientific observations belied the political motivations of planning decisions and an equally unfounded conviction of the universal validity of Western science and denied logic to any other decision-making process.

Scientific collection of demographic data and statistical analyses of the numbers played a central role both in the setting up of the DIT and in the standards that the DIT designs were expected to follow. The very perception of congestion and classification of a 'slum' were both based on the scientific determination of density. In his *Report on the Relief of Congestion in Delhi*, A. P. Hume, as Special Officer to look into the prevailing conditions in Delhi, noted a sharp rise in the population of the city but with an uneven spatial distribution.[34] The report observed a total increase of 35 percent over the 1911 population and of 27 percent over the 1921 population. The increase in the wards immediately outside the walled city including Subzimandi, Paharganj, and Sadar Bazar was substantially more with an 87 percent increase over the 1911 population and 63 percent over the 1921. Hume noted with concern that by 1936 the density of population in some wards had risen to 490 persons/acre.

Hume's report was to have a very significant influence on the DIT schemes. Hume documented information in fastidious detail and made numerous recommendations based on his 'scientific' study. However, translating the 'scientific' advice into planning policies was not simple. For instance, the report recognized a two-fold problem of congestion – congestion of people in houses, and of houses on land. It also indicated that a large number of people were in immediate need of better accommodation in the existing settlements within and outside the walled city. Rather than putting in place a physical, social, and economic infrastructure that would allow communities to settle lands outside the walled city, or create incentives for new migrants to locate themselves outside the already congested nucleus, the DIT hoped to cultivate perfectly controlled visions of a European inspired modernity. With little expectation of actual decongestion, DITs numerous projects envisioned impeccably ordered 'modern' enclaves on vacant or thinly populated lands outside the congested center. Contradictions were also evident in the biased interpretations of seemingly neutral data. The report identified several well-defined 'slum areas' of 'the meanest type' and Hume portrayed the city as abounding in 'insanitary lanes and dwellings constituting a menace to the public health of the whole urban area of Delhi.'[35]

At the same time, the report revealed that the middle classes and the lower middle classes constituted the largest section of the walled city with a few who were destitute. Instead, the settlements that had sprung up to the west of the walled city housed a larger number of the needy. Despite all indications that the spontaneous settlements of Sadar Bazar, Sabzi Mandi, and Paharganj were considerably poorer, more densely inhabited, and less served by city infrastructure than most of the walled city, the focus of the DIT efforts concentrated on decongesting the walled area.

Since one of the primary objectives of the new housing developments was to demonstrate the benefits of scientifically designed environments with optimum densities, officials greatly debated the question of what constituted an optimum or even an acceptable density. Hume's word carried great weight as he argued in his report:

> The standard of overcrowding which should be adopted is necessarily a matter of opinion. I have been influenced by the following standards in force or recommended in other places. In England the 1935 Housing Act has provided a standard for measuring overcrowding, whereby a floor area in a room of 110 sq. feet is the minimum permissible for 2 persons, and a room with a floor area of less than 50 sq. feet would be considered unfit for human habitation. In England therefore, the minimum permissible area, given certain conditions, is 55 sq. feet per person . . . In New Delhi, although the actual minimum permissible space per person is not laid down, the Municipal by-law (no. 28) stipulates that 'no room in a domestic building which is intended to be used as an inhabited room shall have a floor area of less than 90 sq. feet . . .' Assuming that a room of 90 sq. feet floor area, is not ordinarily intended to be occupied by more than 2 persons, the New Delhi standard is equivalent to a minimum of 45 square feet per person. Old Delhi Municipal bye-laws stipulate superficial floor area of not less than 100 square feet, which on the reasoning above, means a minimum of 50 square feet per person . . . In my opinion the final decision, as to which standard to adopt as a 'measuring stick; to measure congestion in Delhi, must be influenced by the conditions of the locality under consideration. Whereas 45, 40 or even 36 square feet per person would be suitable in an area where buildings are well planned and there is proper provision for free access of fresh air, 50 square feet per person is certainly not excessive in the many dismal tenements abutting on the foul, dark, crowded, ill-ventilated and narrow alleys of Delhi city.[36]

That standards from one economic, political, and cultural context were quite arbitrarily transferred to another did not seem to trouble any of the officials. Hume took fifty square feet of living space per person as a minimum. He further established other norms such as a single-storied house should occupy no more than one fourth the size of the lot, and the area occupied by roads, lanes, open spaces, and places of public convenience should be 45 percent of the project area. His calculations corresponded to a density of 120 persons per acre for single-storied constructions. Similarly, in a double-storied building the living space should be three-eighths of the total area of the house resulting in a density of about 180 persons per acre. For a three-storied house the density similarly arrived at was 210 persons per acre. Since Hume saw the walled city as consisting of both two- and three-storied structures, he recommended a figure of 200 persons per acre.[37]

Having assumed ideal densities and compared them with existing ones within the walled area, in his report Hume worked through detailed calculations to establish how many people needed to be removed from the old city and accommodated in extension schemes in order for the concentrations within the walled area to come down to acceptable levels. He declared a standard of no more than 200 persons per acre and anything more he considered to be 'excess.' On the basis of these figures, he proposed solutions to housing the large number of people who would have to be moved out of the walled city to bring the density to acceptable levels.[38] He saw a need to provide a total building area of 1,160 acres sufficient to accommodate 106,000 people.[39] In this pseudo 'objective' approach tightly knit families and cultural communities were reduced to numbers and the complex geography of neighborhoods to undifferentiated territories.

Despite the meticulous efforts to determine scientifically the figures, the final recommendations were quite arbitrary. Hume claimed that the optimum density in his view was 44 to an acre but, for practical reasons, he was going to be satisfied at the moment with a density of 200 persons to an acre. He offered no rationale for either of the two figures. While his calculations showed the need to reduce the population of Delhi city by 138,000 persons to bring down the density, Hume's recommendations for new extension schemes were to accommodate 100,000 persons at the rate of 100 persons per acre. The task then boiled down to finding 1,000 acres of vacant land to accommodate the 'excess' population. His recommendations and reports did not concern themselves with strategies for moving the 'excess' population out of the city or rebuilding communities both within the city and in the extensions. Despite all the apparent concern for systematic design, the amount of area occupied by a unit, and that devoted to roads or open spaces, was not debated or justified.

Providing adequate building area for the 'excess' population from the walled city meant developing to full capacity government lands in the outskirts of Delhi. Additional lands would also be required for which he recommended acquiring 'vacant' lands from private owners. He suggested clearing and rebuilding some depressed 'slum areas' he identified. Built-up property so identified and land still available within the city walls and in the settlements immediately outside included areas in Daryaganj North, Daryaganj South, Garstin Bastion Road, Paharganj, and Sadar Bazar North, all amounted to a total of 26 acres that would accommodate 2,600 persons. By contrast, lands immediately to the West of the walled city had an area of 275 acres for residential development and so could accommodate 275,000 persons making those lands the clear choice for building efforts.[40]

DIT's efforts to develop model dwelling environments included establishing architectural norms and controls. From the beginning the DIT insisted on the necessity of imposing design controls towards improving 'standards of architecture in buildings.'[41] In 1938 the Trust set up a standing sub-committee to advise on architectural questions and pass the type elevations and standard designs that the architecture section prepared under the supervision of an architect with an architectural training from Western Europe. Active members of the sub-committee included an engineer member of the Trust, Lala Sri Ram, one of Delhi's wealthiest industrialists, and Mr. Walter George, a British architect, engaged on the New Delhi building project. The Trust exercised control over buildings either through a lease or by the direct administration of building by-laws.

With the advice of British architects, the DIT formulated normative models for 'improved' architecture in Delhi based on familiar European expressions of modernity, dominant at the time. The controls, containing no explanation of how or from where they were derived, were slightly different for each scheme but shared an overall character. The patterns reflected a curious mix of forms drawn from European spatial practices and European convictions of sanitary science. The layouts, heights of buildings, set backs from streets, space between buildings, locations of stairs, size, and placement of rooms and services, sizes and placement of fenestration, materials and color of exterior finishes, detail of the (minimal) ornamentation – all were specified and carefully monitored by DIT officials. Where the DIT took up both designing and building, the units were to be modular and identical. Houses (and shops) intended to have a similar market value were designed on a modular prototype and grouped together. Simple orthogonal proportions, flat roofs, and a functional layout of rooms built of brick also established detailed façade controls to make the buildings conform to the most recent recommendations of the sanitary engineers. Standardized façade details gave the units a group identity.[42]

An architectural section of the municipality provided free advice to prospective private builders. Detailed drawings were also issued to plot owners for guidance and the results were particularly encouraging for the officials. For the poorer classes, copies of type plans were prepared and sold at a nominal cost (Figure 6.18). The DIT believed that these were commonly used and decreased the frequency with which building applications were rejected. From the DIT's perspective all of these controls helped to elevate the quality of architecture and hence the city. The DIT officials hoped that the public would take more and more advantage of the assistance offered by the Trust to promote the 'general improvement of architectural standards in Delhi.'[43] The new standards were expected to make building designs more scientific, more reasoned and less given to arbitrariness or religious dictum.

Where the DIT only laid out the lots, officials provided architectural guidelines to the builders to make the final settlement more rational. Prior to the commencement of construction, the DIT required lessees and anyone wishing to erect a building to give notice to the Lands Officer of the Trust. Further, they were also expected to submit a detailed site plan at a specified scale, with plans,

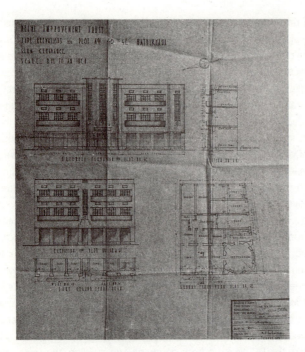

Figure 6.18
DIT, Typical Elevations
for Hathi Khana Slum
Clearance Scheme. The
small lots had shops on
the ground floor and
residences above. The
partial plans showed no
provision for private
courtyards. The
assumption was that the
shops would help to pay
for the project.

elevations, and sections of the proposed structure, and demonstrate its confor-
mity with all Trust by-laws including drainage by-laws. Plans for a residential
building defined every room separately with functional and material speci-
fications for each – the kitchen, the bathroom, corridors, and staircases.

All new structures were expected to meet requirements for light and ventilation for each structure, all determined by Western 'science' that officials
believed had universal validity. The exact basis on which the light and air requirements were formulated were generally vague or absent. A minimum volume of
space was prescribed in front of and to the rear of each structure, called the
'front and rear air planes,' to allow for adequate ventilation of all the rooms.
Similarly, 'light planes' specified the volume and shape of voids between buildings to allow adequate penetration of light into every room. No buildings were
to be erected within 15 feet from the center line of any street as determined by
the Trust, and every building not fronting on a street was to have a permanently
open 'air space' 15 feet wide as part of the building (Figure 6.19). Similarly ten
feet of 'air space' was deemed essential at the rear of the building. Any habitable
room that did not receive light and air from the front or back of the building was
to have one side abutting a permanent courtyard. The Trust even retained the
authority to decide the kind of latrine that was to be constructed (i.e., water
borne or dry; Indian style or Western).[44] After the building section and the lands
department had examined the application, the engineer member of the Trust
inspected it before passing it on to the health member.[45] All of these deliberations completely excluded from consideration the fact that in the hot, dry climate

Figure 6.19
A narrow bazaar street in
the walled city that has
been built up.

of Delhi, customary building practices minimized the direct penetration of
sunlight into the houses, opting instead for shady and breezy courtyards placed
centrally in the dwelling and used as open-air living spaces.

NEGOTIATING HIDDEN AGENDAS: THE POLITICS OF IMPLEMENTATION

The designs and architectural controls may have imagined Indians forming tidy
homogeneous bands of 'poor-,' 'middle-,' and 'upper-' classes, and the scientific

standards assumed people to be undifferentiated beings in a territory, but the politics of implementing the DIT projects and their paradoxical outcomes revealed otherwise. In contrast to the passive subjectivity assumed in the deliberate imposition of modernist forms imagined elsewhere, people sought opportunities to further their interests at a moment of cultural upheaval. In the changing cultural milieu of Delhi's modernity, the idea of private enterprise and maximizing profit had taken root. The astronomical rise in the value of real estate and the creation of land markets in the previous decades brought the tensions sharply into focus. DIT's institutional interests in profiteering, too, conflicted with the stated goals of planning to bring the greatest good for the greatest number.

DIT schemes were undertaken largely on government property such as the Andha Mughal, Western Extension, Arakashan, and Garstin Bastion Road projects. But the DIT also acquired additional lands such as in the Roshanara Extension, Northern City Extension, Delhi Ajmeri Gate Slum clearance, Industrial Area, and Hathi Khana schemes. The lands once acquired or those already in their charge were laid out according to a predetermined plan and the plots then auctioned for leasehold rights. The heavy expense of laying out the extension were to be met from the profits earned. Once the area had been so developed, its maintenance was turned over to the Delhi Municipal Committee (although income from the lands continued to flow to the Government). The Land Acquisition Act of 1894 allowed city officials to compulsorily acquire land from residents for public purposes. In situations where the owners were unwilling to sell or demanded a higher compensation than that offered by officials, the land was compulsorily acquired by enforcing the Land Acquisition Law.[46] However, land acquisition for DIT projects was clearly not for public purposes.

Within just six months of starting its programs, both citizens and officials of the walled city were already disparaging of the DIT's work. The chief criticism was that the DIT only took up Extension Schemes that were self-supporting or likely to yield a good profit. Nothing was done in reality, commentators observed, to remove what the DIT had labeled as 'slums' from inside the city.[47] Critics argued that the DIT's projects were designed to bring in substantial profits to the imperial government. Since the DIT was not under the local city government, its finances were directly under the national government rather than the city.

'Slum clearance' schemes were one of the DIT's main responsibilities. Even when the DIT undertook 'slum clearance,' critics accused them of following an incorrect sequence of activities. The way most of the schemes were to proceed was that an area would be identified and the properties acquired. The owners of the 'slum' sites were to be paid a minimum compensation and building sites allotted elsewhere to the original residents. The 'slum' land itself was then to be improved and provided with all essential services according to a sanctioned layout plan. The newly developed land was then to be leased out to other tenants on long-term leases or were sold by public auction. In the process, a 'slum' would be removed, a new sanitary colony would be established, and the DIT would have gained a considerable amount of money. In common practice, the DIT first evicted poor 'slum' dwellers before they even acquired the property. Only after they had acquired, improved, and sold the properties at a considerable profit did the DIT take up re-housing for the displaced. As a consequence, the poor were pushed to the outskirts of the new developments (or forced to huddle together in other 'slums') with no alternative accommodation, let alone economic and social networks.

In 1940 'rehousing' schemes were introduced into the repertoire of DIT projects as a separate category. Rehousing projects were to be state-subsidized schemes to accommodate the poor and the dispossessed forced out of the 'slum' redevelopment. The idea was for the benevolent state to take care of 'people of the poorest class dispossessed as the result of operations undertaken by the Trust.'[48] However, the re-housing schemes were designed to be financially self-sufficient, inadequate for the families dispossessed and slow to be implemented. Even where they had been built, they were often constructed as rental properties out of reach for the poor tenants. Compensation for the acquisition of property was only due to the owners.

While maximizing monetary returns from the Government lands, as an arm of the imperial Government, the DIT was careful to protect Government interests in retaining proprietary titles to the lands through long-term leases, selling few lots outright. Critics accused the DIT of profiteering. Each year the expenditure of the DIT was considerably less than the income it had earned.[49] In contrast, the expenditure on re-housing schemes was exactly equivalent to the receipts most of which were in the form of Government loans and subsidies. This meant that the surplus income earned by the Trust's improvement projects was not being put back into housing. Rather, the re-housing account was entirely separate.

The DIT projects served to open up new properties to an already bullish land market. Economic transformations freeing capital made it possible for investors, both big and small, to seek out assets to invest in. Land speculation became rampant. Since speculation further raised land prices, making it difficult for the DIT to acquire properties for development or to make a substantial profit from them, officials attempted in vain to use legal instruments to fix prices. In this manner, the DIT's programs for developing large estates embodied the contradictory goals of stimulating private capital while controlling it.

On the one hand, Hume clearly stated the official policy of encouraging private capital so that '. . . extension schemes must be expedited and reasonable facilities given to private capitalists to develop land outside the city.'[50] On the other hand, when a DIT scheme was still at a conceptual stage, a notification was usually issued under the Land Acquisition Act. Such a notification fixed land prices and prevented speculation before the scheme was brought to the ground and the negotiations for acquisition completed, otherwise land prices would skyrocket making the project not viable.[51] Officials feared that without such a notification speculators would endeavor to take advantage of any scheme that the government approved for the city.

Regardless of the confidentiality of the schemes, Delhi's petty capitalists learned of proposed projects even while they were in the earliest stages of discussion. The speculation that followed drove the prices of land up before any notification could go into effect.[52] Even before the DIT was actually established, A. P. Hume, as special officer appointed to study the relief of congestion in Delhi, noted:

> The public are aware that there is a definite intention on the part of the Municipality to launch a comprehensive extension scheme; they are also aware that an officer has been appointed by the Govt. of India to examine the problem of congestion and its relief. I have now myself verified the fact that during the last few months there has been considerable increase in the activities of speculators at various points on the west of the city . . . During a recent inspection, I found the agent of a private land-owner sitting under a tree on the Grand Trunk Road near the Najafgarh drain, with a register in his hands, awaiting bidders for a plot of land. He told me that he had been there a month and had so far refused a bid of Rs.4,600 for 1,700 sq. yds. of land. This is the equivalent of Rs.2-20-0 a square yard. The revenue authorities tell me that the general accepted rate for land of this kind is about Re. 1/- a square yard . . . I may mention the case of a certain colonisation company, which has recently sold land on the Grand Trunk Road at a price of Rs.2/8/- per sq. yd . . . The fact is that land-owners anywhere in the neighborhood of the Grand Trunk Road beyond Subzimandi are fully alive to the possibility of making their fortune, and many have already gone a good way to doing so. Not only will the effect of such speculation be to make the cost of acquisition of land for city extension in this neighborhood unrenumerative, if not prohibitive, but also the growth of numerous private unconnected colonisation schemes must render the task of framing a comprehensive extension plan utterly impossible.[53]

Residents were also aware of other monetary benefits they could derive from the redevelopment efforts that they had scant respect for to begin with. Where large-scale land acquisition was involved, a majority of the owners were generally dissatisfied with the amount of compensation and appealed to a tribunal set up by the DIT for granting awards. For instance in the Roshanara Extension project, land was acquired by compulsion from 23 owners and 21 of them appealed to the tribunal.[54] One property owner in the Roshanara scheme, whose lands the Trust attempted to acquire filed a suit in the civil courts seeking a permanent injunction to restrain the Trust from acquiring his land. Several other property owners in the Roshanara and Northern City II extension and Hathi Khana slum-clearance schemes requested the Trust to abandon the acquisition of their properties. In response, DIT was obliged to negotiate with them over their properties and compensations. In some cases, DIT was forced to exempt the property from acquisition. Those whose properties had been exempt were required to pay the DIT a substantial sum (equivalent to the estimated value of the land after redevelopment). Yet, even with the payments, most property owners preferred to remain in their old locations rather than allow their entire properties to be acquired and move to new locations, thus complicating matters for the DIT. The response of the citizenry was clear: people were unwilling to allow the Trust to acquire their properties towards an 'improved' city. The property owners did not see their own living conditions as improved by accepting compensation and moving elsewhere. Yet, they engaged with the economic and legal modernization enough to know how to maximize their individual gain.

'SCIENCE' AND SIGNS OF MODERNITY

In the end, a particular take on 'science,' with its aura of objectivity, was instrumental in the colonial officials' (and gradually of Indians educated and acculturated in Western ways of thinking) rejection of customary spatial practices and built forms as 'slum'-like in favor of other practices and forms that resembled European modernisms, reassuring in their visual completeness. If European art and literature had helped to create among Europeans an identity of historic Delhi as picturesque and exotic, mired in superstition, European 'science' constructed it as destitute and desperate in a manner that was convincing for both Europeans and Western educated Indians. Grassy lawns (even the name Champs de Mars), new types of markets, the planar street volumes, the rhythmic and modular architectural patterns, the affluent homes with European living influences were all distinct from the customary spatial and cultural arrangements in the walled city as well as being gainful business propositions for the DIT. Spatial forms that at least looked like the modernisms of Europe implicitly expressed the hope of achieving it – whether or not it was actually possible. This was, perhaps, the most lasting legacy of the DIT (Figure 6.20).

Local ways of living and working, together with people's social networks, economic interdependencies, and cultural significance, were irrelevant for the new designs (Figure 6.21). Extended families were not factored in nor was room assigned for mosques or temples. Regardless of (very low) car ownership at that time, streets marched across the landscape in straight lines and some leaning curves. A new centralized building process, rigid and unyielding, expected to put down completed forms and spaces which would be inhabited as they were built, replacing a more flexible and negotiated approach that responded to constant change. Yet, despite all attempts to create a visible distance from the existing cityscape of the walled area, in Delhi's planned neighborhoods, the resemblance to European forms was more implied than real. The density that the DIT followed was of 100 persons/acre in the planned extensions of Delhi, while 20 persons/acre was determined as appropriate for the development of Greater London.[55] High densities (relative to European standards), brick and plaster construction with flat roofs, covered verandahs on upper levels, openings with lattice work, courtyards, multipurpose rooms, detached bathrooms, and Indian-style toilets crept into the DIT's dwelling unit designs. Although some aspects of the DIT projects may have had in their initial conception a closer likeness to European models, in their adaptation to local context and in their inhabitation, they were soon indigenized.

The vision of model living that the projects presented, one that officials believed was universally ideal, was unappealing to the residents of the so-called

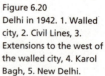

Figure 6.20
Delhi in 1942. 1. Walled
city, 2. Civil Lines, 3.
Extensions to the west of
the walled city, 4. Karol
Bagh, 5. New Delhi.

Figure 6.21
Women artisans continue to work in their homes. This kind of piecework or subcontracting in the context of tight social networks meant that women, even those in *purdāh*, were active participants in economic production.

'slums' in the walled city. Five years after DIT's inception in 1936, only 242 houses had been completed and five years later only 104 of them had been occupied. Residents displayed their disregard for and disagreement with the DIT projects in their lack of cooperation in forfeiting private land for Trust schemes, in their reluctance to inhabit the projects, in persistent land speculation, and through formal protests. Instead of decongesting the areas that officials labeled overcrowded, fresh categories of people moved into the new planned extensions. An army of immigrants had come to Delhi to work as menial labor to construct the capital complex and then stayed on. Also included were the petty entrepreneur, the worker, the trader, and the person-on-the-street who migrated to Delhi from across northern India, enticed by the opportunities the fast-growing city offered. This motley group, already displaced and disconnected, seeking to reinvent themselves, came to occupy many of the planned extensions. It was not that the residents perceived conditions in the most crowded parts to be healthy or ideal but rather, that the official solutions were less reasonable.

The new housing developments on the fringes of Old and New Delhi were meant to create ideal environments for the consummate citizens of British India. Prevailing environmental determinist views reinforced the idea that an orderly and sanitary environment would create orderly and healthy citizens who owed allegiance to the nation rather than the community. However, the British had multiple hidden agendas that complicated their stated intention of 'improvement' towards their own image. First was the motivation of an increasingly resource-starved government to raise revenue from its holdings that could be made to yield high returns. This meant the regular monitoring and managing of rents and leases to protect the vast and valuable government land holdings around the walled city from ad hoc settlement by those they considered as 'squatters.' The rapid development of Sadar Bazar, Paharganj, and Sabzimandi to the West of the city was evidence that spontaneous and irregular development had begun to spill beyond the walls and would spread quickly, threatening the society and space of New Delhi. Second, the British had a particular architectural vision of modernity in Delhi that was based on the normative ideals of the metropole. Applying 'modern' methods of administration and government by law had not yielded the desired outcome of taming the walled city to conform to that image. With New Delhi as a testament to their authority and superior accomplishments, the defiance of 'old' Delhi's uncontrollable built form, together with its inhabitants, was a continuing embarrassment for the British. Third, the colonial state wanted to present itself as a benevolent government committed to advancing the welfare of citizens but individual officials were faced with choosing between their multiple allegiances and the opportunities for personal gain. Finally, having built a brand new city that supposedly symbolized progress, and 'rational' governance and equal justice, it aspired towards a society of citizens who were good workers, healthy, morally upright, and obedient during a time of growing nationalism in India.

From the government's perspective, the planned extensions were meant to be exemplars of controlled growth. Intended to represent its version of urban and social modernity and the kind of progress possible under colonial rule, the housing schemes were meant to create model living environments through a rational planning process and present a vision of unity and stability. Against the background of poverty in India at the end of the First World War, the political and economic upheavals of the Second World War, the growing strength of the

Indian National Congress and Indian nationalism, and Hindu–Muslim conflicts, the carefully controlled landscapes of the DIT projects created an image of enduring stability that did not exist.

The residents for their part, however, were not passive recipients of these 'civilizing projects.' As they struggled to find a place for themselves in the tumult of economic and political change, citizens responded variously by maximizing personal gain, making their homes secure, predictable, and productive in their own social and cultural terms. Those who could took advantage of the new opportunities to make financial gains through investment in real estate. As they claimed public space, added to or modified their buildings, residents also used their own logic to develop a set of spaces most functionally advantageous to them and that offered continuity to their existing socio-economic structures and culturally familiar ways of living. However, with reduced community control, in focusing on private gain, they sometimes sacrificed public good. Faced with the rules and regulations of a new administrative and legal system, residents were quick to understand them and find ways of working them to their advantage. The rapid and uncontrolled growth of the urban fabric was also evidence of increasing investment and the growing power of petty entrepreneurs. Nominally following the law or manipulating it, appropriating space by stealth, negotiating compensations, pressurizing inspectors, screaming injustice and seeking protection of the law were only some of the many different methods that people used to confront the government and drive a compromise, even if it was not the outcome residents desired. Those who eventually did settle in the new developments adapted the space to suit their way of living. While some residents became convinced of the virtues of Western science, others ignored or resented the changes they were expected to make in their daily lives to accommodate the new spaces. Instead, they adapted and changed as it suited their needs and priorities (Figure 6.22). Where the tidy rows of houses did develop, personalized and added to they obscured the chaotic and informal processes that led to their creation. In their unpredictable and negotiated outcome, the planned extensions developed from building processes that partially resembled those already existing in Delhi.

The assumption that good design and effective planning could be accomplished by the simplistic application of 'scientific' formulae assumed to be universally valid was in itself erroneous. Although the calculations and by-laws themselves appeared very rational, the analytical basis for their prescriptions was not. As with Hume's estimates of acceptable densities, the ideal densities, 'air planes,' and 'light planes' were all quite arbitrary and had their origins and values in the totally different cultural and social milieu of the metropole. The narrow scientism of the officials neglected to understand the cultural value of dwelling and community. In emphasizing the numerical values of density, size, and stories, colonial officials ignored the totally different cultural, social, and economic conditions which governed people's lives, the significance of extended families, community networks, their location near mosques and temples, and the possibilities of economic production for residents in determining the appropriateness of

Figure 6.22
The DIT development of
Western Extension Karol
Bagh. Note that the
streets are narrow but
paved and rectilinear.
Apartments with shared
stairwells were the norm.
Over the years owners
have modified the
designs. Encroachment
on to the public street is
visible for some of the
buildings.

their dwellings. For inhabitants of the old city, living in propinquity with family and community, whether religious, caste, sect, or occupational, was central to their survival and prosperity. Customary house designs in what officers saw as 'congested' quarters of the old city also supported home-based industries that included the labor of women and older children. The new designs as well as their location outside the city required the separation of home from work and daily

Figure 6.23
Kamala Market
clocktower.

transportation beyond their means. Further, the creation of modular units grouped into income categories assumed cultural homogeneity and harmony within each of the bands. Far from homogeneity, in Delhi's society occupation, caste, sect, ethnicity, and religion defined people's identities to create a complex diversity that forms of European modernism could hardly suppress. Finally, the residents found community policing, oversight by neighbors whom they knew, to be a far greater source of security than surveillance by the agents of a government they did not trust.

The colonial agenda of absolute control was to be well served in the layout of the DIT projects. Wide, orthogonal streets, clear boundaries, modular lots and buildings, and the frequent absence of internal courtyards created an environment that was more transparent than the one in the walled city and hence it was easy for officials to police deviant behavior and insurgency. DIT and its redevelopments helped to justify the penetration of even the most opaque neighborhoods in the walled area where official notification of rebuilding enabled surveyors to intrude into private properties and carry out detailed surveys as well as note suspicious activities and materials. Most significantly, the flagship layouts of the DIT zoned out prostitution, gaming houses, bars, and other activities officials considered injurious either physically or morally. (Ironically, in postcolonial Delhi, many of the planned residential neighborhoods meant to nurture model citizens became centers of subversive activities.)

In the end many of the DIT projects were at least partially completed – some more than others. The designs were modified, scaled back, compromised, and adapted in many instances. And most took several years of planning and negotiation before they could even begin, let alone be completed. However, the idea that an architecture and urban design that resembled those of European modernism would eventually result in a similar form of modernity was a very powerful one (Figure 6.23). It was not only the British who were responsible for declaring their own version of modernity to be the only valid one; Indian nationalists, increasingly powerful players in the movement for independence, were equally adamant about their own version. After India gained independence in 1947, the work of the DIT was given over to the newly established Delhi Development Authority which brought to fruition some of the DIT projects. But in the years preceding it, the center of Indian political leadership in Delhi had moved out of the walled city to the Civil Lines and the newly developed estates in and around New Delhi. In a curious inversion where the familiar became strange and the strange became familiar, spaces meant to define ideal subject-hood of the British Empire became spaces for nurturing a new independent republic.

Chapter 7: Recovering an Urban Past

Delhi, the walled city, rich with building traditions, and for Europeans, the quintessential Oriental landscape, encountered dramatic cultural upheavals in the nineteenth and early twentieth centuries. Reason, science, and the universals of modernism in Europe arrived in India along with an authoritarian imperialism and exploitative capitalism. For their own economic and political ends, the new regime introduced, encouraged, and imposed modernisms which had arisen under different circumstances in Europe and which were presented as the only legitimate expressions to which Indians might aspire. The British brought to Delhi institutions (municipal governance), spatial forms (wide boulevards, house-in-a-garden), technologies (railways, sanitary reform), and concepts (land as commodity, private/public divide) imagined elsewhere and with the expectation of replacing those that existed. Over almost a century from 1857 to 1946, the city grew enormously, though with its urban form remarkably altered. However, if the objective was to achieve a built form and spatial culture that was 'modern' from the perspective of Europe, Delhi, a patchwork of many different landscapes, had only partially succeeded.

From a city entirely contained within its walls and with a dense organic fabric, Delhi had spread to several miles beyond, including in its boundaries the magnificent new capital complex of New Delhi. With narrow winding lanes, mansions with large courtyards, and dense clusters of smaller dwellings, Delhi's urbanism, until the middle of the nineteenth century, had a legible formal character, a grand palace, glittering bazaars, vibrant squares, streets lined with hawkers and vendors, and a multitude of mosques, temples, and tombs. Outside the walls were villages, estates, orchards, and gardens that supported the intensity of urban life within. After the East India Company's conquest of the city in 1803, the Mughal emperor remained a titular head until the British Imperial rule was established in 1857. Early British influence had brought a church, infantry barracks, and some large houses in the northern and eastern parts of the city. Yet, despite these changes, dramatic transformations in the space and culture of the city did not take place until the latter half of the nineteenth century.

Figure 7.1
A sidewalk appropriated for binding and selling calenders and small posters printed at a nearby press. The building behind is a turn of the century school that proclaims its Western orientation with its Grecian columns.

In the decades following 1857, many European buildings developed in the northern parts of the city, particularly around Kashmiri Darwaza. An extensive European enclave, the Civil Lines, was established to the north of the walled city; new institutions (colleges, hospitals, hotels), military barracks, and bungalows dotted the landscape. Bungalows in the Civil Lines lined broad regular streets in tidy lots. Large, low, and sprawling structures set in gardens, they stood in contrast to the dense network of walled compounds in the indigenous settlement.

The British also undertook drastic demolitions of entire neighborhoods within and around the palace in Delhi after the First War of Independence. During the subsequent decades a new town hall building, a clock tower, and a statue of Queen Victoria supplanted a vast *serai* and market in the central square of the city. A museum, hotels, hospitals, schools, and banks were other new buildings developed in the city. Large areas were cleared to make room for the railroad which entered the city in 1867. Streets were widened and others carved anew to allow the more efficient movement of vehicles. Bridges, roads, factories, mills, and large-span warehouses of steel construction were all new building forms in Delhi. A water-supply system, engineered solutions for sewage and garbage disposal, and electric lighting were all evidence of technological advances. Newly introduced neoclassical and beaux-arts influences in building façades and street design combined with a flood of new building materials from Europe such as glass, ceramic tiles, and wrought iron to change the image of the streetscape. Furnishings and décor of the interior spaces of Indian homes also changed with sofas, chandeliers, mirrors, and other European influences displaying new materials and more Westernized ways of living.

By the early twentieth century, an extraordinary growth in commerce and population was evident in Delhi, one that only escalated with the building of the sprawling new capital of New Delhi to the south. While the dense organic pattern of the walled city spilled over into a few small settlements to the west of the city, by the middle of the twentieth century the vast agricultural estates in the surrounding region had been turned into a number of planned residential neighborhoods. As low-density single-family units or higher-density multi-family houses, every last construction detail of the structures had been predetermined in many areas and in others building codes and guidelines regulated the built form. For those observers who shared Europe's claim to a universal standardized modernity, whose expressions resembled the familiar modernisms of home, these developments in Delhi were seen as signs of progress.

Striking as these changes were, after nearly a century of turmoil, by 1946 the architecture and urbanism of Delhi remained patchy and at best 'incomplete.' In its transformation into a 'modern' city in the European mold its status was only tentative. Even where formal elements resembled those of Europe, in a reconstituted context the spatial culture – use, meanings, and practices – in which the buildings were embedded, differed significantly. The built form had not simply exchanged one kind of fixed-place and context-based character for another, more 'universal' one based on self-conscious forms of modernism imagined as complete elsewhere. Nor did the modifications uniformly affect all parts of the city. Instead, the interventions had rebuilt the northern and eastern portions of the walled city, providing those parts with greater access to new roads, buildings, electricity, new drains, and other services. And new water supply and sewage systems supported the Civil Lines and military barracks more than the population in the walled city. Meanwhile, a building moratorium had frozen the footprint of the buildings and streets in the southern two-thirds of walled Delhi. As a consequence, that portion of the city to the south of Chandni Chowk and west of Faiz Bazaar had become more crowded and illegal developments had proliferated. This was also the case with the settlements just outside the Western walls. Based on various surveys and statistics, officials had classified some of them as blighted and their residents as squatters. Moreover, what was to become of increasing importance in the years to come, with the building of the imperial city and the new neighborhoods, residents of New Delhi began to perceive the walled city of what was now called 'Old Delhi' as a quaint and crowded relic, an embarrassment to the empire's modernist ambitions.

The formal changes during a period of a century were perhaps less remarkable than those in the meanings and significance of space. The commodification of property and the creation of a market in land had transformed their hereditary status. As an exchangeable economic resource, mansions and homes had become functional structures to be bought, sold, converted into shops, warehouses, factories, or rental apartments. Symbolically, land and property, in its arrangement and predictability of value, went from a system of representing the feudal power of princes to one of signifying rationalism, efficiency, and technological progress. New definitions of what was public and private were overlaid on existing structures of space and society. Buildings nested in one kind of customary spatial and cultural hierarchy now acquired new meanings in another. Public spaces, once the locale of noisy and ritualized public interaction, processions, trade, riots and conflicts, were expected to conform to official perceptions of order. While the commodification of private property and municipalized city governance meant redefining the boundaries of property and of communal authority, people continued to encroach on public space and build stealthily in defiance of municipal regulations (Figure 7.1). Efforts to rationalize and modernize the city through municipalization had resulted in the opposite effect, the preservation of an older street pattern that the British found both disorderly and threatening. With the mapping, policing, and regulation of ownership, interventions initially aimed at modifying the layout and form of streets and houses in the end resulted in controlling the relationship of people to property as well as the organization of communal life.

New Delhi, the capital of the British Empire in India, was conceived and built on vast estates outside the walled city. It had a separate budget, a novel design, and a discrete administration to govern it. A new railway station was built expressly to serve the new capital. Adjacent to the walled city and its spontaneous extensions, on vast tracts of agricultural land acquired and owned by the government, the new city's layout was an ironic and also arrogant commentary on the old one. In all its imperial majesty, New Delhi was designed and built to accommodate military pageants, grand displays, bureaucratic order, new modes of trade, business, and administration. It included a large retail and office complex, novel and organized forms of leisure activities such as a golf course, polo and horse-racing fields, clubs, and a rigid spatial hierarchy of residences – both British and Indian – for those in the service of the empire. Imagined as an aesthetic diagram, the idealized city hoped to exclude vice and deviance by making no spatial provision for them and, in this way, sculpt a new society. Richardson had imagined Hygiea as a place that contained no saloons and no gaming houses.[1] New Delhi was also a city with no room for the marginal: the prostitute, the gambler, the homeless, the itinerant, the infirm or even any kind of industry or workshops. These were all banished to the less rigid, less visible, and more negotiable by-lanes of the old city and its extensions, Sadar Bazaar, Paharganj, and Sabzi Mandi. Yet, despite their apparent differences, the old and the new cities were bound together by a common land market, shared infrastructure, taxation, regulation, and revenues from the vast government land holdings, while the planned residential developments of the Delhi Improvement Trust mediated the space in between.

The destruction of existing political and economic structures and the creation of new ones altered the very basis of the city and its built environment. Rapid growth in communication networks, travel, international commerce, and colonialism itself contributed to the availability of European technologies, scientific achievements, and new products and materials everywhere. The daily processes of negotiating and city building were central to the making of Delhi's indigenous modernities. Grand universalizing concepts and trenchant local traditions were mediated on the ground by individuals who acted in their many capacities and with their diverse interests as colonial masters, bureaucrats, petty administrators, city officials, local elites, ordinary residents, real-estate investors, speculators, wealthy shop owners, small businesses, petty traders, sanitary workers, daily wage-earners, members of religious groups, and numerous others. There were those, both European and Indian, who supported and actively sought to bring about what they saw as the triumph of Western science over faith, customary practice, and superstition. Conservatives, fearful of questioning and of innovation, rejected the rule of reason. But most used the potential for change to improve their own social and economic positions in ways they saw fit.

Ordinary residents were not passive recipients of what colonial officials imagined were 'civilizing' projects of a universal modernity. Local people, as they struggled to find a place for themselves in the turmoil of economic and political transition, responded in various ways. They maximized personal profit and sought to make their homes and futures secure and predictable in their own terms. Those who could took advantage of the new opportunities for financial gain. As they claimed public space, and modified their houses, residents used their own logic to develop spaces functionally advantageous to them and offering continuity to their communal way of living. Organized petitions, demonstrations, delays, non-cooperation, disobedience, vandalism, and non-compliance were tactics used to confront the Government and to drive compromises even if they were not the outcome residents desired.

Policing and surveillance took on a new significance. Colonial rulers, city officials, and the police watched people's behavior for signs of insurgency. They guarded property boundaries from squatting and appropriation, monitored births and deaths, sickness and disease, and inspected buildings for endangering the health of inhabitants in the neighborhood. Wide straight streets and a tidy, transparent, and predictable built form allowed for easy scrutiny. While this was more easily accomplished in the new planned enclaves, the inner streets of the walled city were harder to observe. Through legal codes and policing, the city administration of Delhi attempted to coax the irregular structures, narrow winding lanes, and introverted courtyard houses to become transparent and to reveal.

Fundamental to Delhi's indigenous modernities were the multiple perceptions that often contradicted the many realities. The dominant view that the people of Delhi, their way of living and building, were static and steeped in superstition formed the very basis of colonial interventions, the objective of which was to bring about transformation. Scientific statistics of improvements in health conditions and the introduction of a carefully engineered infrastructure did not alter the conviction of Europeans that the densely populated indigenous city was both a 'slum' and a source of disease. Officials attributed poverty to the walled city and overlooked an increasingly prosperous entrepreneurial class there even though their own surveys showed that the poorest communities more extensively inhabited settlements outside the city walls. Fearful of a renewed insurrection colonial officials imagined a lack of security in the walled city that was, in their eyes, mysterious and unpredictable. Paradoxically, where there was no criminal intent, European observers attributed a romantic naiveté to the people and historic built forms of Delhi. The mystique of 'timeless tradition' obscured the reality of the residents' engagement with modernity and the global politics of colonialism. As Ashish Nandy has pointed out, the perceptions of those in power, socially and culturally constructed and construed as they may have been, were eventually to become internalized by the subjugated.[2]

Reason as the outgrowth of Enlightenment rationalism also originated in a specific social and geographical context. Having acquired the status of a universal truth above all others, and pitted as it was against faith and superstition, in the hands of the powerful, the particular concept of rationality became an instrument of domination. When those in power recognized the dominant forms of European modernity as the only valid forms of science and reason, they simultaneously cast all others as devoid of both. Logic, reasoning, and scientific traditions were not absent in Delhi before the British arrived: they were culturally conditioned and did not carry with them the burden of making progress or claim to be objective. The organic layout and incrementally developed structures of the walled city were neither accidental nor disorderly. Rather, the built form was a reasonable response to existing social and functional needs, to climate, and to available resources, materials, and technology. People built and used space in ways that responded to indigenous notions of identity, social functions and behavior, and spatial assumptions. Yet it was the European perception of disorder that prompted the 'civilizing mission' of 'modernizing' the city along lines familiar to those who claimed the authorship (and authority) of a universal modernity. However, many inhabitants of the city saw their various traditions, such as inherited building practices, not as superstition but rather as embodying cumulative knowledge. For many, the wholesale rejection of this accumulated understanding of generations was in itself a contradiction of locally perceived reason. People with varying levels of needs, skills, economic and political power, social standing, ambition, and risk-taking abilities responded to the rapidly changing circumstances in ways that served their best interest. The many different viewpoints among the residents operated each according to its own logic (Figure 7.2).

Indigenous modernities in the built environment was not a colonial conspiracy or an architecture of resistance. Although the British were certainly responsible for introducing certain forms and spatial practices, Indians were equally imbricated in supporting the dominant narrative of European modernity. Whether motivated by a desire to share the might of the rulers, keep up with the times, or to exploit a new opportunity, some Indians accepted the idea of a superior Western science and technology. As officials in the colonial regime, reformers, educators, and nationalists, Indians helped to reify European accounts as the only version of modernity and aspired to share in the heroic endeavor. The Indian National Congress was formed in 1885 and the period until India's independence in 1947 saw the rise of Indian nationalism. However, this growth of nation-

Figure 7.2
Entrance to a mid-
nineteenth century
haveli. Old buildings in
an altered context imply
new meanings for the
same spaces.

alism did not question the validity of received narratives of modernity, particularly its various expression in architecture and urban design.[3]

The British introduced Delhi to the apparatus of European urbanism: the idea of a city as a functional and efficient machine for producing healthy, loyal, and morally upright subjects of the empire. The domination of the population was to be through the means of technology. Consumed by empire building, colonial officials co-opted the project of modernity to become an instrument for domination: the space of buildings and cities themselves became technologies of production and control. Interventions such as municipal strategies in regulating buildings and open space, rebuilding, introducing municipal infrastructure, demarcating boundaries between the private and public, surveillance, and the development of new residential enclaves all reflected a mechanistic view of urbanism. The powerful appropriated the right to command the city as a machine, working towards their own ends. The language of 'improvement' masked political and profit motivations of the interventions. However, such a functional view of the city failed to recognize that for local residents (including those charmed by the power of Western science) space also had symbolic significance and was a result of a complex network of social relationships.

The plural expressions of Delhi's modernity also expressed the contradictions inherent in the planning interventions. The idea of encouraging private enterprise assumed that individuals would act rationally to maximize personal gain, regardless of their community. However, in Delhi, community pressures and mores helped to provide and maintain 'public goods' such as public spaces and streets, adequate light and ventilation for neighboring structures, safety, and the application of minimum standards of health as prescribed by traditional medical sciences. Community elders, heads of extended families and of religious sects, and also nobility, mediated conflicts and worked out compromises. In the reconstituted social structure and new form of urban governance, the administrative apparatus of the municipality sought to replace existing communal hierarchies and wrest power from the elders. Yet the new institutions and holders of authority were not effective in providing and protecting 'public goods' such as public space. As the persistence and even uncontrolled proliferation of illegal building activity in Delhi was to show, disbanding local communities was to prove detrimental to the city's built form.

The dramatic transformation of Delhi's landscape over a century was the consequence not of a single powerful encounter but of numerous daily events, each with varying outcomes. Official action to refashion and reform space and society, the chaotic destruction and building anew of social institutions and what had been shared spatial meanings, people's responses to the changing conditions and the imposed order – these were all factors that influenced the form and significance of the built environment in Delhi.

Dominant discourses of reason, science, and rationality as universal located them outside the particularities of place and culture. This allowed the 'project of modernity,' with its supposedly liberating and transforming agenda, to become, in the hands of colonial authorities, an instrument which, while furthering the goals of colonialism, reinforced fundamental inequities. The rejection of existing spatial and institutional structures assumed that there was only one right way to do things. From this perspective, prevalent practices of building and inhabiting space were to be conquered and replaced with new beliefs and practices. In this context, municipal strategies worked to disband the very institutions that supported existing building processes. While putting in place a codified, formal, and transparent structure for urban development, the efforts failed to recognize the plural processes and spatial practices operating at the levels of community and custom. The colonial imperative to dominate combined with the mastery of technology. Together they failed to acknowledge alternative traditions of science and rationality and see them as culturally rooted. As a consequence, indigenous institutions, traditions, and knowledge became marginalized and invisible in the city's development but never completely erased.

Despite official claims to scientific reason and objectivity in the identification of problems in Delhi and their methods to resolve them, decisions and policies were influenced by the local: the political motivations of individual officials, their prejudices, cultural perceptions, practical concerns, available resources, and human weaknesses all influenced state actions. Importing advice and experience from Britain, however, helped to legitimize the projects.

Throughout the book, I have focused on the lesser-known buildings and ordinary architecture of a city that many have assumed to epitomize the indigenous and the vernacular. These remind us that the transplantation of practices, built forms, and materials of European modernism happened in many complex ways and in many unexpected places. The varied landscape of the city tells a story of the processes by which these unfamiliar forms became situated and contextualized as expressions of indigenous modernities.

The cultural milieu of modernity in Delhi in the nineteenth and early twentieth centuries was distinct from those of major urban centers in Western Europe at the time. The historical events preceding the cultural upheaval, and the social, economic, and political context within which it occurred, were particular to the place. As modernity and colonialism each constituted the other in Delhi, the emergent forms were not the replicas of imagined ones in the distant metropole. With a different starting point, and an entirely different social and spatial structure, the expressions and experiences of modernity in Delhi were particular to the time and place and different from those of cities in Western Europe. On the one hand was a whirlwind of economic and political change, on the other were inherited ways of living and building, hierarchy, status, and allegiances that continued to structure daily life. Mediating between them were European officials and Western-educated Indian elites aspiring for the benefits of what they believed was 'universal' 'science' and 'reason'. These included self-serving officials exploiting existing hierarchies and allegiances for their own profit, mid-level bureaucrats and administrators, as well as subversive inhabitants. I think of the encounter not as a single dramatic moment but rather as a vast array of numerous ordinary events with a multiplicity of diverse outcomes.

British colonialism's grand plan of conquering what they saw as myth, religion, and superstition with the power of 'science' and 'universal reason' did not come to pass in the way they had imagined it in Delhi. Although scientific classification, efficiency, and utilitarian principles were at the heart of the urban projects and interventions, other objectives and factors complicated the mission. The government's ambition to promote commerce and free enterprise, desire to know and manage its territories, its aspirations as a property owner to maximize financial returns, its efforts to effectively police insurgent subjects and its properties, and the residents' differing interests in subverting, appropriating, and co-opting were all events and limitations particular to Delhi's circumstances that were at odds with the liberating intent of modernization.

Customary spatial practices, local culture, and local knowledge did not continue unchanged either. In the tumultuous environment of renovation, existing ways of building and inhabiting space also came under questioning. In the moment of disarray, accepted ways of buildings and shared spatial meanings were reconstituted to accommodate the changing economic and political conditions of the city. The development of a more simplified, functional, and efficient *haveli*, or constructing additions to homes in stealth were reasonable responses based on a different logic and alternative social networks of neighborhood and community operating in a new context. However much the state attempted to define people's relationship to the past, different groups of people had their own memories, imaginations, and visions of a better future. For them, new conditions demanded new solutions. Building, city, and landscape were to be imagined differently. But the imagination of Indians was overwhelmed with forms of European modernity and the memory of associations with customary older ones. Unable to completely reject one or surrender fully to the other, they melded into internally divided indigenous modernities.[4]

As long as one positions oneself to equate particular forms that arose in Europe to modernity, all other forms in comparison will appear only transitory, incomplete, inadequate, or enduringly 'traditional.' All other constructs will remain 'not-modern,' a binary state necessary to support the universal validity of certain forms. However, a relocated position to view modernity and colonialism as fundamentally connected, where the two are integrally linked, would accept modernity as a global project from the beginning. As culturally constructed oppositions, 'modern' and 'traditional' are not inherent features of a built form. From this perspective, all modernities are indigenous and all its expressions equally valid. Acknowledging the plurality of modernities legitimizes its many interpretations. We would then cease to aspire for and lament over an imagined universalism or romanticize about a built environment imagined and fixed as 'traditional.'

The remarkable features of Delhi's modernity were the circumstances of its arrival, its imposition by colonial forces, and its adaptation to local conditions. This indigenization was implicitly a critique of particular forms of modernity being idealized as universal and liberating in the dominant view without being self-conscious. It was a celebration of the city's uniqueness without being romantic, and anti-imperial without parading as nationalistic. What made a city like Delhi modern was not the modern technologies of space that the British introduced nor was the city cast in myth and rigid traditions. It was not a simple tale of the victory of one over the other but a complex and nuanced history of conflict and negotiation. The compromises helped to humanize and integrate the brutal and dislocating effects of modernity as a destructive/creative force under an authoritarian regime.

Having studied the disjunctive course of architecture and urbanism in one city for almost a century, what should one say about its future in that city – or in other cities? Those who had hoped that built forms that had once represented the antithesis of modernism imagined in the mythical West might ask, will 'traditional' urbanism ever complete its transition to resemble entirely the modernism of 'the West'? To them I would respond, will the idealized modernism ever become a reality even within 'the West'? All idealizations of modernities are, in the end, indigenized in their actualization. All modernisms are the consequence of negotiations of an imagined ideal with the particularities of a place and its socio-political context, and hence are *indigenous modernities*. If nineteenth- and twentieth-century architecture and urbanism of the imagined 'West' are expressions of their indigenous modernities, then why must the built forms and meaning of other places be expected to struggle hard to achieve them – and always fail. Indigenous modernity everywhere is the result of a constant search to modernize in the mold of the idealized original. It is an architecture and urbanism that is in constant juxtaposition and never at ease. If the course of modernity is a constant cycle of destruction and creation, and tradition, too, is subject to reason, adaptation, and change, then the historical route of the one is intimately linked to that of the other. The unsettling concept of indigenous modernity offers the possibility of recovering a past from which we might better understand the trajectory of its development in postcolonial architecture and urbanism – and better direct it. The indigenous modernities of a city's past are not just history, but also the present as well as the future.

Notes

1 INTRODUCTION; BECOMING 'MODERN'

1 Dipesh Chakrabarty, 'Postcoloniality and the Artifice of History: Who speaks for "Indian" pasts?' In *Representations*, Vol. 37, Winter 1992, p. 21.

2 Arjun Appadurai, *Modernity at Large: Cultural Dimensions of Globalization*. Minneapolis, MN: University of Minnesota Press, 1996, p. 3.

3 Dipesh Chakrabarty, Partha Chatterjee, Ranajit Guha and Gayatri Chakravorty Spivak, Gyan Pandey and Sumit Sarkar, have proposed in different ways that 'failure,' and 'incompleteness' is the central problematic in the historiography of modern India. See, Ranajit Guha and Gayatri Chakravorty Spivak (eds), *Selected Subaltern Studies*. New York: Oxford University Press, 1988.

4 The events surrounding the revolt, its reprisal, the causes, the participants, and the strategies have all been copiously debated by historians of modern India. See, for instance, Sir John William Kaye, *Indian Mutiny of 1857*. Edited by Bruce Malleson. Fourth revised edition. London: R. J. Leach, 1993. First published as *A History of the Sepoy War in India, 1857–58*. London: W. H. Allen, 1864–76; Sangat Singh, *Freedom Movement in Delhi*. New Delhi: Associated Publishing House, 1972. For personal accounts of the events surrounding the 1857 siege see Alexander Llewellwyn, *The Seige of Delhi*. London: Macdonald and Jane, 1977; Charles John Griffiths, *A Narrative of the Siege of Delhi, with an Account of the Mutiny at Ferozepore in 1857*. Edited by H. J. Yonge. London: John Murray, 1910; Kaye, op. cit.; Charles Theophilus Metcalfe, *Two Native Narratives of the Mutiny in Delhi*. Westminster: A. Constable, 1898. Sumit Sarkar, has observed that India witnessed the greatest transition in the country's history from 1885–1947.

5 C. A. Bayly's remarkable history of north Indian cities shows the rise of professionalized trade since the late eighteenth century. C. A. Bayly, *Rulers, Townsmens, and Bazaars: North Indian Society in the Age of British Expansions, 1770–1870*. Cambridge, U.K.: Cambridge University Press, 1983.

6 I see Delhi as multiple overlapping landscapes after Italo Calvino. See, Italo Calvino,

Invisible Cities. Translated from the Italian by William Weaver. New York: Harcourt Brace Jovanovich, 1978, first published c.1974.

7 The Daniell brothers painted several popular aquatints of the exotic, the picturesque, and the sublime in India since the late eighteenth century. The views of Delhi too represented the mystical and beautiful Orient in the grand monuments and ethereal ruins. See Mildred Archer, *Early Views of India: The Picturesque Journeys of Thomas and William Daniell 1786–1794*. London: Thames and Hudson, 1980.

8 Emily Eden, *Up the Country: Letters Written to Her Sister from the Upper Provinces of India*. Edited by Elizabeth Claridge. London: Virago, 1983, pp. 94–95. First published 1866.

9 *Illustrated London News*, August 29, 1857, p. 210.

10 Jurgen Habermas, 'Modernity – An incomplete Project.' In Hal Foster (ed.), *The Anti-Aesthetic: Essays on Postmodern Culture*. Port Townsend, WA: Bay Press, 1983, pp. 3–15.

11 See, for example, Kenneth Frampton, *Modern Architecture: A Critical History*. London: Thames and Hudson, 1985, c.1980.

12 For another perspective on the development of European modernity and its relationship to colonialism see also Paul Rabinow, *French Modern: Norms and Forms of the Social Environment*. Cambridge, MA: MIT Press, 1989.

13 Sir Banister Fletcher, *A History of Architecture on the Comparative Method for the Student, Craftsman, and Amateur*. London, Batsford; New York, Scribner's sons, 1905. 5th edition, rev. and enl. by Banister F. Fletcher; and Eugene Emmanuel Viollet le Duc, *The Habitations of Man in all Ages*. Translated from the French by Benjamin Bucknall. Ann Arbor, MI: Gryphon Books, 1971. Facsimile reprint of the 1876 edition. For instance, Fletcher (pp. 603–604) says in his introduction to the 'non-historical' styles:

> The non-historical styles – Indian, Chinese, and Japanese, and Central American – are those which developed mainly on their own account and exercised little direct influence on other styles. They can thus be studied independently, and need not interrupt the story of the evolution of European Historical Architecture dealt with in Part I, which would probably be the case if they were placed in their chronological order. The position which they should occupy in a History of Architecture is, however, a matter of doubt, but it is thought that by keeping them quite separate from the historical styles, it will make for greater clearness to the student . . . The study of Indian, indeed of all Eastern art enlarges the view, since it presents many novel forms to which one is unaccustomed, and which, doubtless because of their unusual character, often strike one as ugly or *bizarre*.

14 Sibel Bozdogan has noted that 'Modern' has been assumed to be an exclusively European category that non-Western others could import, adopt or perhaps resist but not reproduce from within, or make their own. Sibel Bozdogan, *Modernism and Nation Building: Turkish Architectural Culture in the Early Republic*. Seattle, WA: University of Washington Press, 2001. Partha Chatterjee has also observed, 'History it would seem, has decreed that we in the postcolonial world shall only be perpetual consumers of modernity.' Partha Chatterjee. *Nation and its Fragments: Colonial and Postcolonial Histories*. Princeton: Princeton University Press, 1993.

15 Dilip Gaonkar and others discuss the idea of alternative modernities in Dilip Paramesh-
    war Gaonkar (ed.), *Alternative Modernities*. Durham, NC: Duke University Press, 2001.
    See also, Dipesh Chakrabarty. *Habitations of Modernity: Essays in the Wake of Subal-
    tern Studies*. Chicago: University of Chicago, 2002.

16 Charles Baudelaire, *Selected Writings on Art and Artists*. Translated with an introduc-
    tion by P. E. Charvet. Cambridge, U.K.: Cambridge University Press, 1981; Octavio
    Paz, *Convergences: Essays on Art and Literature*. Translated from the Spanish by
    Helen Lane. San Diego: Harcourt Brace Jovanovich, 1987.

17 Marshall Berman, *All that is Solid Melts into Air: The Experience of Modernity*. New
    York: Simon and Schuster, 1982. .

18 Harvey David, *The Condition of Postmodernity: An Enquiry into the Origins of Cultural
    Change*. Oxford, U.K.: Basil Blackwell, 1989. See also, David Harvey. *Paris Capital of
    Modernity*. London, New York: Routledge, 2003.

19 Marshall Berman refers to this distinction as being the interplay of the social processes
    of becoming (modernization) and the visions and values nurtured by this (modernism);
    Hilde Heynen refers to them as the programmatic and transitory aspects of modernity.
    Anthony King has referred to a 'particular materialization' of a set of economic and
    social relationships. Berman, op. cit. Hilde Heynen, *Architecture and Modernity: A Cri-
    tique*. Cambridge, MA: MIT Press, 1999. Also see Huber-Jan Henket and Hilde Heynen
    (eds) *Back from Utopia: The Challenge of the Modern Movement*. Rotterdam: OIO,
    2002. Anthony D. King, 'The Times and Spaces of Modernity' in *The Spaces of Global
    Cultures: Architecture, Urbanism, Identity*. London: Routledge, 2004.

20 Artistic and literary movements including the Modern Movement in architecture are
    encompassed in my use of *modernism*. Le Corbusier, as a leading protagonist of the
    Modern Movement, believed that Modern Architecture was a celebration of the
    machine age. See, among others, Eric Mumford, *The CIAM Discourse on Urbanism,
    1928–1960*. Cambridge, MA: MIT Press, 2000; and Adolf Max Vogt, *Le Corbusier, the
    Noble Savage: Towards an Archaeology of Modernism*. Trans. by Radka Donnell.
    Cambridge: MIT Press, 1998.

21 Dell Upton has expressed his hope that '. . . [the] line between vernacular and acade-
    mic architecture will be erased and the vernacular-academic dichotomy will be
    replaced by a much more complex paradigm that recognizes change and stasis, diver-
    sity and conflict, pattern and discontinuity in all varieties of architecture.' Dell Upton,
    'Outside the Academy: A century of vernacular architecture studies, 1890–1990,' in
    Studies in the History of Art, Vol. 35, 1990, pp. 199–213.

22 I refer here to the discourse in critical regionalism that has provided a basis for a
    significant move, especially outside the conventional West, to develop regional identi-
    ties within an accepted framework of modern architecture. The theoretical work of
    Alexander Tzonis and Liane Lefaivre, and Kenneth Frampton have provided the under-
    pinnings for such design. For a postcolonial critiques of critical regionalism see
    Gülsüm Baydar Nalbantoglu and Wong Chong Thai, *Postcolonial Space(s)*. Princeton,
    NJ: Princeton Architectural Press, 1997 and Keith L. Eggener, 'Placing Resistance: A
    Critique of Critical Regionalism.' In *Journal of Architectural Education*, Vol. 55, no. 4,
    May 2002, pp. 228–237.

23 Shirine Hamadeh has correctly pointed out that the very conceptualization of a 'traditional' city as the indigenous city was in relation to the 'modern' city of the French
colonizers. My interest is in the ways the categories infiltrate each other so that
neither form is completely one or the other. Shirine Hamadeh, 'Creating the Traditional City: a French Project.' In Nezar Alsayyad (ed.), *Forms of Dominance: On the
Architecture and Urbanism of the Colonial Enterprise*. Aldershot: Avebury, 1992, pp.
241–260. For a discussion of the concept of 'traditional' see, Nezar Alsayyad. *The End
of Tradition?* London, New York: Routledge, 2004.

24 For instance, Gyan Prakash has argued that that while science represented freedom of
thought, the British used it to practice despotism. Seizing on this contradiction, many
of the colonized elite began to seek parallels and precedents for scientific thought in
India's own intellectual history, creating a hybrid form of knowledge that combined
Western ideas with local cultural and religious understanding. Their work disrupted
accepted notions of colonizer versus colonized, civilized versus savage, modern versus
traditional, and created a form of modernity that was at once Western and indigenous. Gyan Prakash, *Another Reason: Science and the Imagination of Modern India*.
Princeton, NJ: Princeton University Press, 1999.

25 Homi K. Bhabha, *The Location of Culture*. London, New York: Routledge, 1994, p. 2.

26 The asymmetrical power relations are both within a local society and part of global
differences in power. Sherry Ortner has noted that the strategies for furthering interests by a group of people are based on assumed patterns of relations. She observes,
'when the context of these traditional relations are altered, then strategies too
change as do the relationships.' Sherry Ortner, 'Theory in Anthropology since the
Sixties.' In Nicholas B. Dirks, Geoff Eley, and Sherry B. Ortner (eds), *Culture/Power/
History: A Reader in Contemporary Social Theory*. Princeton, NJ: Princeton University
Press, 1994, pp. 372–411.

27 Ronald B. Inden, *Imagining India*. Oxford, U.K.: Basil Blackwell, 1990.

28 See for instance, Sir Alexander Cunningham, *Four Reports Made During the Years,
1862–63–64–65*, 2 Volumes, Delhi: Indological Book House, 1972. The Archaelogical
Survey of India produced numerous studies such as: Archaeological Survey of India,
Report for the Year 1871–72: Delhi by J. D. Beglar; *Agra* by A. S. L. Carlyle, under the
Superintendence of Maj. Gen. A. Cunningham. Vol. IV. Varanasi: Indological Book
house, 1966. First published, Calcutta: Office of the Superintendent of Government
Printing, 1874.

29 James Fergusson, *History of Indian and Eastern Architecture*. Delhi: Munshiram
Manoharlal, 1967. Rev. and edited, with additions [on] Indian architecture by James
Burgess, and Eastern architecture by R. Phene Spiers. First published in 1876. See also
Catherine Asher and Thomas R. Metcalf. *Perceptions of South Asia's Visual Past*. New
Delhi: IBH Pub., *c.* 1994.

30 For a detailed discussion of British imperialist historiography of Indian architecture see
Jyoti Hosagrahar, 'Teaching Architectural History in South Asia: Looking Back, Moving
Ahead: History and Modernization in South Asia.' In the *Journal of the Society of
Architectural Historians*, Vol. 61, No. 3, September 2002.

31 Ibid.

32 Some of the works on British imperialism and built form have been insightful in their analysis of culture and power. See, Thomas R. Metcalf, *An Imperial Vision: Indian Architecture and Britain's Raj*. Berkeley: University of California Press, 1989; Robert Grant Irving, *Indian Summer: Lutyens, Baker and Imperial Delhi*. New Haven, CT: Yale University Press, 1981; Anthony D. King, *The Bungalow: The Production of a Global Culture*. London: Routledge and Kegan Paul, 1984; Anthony D. King, *Colonial Urban Development*. London: Routledge and Kegan Paul, 1976. Others in this genre include, Sten Nilsson, *New Capitals of India, Pakistan and Bangladesh*. Trans. Elisabeth Andreasson. Lund: Scandinavian Institute of Asian Studies, 1973; Peter Scriver, 'Rationalization, Standardization, and Control in Design: A Cognitive Historical Study of Architectural Design and Planning in the Public Works Department of British India, 1855–1901.' Ph.D. dissertation, Delft Technical University, 1994; Philip Davies, *Splendors of the Raj: British Architecture in India, 1660–1947*. London: J. Murray, 1985; Mariam Dossal, *Imperial Designs and Indian Realities: The Planning of Bombay City, 1845–1875*. Bombay: Oxford University Press, 1991. Studies of the modern movement include, Vikram Bhatt and Peter Scriver, *After the Masters*. Ahmedabad, India: Mapin, 1990; Norma Evenson, *Indian Metropolis: A View Toward the West*. New Haven: Yale University Press, 1989; and Rahal Mehrotra (ed.) *South Asia: World Architecture 1900–2000: A Critical Mosaic*. Vol. 8, Wien: Springer, 2000.

33 Nuanced readings of cities are offered by scholars from many fields including historians, geographers, art and architectural historians. A few books of this genre are: Carl E. Schorske. *Fin-de-Siècle Vienna: Politics and Culture*. New York: Knopf, 1979; Timothy J. Clark. *The Painting of Modern Life: Paris in the Art of Manet and His Followers*. Princeton, NJ: Princeton University Press, 1984; David Harvey, Paris, *Capital of Modernity*. New York, Routledge, 2003; Kay Anderson, *Vancouver's Chinatown: Racial discourse in Canada, 1875–1980*. Montreal: McGill-Queen's University Press, 1991; James Borchert, *Alley Life in Washington: Family, Community, Religion and Folklife in the City, 1850–1970*. Urbana, IL: University of Illinois Press, 1980; Christine Stansell, *City of Women: Sex and Class in New York, 1789–1860*. New York: Knopf, 1986; Elizabeth Blackmar, *Manhattan for Rent, 1785–1850*. Ithaca, NY: Cornell University Press, 1990; June Manning Thomas, *Redevelopment and Race: Planning a Finer City in Postwar Detroit*. Baltimore: Johns Hopkins University Press, 1997; Elizabeth C. Cromley and Carter L. Hudgins. *Gender, Class, and Shelter*. Knoxville: University of Tennessee Press, c.1995.

34 Studies of nineteenth- and early twentieth-century architecture and urbanism outside the commonly accepted boundaries of the West include those on Eastern Europe and Russian constructivist architecture such as the work of Akos Moravanzsky, Rostislav Svacha, and William C. Brumfield. Western Europe's colonization of Asia and Africa has been central to studies of architecture and urbanism in the latter continents. The works of Thomas Metcalf on India, of Gwendolyn Wright on French Colonial architecture, and of Zeynep Celik on colonial Algiers are insightful for their analyses of the insidious ways that authority and power are expressed in the colonies. Eleni Bastea, Sibel Bozdogan, Patricia Morton, and Vikramaditya Prakash have made significant contributions to thinking about modernity, nationalism, and identity in relation to

architecture. Along with Jeffrey Cody, Abidin Kusno, Mia Fuller, Gulsum Nalbantoglu, and Wong Chong Thai they have also begun to explore postcolonial interaction of East and West in architecture. Edited collections, one by Robbie Goh, et al. and another by Ryan Bishop, et al., explore new ways of understanding the complex urbanism of Southeast Asian cities. Rostislav Svacha, *Architecture of New Prague, 1895–1945*. Trans. Alexandra Buchler. Cambridge, MA: MIT Press, 1999; Akos Mora-vanszky, *Competing Visions: Aesthetic Invention and Social Imagination in Central European Architecture, 1867–1918*. Cambridge, MA: MIT Press, 1998; William C. Brumfield, Origins *of Modernism in Russian Architecture*. Berkeley: University of California Press, 1991; Metcalf, op. cit.; Gwendolyn Wright, *Politics of Design in French Colonial Urbanism*. Chicago: University of Chicago Press, 1991; Zeynep Celik. *Urban Forms and Colonial Confrontations: Algiers under French Rule*. Berkeley: University of California Press, 1997; Eleni Bastéa, *The Creation of Modern Athens*. Cambridge, U.K.: Cambridge University Press, 2000; Sibel Bozdogan, *Modernism and Nation Building: Turkish Architectural Culture in the Early Republic*. Seattle: University of Washington Press, 2001; Patricia A. Morton, *Hybrid Modernities: Architecture and Representation at the 1931 Colonial Exposition*, Paris. Cambridge, MA: MIT Press, 2000; Vikramaditya Prakash, *Chandigarth's Le Corbussiér: The Struggle for Modernity in Postcolonial India*. Seattle: University of Washington, 2002; Jeffrey W. Cody, *Exporting American Architecture, 1870–2000*. London: Routledge, 2003; Mia Fuller. *Moderns Abroad: Italian Colonial Architecture and Urbanism*. London: Routledge, forthcoming. Abidin Kusno, *Behind the Postcolonial: Architecture, Urban Space, and Political Cultures in Indonesia*. London: Routledge, 2000. Gülsüm Baydar Nalbantoglu and Wong Chong Thai, op. cit. Robbie B. H. Goh and Brenda S. A. Yeoh. *Theorizing the Southeast Asian City as Text: Urban Landscapes, Cultural Documents, and Inter-pretive Experiences*. World Scientific Publishing, 2003; Ryan Bishop, John Phillips, and Wei-Wei Yeo (eds). *Postcolonial Urbanism: Southeast Asian Cities and Global Processes*. London, New York: Routledge, 2003; Ryan Bishop, et al. (eds) *Beyond Description: Singapore Space Historicity*. London: Routledge, 2004. See also Brenda Yeoh, *Contesting Space: Power Relations and the Urban Built Environment in Colonial Singapore*. Kuala Lumpur: Oxford University Press, 1996; Robert K. Home, *Of Planting and Planning: The Making of British Colonial Cities*. London: Spon, 1997; King, 1976; Irving, op. cit.; Nezar Alsayyad (ed.), *Forms of Dominance: On the Architecture and Urbanism of the Colonial Enterprise*. London: Avebury and Gower House, 1992; William Stewart Logan, *Hanoi: Biography of a City*. Seattle, WA: University of Washington Press, 2000; Jean-Louis Cohen and Monique Eleb, *Casablanca: Colonial Myths and Architectural Ventures*. New York: Monacelli Press, 2002; Lawrence J. Vale, *Architecture, Power, and National Identity*. New Haven, CT: Yale University Press, c.1992; Nihal Perera, *Society and Space: Colonialism, Nationalism, and Postcolonial Identity in Sri Lanka*. Boulder, CO: Westview Press, 1998; Zeynep Kezar, 'Contesting Urban Space in Early Republican Ankara.' In *Journal of Architectural Education*, Vol. 52, No. 1, September 1998, pp. 11–19; Swati Chattopadhyay, 'Blurring Boundaries: The Limits of "White Town" in Colonial Calcutta.' In *Journal of the Society of Architectural Historians*, 2000 June, Vol. 59, No. 2, pp. 154–179. Zeynep Celik, Hilde Heynen and Andre Loeckx (eds), 'Patterns of Displacement.' In *Journal of Architectural Education* (Vol. 52, Nos 1 and 2, 1998) contains articles on issues of ambivalence and displacement (in the built form) as a material expression of cultural dislocation brought about by modernity.

35 Arjun Appadurai, *Modernity at Large: Cultural Dimensions of Globalization*. Minneapolis: University of Minnesota Press, 1996; Douglas Haynes and Gyan Prakash (eds), *Contesting Power: Resistance and Everyday Social Relations in South Asia*. Berkeley: University of California Press, 1992. Gyan Prakash (ed.), *After Colonialism: Imperial Histories and Postcolonial Displacements*. Princeton, NJ: Princeton University Press, 1995; Gyan Prakash, *Another Reason: Science and the Imagination of Modern India*. Princeton, NJ: Princeton University Press, 1999; Homi Bhabha, *The Location of Culture*. London: Routledge, 1994; Homi Bhabha, *Nation and Narration*. New York: Routledge, 1990; Ranajit Guha and Gayatri Chakravorty Spivak (eds), *Selected Subaltern studies*. Oxford, U.K.: Oxford University Press, 1998; Ranajit Guha, *Dominance without Hegemony: History and Power in Colonial India*. Cambridge, U.K.: Harvard University Press, 1997; Bernard S. Cohn, *Colonialism and its Forms of Knowledge: the British in India*. Princeton, NJ: Princeton University Press, 1996; Nicholas B. Dirks, *Castes of Mind: Colonialism and the Making of Modern India*. Princeton, NJ: Princeton University, 2001; Dirks et al., op. cit.; Chatterjee, op. cit.; Partha Chatterjee and Anjan Ghosh (eds), *History and the Present*. Delhi: Permanent Black, 2002; Dipesh Chakrabarty, *Provincializing Europe: Postcolonial Thought and Historical Difference*. Princeton, NJ: Princeton University Press, 2000. Arjun Appadurai. *Globalization*. Durham, NC: Duke University Press, 2001; Chakrabarty, op. cit.

36 Sir Sayyid Ahmad Khan first published a detailed work on Delhi's buildings, in 1854. Sir Sayyid Ahmad Khan, *Asarussanadid*. (Description of Historical Buildings and Monuments of Delhi). Edited by Khaliq Anjum. New Delhi: Urdu Akadmi, Delhi, 1990. First published, Delhi: Matba-'yi Sultani, 1854. 2 Vols. European accounts that followed, too, focused on the monuments. See for instance, H. C. Fanshawe, *Delhi Past and Present*. London: J. Murray, 1902; and Stephen Carr, *Archaeology and Monumental Remains of Delhi*. Allahabad: Kitab Mahal, 1967. First published 1876. James Fergusson's detailed work on Indian architecture was accepted as canonical for more than a century after it was first published. See Fergusson, op. cit.; Percival Spear, *Twilight of the Mughals*. Cambridge, U.K.: Cambridge University Press, 1951; Percival Spear, *Delhi: Its Monuments and History*. Bombay: Oxford University Press, 1943; Shama Mitra Chenoy, *Shahjahanabad, a City of Delhi, 1638–1857*. New Delhi: Munshiram Manoharlal Publishers, 1998; Anisha Shekhar Mukherji, *The Red Fort of Shahjahanabad*. Delhi: Oxford University Press, 2002.

37 Historical accounts such as Mirza Sangin Beg, *Sair-al-manzil* (A Tour of the Buildings). Lahore: 1828. Bashiruddin Ahmad Dehlavi, *Vaqiat-i darul-hakumat-i dihli*. (A History of the Buildings of Delhi). New Delhii: Urdu Akadmi, 1990, 3 vols. First published, Agra: Shamsi Press, 1919; Vali Ashraf Sabuhi Dihlavi, Dilli ki cand 'ajib hastiyan (A Few Remarkable Characters of Delhi). Lahore, 1963 first published c.1930; Maheshwar Dayal, *Rediscovering Delhi*, Delh: S. Chand 1975; Maheshwar Dayal, *Dilli jo ek shahar hai* (The City that is Delhi). Delhi: Hindi Academy, 1991. These works have been very helpful in my study of Delhi.

38   Maulvi Zafar Hasan and Page, J. A. *Monuments of Delhi: Lasting Splendour of the Great Mughals and Others*. New Delhi: Aryan Books International, 1997. First published 1916. Ratish Nanda, Narayani Gupta, and O. P. Jain, *Delhi, the Built Heritage: A Listing*. New Delhi: INTACH, 1999.

39   Two recent works that analyze the morphology of Mughal Delhi are: Stephen P. Blake, *Shahjahanabad: The Sovereign City in Mughal India, 1639–1739*. Cambridge, U.K.: Cambridge University Press, 1991; Ehlers Eckhart and Thomas Krafft (eds), *Shahjahanabad/Old Delhi: Tradition and Colonial Change*. Stuttgart: Franz Steiner Verlag, 1993. The latter also chronicles some aspects of the city's evolution. Among those who have been concerned with the problems of the walled city are: Patwant Singh and Ram Dhamija (eds) *Delhi, the Deepening Crisis*. New Delhi: Sterling Publishers, 1989; Ajay K. Mehra, *Politics of Urban Redevelopment: A Study of Old Delhi*. New Delhi: Sage Publications, 1990. Some in recent years have attempted to bridge this gap. See for instance, Balmiki Prasad Singh and Pavan K. Varma, *The Millennium Book on New Delhi*. New Delhi: Oxford University Press, 2001; and Rahul Mehrotra, *Evolution, involution and the City's Future: A Pespective on Bombay's Urban Form*.' In *Marg*, 1997 September, v. 49., no. 1, pp. 14–33,

40   Narayani Gupta, *Delhi Between Two Empires, 1803–1931: Society, Government and Urban Growth*. Delhi: Oxford University Press, 1981.

41   Maheshwar Dayal, Alam men intikhab, Dilli. (Civilization of Delhi Through the Ages). New Delhi: Urdu Akad mi, Delhi, 1987; Dayal, op. cit.

42   Irving, op. cit.; Evenson, op. cit.; Metcalf, op. cit.; King, op. cit.; Nilsson, op. cit.

2 FRAGMENTING DOMESTIC LANDSCAPES: FROM MANSIONS TO MARGINS

1   Widely used as the term is, a precise definition of *haveli* is hard to come by. A dictionary defines a *haveli* as a mansion or a spacious house (Bashir Ahmad Qureshi (ed.), *Standard Twentieth Century Dictionary: Urdu into English*. Revised by Abdul Haq. Delhi: Educational Publishing House, 1991, p. 279). Rory Fonseca considers contemporary *haveli* in Delhi as houses with introverted gardens ('The Walled City of Old Delhi,' in *Shelter and Society*, edited by Paul Oliver. London: Barrie and Rockliff, 1969. Varma and Shanker have interpreted *haveli* to mean mansions, including those built by the British, that did not have interior courtyards (Pawan Varma and Sandeep Shanker. *Mansions at Dusk: The Havelis of Old Delhi*. New Delhi: Spantech Publications, 1992). I use the words 'haveli' and 'mansion' interchangeably. See Varma and Shanker for a photographic documentation of the contemporary condition of some selected *haveli*. See Sarah Tillotson for a general sociological study of *haveli* life in Rajasthan India (*Indian Mansions: A Social History of the Haveli*. Cambridge, U.K.: Oleander Press, 1994).

2   Francois Bernier, *Travels in the Mogul Empire, A.D. 1656–1668*. Second edition revised by Vincent Smith, based on Archibald Constable's revision of Irving Brock's translation. New Delhi: Low Price, 1989, pp. 247–248. First published 1670. Paris, 2

volumes. *Amīr* refers to a rich person, a ruler, a governor or a prince commander (Qureshi, op. cit.). *Umrāh* is the plural form of *amīr*.

3   In his study of Delhi in the seventeenth century, Stephen Blake has argued that the *haveli* were designed as mini-fortresses on design principles similar to that of the King's palace in Delhi. I regard the fortifications as symbolic since many multi-unit mansions did not have clearly articulated physical boundaries. However, the core of the larger *haveli* were, as Blake suggests, organized along the lines of the King's palace. See Stephen P. Blake, *Shahjahanabad: The Sovereign City in Mughal India, 1639–1739*. Cambridge, U.K.: Cambridge University Press, 1991.

4   Dargah Quli Khan, *Muraqqa'-e-Dehli: The Mughal Capital in Muhammad Shah's time*. Personal diary of Dargah Quli Khan for the period, 1737–41. Edited and translated from the Persian by Chandra Shekhar and Shama Mitra Chenoy. Delhi: Deputy Publications, 1989, p. 61. First edited and published, 1926.

5   *Jharokā* are elaborately carved enclosed balconies to screen aristocratic women from public view as they watched ceremonies. *Jāli* are lattice-work screens of stone or wood.

6   C. A. Bayly, *Rulers, Townsmen and Bazaars: North Indian Society in the Age of British Expansions, 1770–1870*. Cambridge, U.K.: Cambridge University Press, 1983.

7   Qamr al-Din Khan was a *wazir* in the Mughal court from 1724–48. My interpretation of Qamr-al-Din Khan's *haveli* is based on an Urdu map of Delhi around 1850 (OIOC, 1659) and period descriptions from travelogues and historical accounts including: Ehlers Eckhart and Thomas Krafft (eds), *Shahjahanabad/Old Delhi: Tradition and Colonial Change*. Stuttgart: Franz Steiner Verlag, 1993; Descriptions in Bernier, op. cit.; William Franklin, 'An Account of the Present State of Delhi,' *Asiatick Researches*, Vol. 4, 1795; Blake, op. cit.; Mirza Sangin Beg, *Sair-al-manzil* (A Tour of the Buildings), Lahore: 1828. Original Manuscript 1762; Dargah Quli Khan, op. cit.; Shamim Ahmad, *Marhum dilli ki ek jhalak* (A Glimpse of Delhi's Past), Delhi: Idarah-yi adabiyat-i Dillir, 1965; Mirza Mohammad Hadi Ruswa, *Umrao jan ada*. Translated as *Courtesan of Lucknow*, by Khushwant Singh and M. A. Husaini. Lahore: Book Centre, 1974.

8   Maulvi Zafrur Rehman Dehlavi, *Farhang-i istilahat-i peshavaran*.(A Technical Dictionary of Handicraft Occupations), Vol. I. Hyderabad, India: Anjuman Taraqqi Urdu, 1940; James Forbes, *Oriental Memoirs: A Narrative of Seventeen Years Residence in India*. Second edition by his daughter, the Countess de Montalembert. London: R. Bentley, 1834. First published, London: White, Cochrane & Co., 1813.

9   Urdu map, c.1850 (OIOC, X/1659) and Dehlavi, op. cit. Livestock were maintained in close proximity to living quarters even as late as the end of the nineteenth century. Colonial officials found the presence of cows and goats within the city very offensive. They tried incentives as well as penalties to remove them outside the city walls, but with partial success. See for instance, papers related to 'The Imposition of Tax on Milch Cows.' Commissioner's Office, Delhi Division, File # 39, Carton Box # 47, 1890 DSA).

10 A palanquin was placed on top of an elephant. *Ammari* and *rath* were ceremonial chariots. See Dehlavi, op. cit.; Franklin, op. cit.

11 'Bayaz-i khushbui,' Persian Manuscript Collection, (E 2784, OIOC, fols. 108a-11a) as quoted in Blake, op. cit., p. 45.

12   Archaeological Survey of India, *List of Mohammadan and Hindu Monuments, Delhi Province: Shahjahanabad*, Vol. I, Calcutta: Superintendent of Government Printing, 1916.

13   Forbes, op. cit., 1813. Hameeda Khatoon Naqvi has suggested that Delhi in the seventeenth century consisted of caste and occupation-based neighborhoods or *mohalla* and the elaborate houses of the nobility (Hameeda Khatoon Naqvi, *Urban Centers and Industries in Upper India, 1556–1803*. Bombay: Asia Publishing House, 1968). Blake, op. cit., contests this notion and argues that the patron–client relationship between the princes and the artisans was the primary force in organizing neighborhoods. He suggests that the elite quarters were the primary institutions in Mughal Delhi, and that the mansions of the *amīr* centered, structured and held together sectors of the city. My analysis of the urban form of Delhi today and of the accounts of seventeenth-century travelers leads me to support the latter argument. The communities of artisans, soldiers, servants, and professionals in the service of the *amīr* formed the neighborhood in and around the *haveli*. The subsequent rise of professionalism and mercantile trade contributed to the formation of enclaves based on craft specializations.

14   A *jāgirdār* was a person who held the right to a *jagīr*. In his treatise on the land systems of British India, B. H. Baden-Powell described a *jagir* as 'an assignment of land rights to a chief or a noble, to support troops, police or for a specific service; to maintain the state and dignity of the grantee; or sometimes to encourage the colonization and population of a jungle tract. The grant may include a right in the soil, originally for life but often became permanent and hereditary.' B. H. Baden-Powell, *The Land Systems of British India: Being a Manual of the Land Tenures and of the Systems of Land-Revenue Administration Prevalent in the Several Provinces.* New Delhi: Low Price Publications, 1990, Vol. III, p. 605. First published, Oxford: Clarendon Press, 1892.

15   A history of the Jain family narrated by Premchand Jain (Delhi, March 1993), and a history of Delhi narrated by Tanveer Ahmad Alvi (Delhi, Jan. 1992). Also see Bayly, op. cit.

16   Map entitled 'Jaghirs and Possessions of Petty Native Chiefs in Delhi Territory,' Dated 1872 (NAI), shows the ownership of vast estates around Delhi. The use of Nawab or Rajah before a name was an honorific title indicative of a ruler. In addition to land, the Mughal Emperor conferred titles on people for their services and accomplishments. Sometimes petty rulers had through various treaties become part of the Mughal Empire but retained their titles and holdings. I came across a variety of honorific titles in the documents but no evidence of equivalencies for them in terms of land or rank. Here I include such petty rulers in my use of the word aristocrats or nobility. The word *amīr* would also include most holders of substantial property, rank, and titles.

17   Musavvir Muhammad, Urdu map of Delhi, 1843, written and drawn in pencil, private collection of Farid and Sajda Beg, Delhi. Though the map is dated 1843 the absence of British military structures to the north or south of the royal palace suggests that the map was originally drawn much earlier, probably before British occupation in 1803.

18   Even today, many neighborhoods and streets in the old city continue to carry the

names of historical figures. See Maheshwar Dayal, *Dilli jo ek shahar hai* (Delhi that is a City). Delhi: Hindi Academy, 1991.

19 Major H. C. Beadon, *Final Report of the Third Regular Settlement of the Delhi District. 1906–1910*, Lahore: Civil and Military Gazette, 1910, p. cxlvii.

20 Jain, op. cit.

21 P. Hardy, 'Ghalib and the British,' in *Ghalib: The Poet and His Age*, edited by Ralph Russell. London: Allen and Unwin, 1972. Also see Varma and Shanker, op. cit., and Mirza Asadullah Khan Ghalib, *Ghalib ke khutut* (1797–1869) (Letters of Ghalib). Edited by Khaliq Anjum. New Delhi: Ghalib Institute, 1984–93.

22 *Ra'īs* refers to an aristocrat (*Concise Twentieth Century Dictionary: Urdu to English*. Compiled by Makhdoom Sabri. Delhi: Educational Publishing, 1985). Although *amīr* and *ra'īs* seem to be synonymous terms their distinction lie in their use. *Amīr* generally indicates a princely noble while *ra'īs*, a term more frequently used in nineteenth-century Urdu literature, indicates a person of the land-owning class. I see them as indicative of new concepts of social class emergent at the time.

23 Analysis is based on a detailed examination of the maps and ledgers of the *Wilson Survey* of 1910–12 maps of Delhi, and an Urdu map of Delhi (OIOC, X/1659). The British appropriated many of Nawab Bangash's key city properties in 1857.

24 The Khazanchi *haveli* is one of the more substantial ones that remain today with a main courtyard that has not yet been greatly rebuilt. Among other sources, my interpretation of the Khazanchi Haveli is based on descriptions of similar *haveli* in Vali Ashraf Sabuhi, *Dilli ki cand 'ajib hastiyan* (A Few Amazing Personalities of Delhi). Lahore, 1963. First published c.1930; Bashiruddin Ahmad Dehlavi, *Vaqiat-i darul-hakumat-i dihli* (A History of the Buildings of Delhi). New Delhi: Urdu Akadmi, 1990, 3 vols. First published Agra: Shamsi Press, 1919; Ahmed Ali, *Twilight in Delhi*. New Delhi: Sterling Publishers, 1973; Maheshwar Dayal, *Rediscovering Delhi*. Delhi: S. Chand, 1975; and oral histories as narrated by Dwijendra Kalia (Delhi, April, 1993), Vidhu Khanna (Delhi, May 1992), Tejasna Dhari (Delhi, Feb., 1993), Tanveer Ahmad Alvi (Delhi, Sept., 1992), Khaliq Anjum (Delhi, Sept., 1992), and Saeed Khan (Delhi, Sept., 1992).

25 Custom demanded that women (especially of Muslim households) in *purdāh* secluded themselves from public view. They moved out of their quarters only if necessary and then they traveled escorted. At such times, wealthier women traveled in enclosed palanquins and lesser ones with long, dark veils. The *zenānā* or *zenānkhānā* was the women's quarters in a *haveli*. Typically, the *zenānkhānā* consisted of a courtyard and rooms around it. This courtyard was located in the most private part of the house and did not have direct entry from a main thoroughfare or bazaar street.

26 Dehlavi, op. cit.

27 Mrs. B. Mir Hasan 'Ali. Observations on the Mussulmauns of India: Descriptive of their Manners, Customs, Habits, and Religious Opinions; Made During a Twelve Years Residence in their Immediate Society. Second edition with notes and introduction by William Crooke. Delhi: Deep Publications, 1975. First published, 1832, p. 173.

28 Sabuhi (op. cit.) portrays this powerfully in his short stories (see n. 24). While the King or the great *amīr* controlled some markets, artisans specializing in particular occupa-

tions dominated certain areas. Bayly (op. cit.) has concluded that artisans' guilds and traders' associations became increasingly powerful from the late eighteenth century.

29 Fictional though the works are, the settings and descriptions are reflective of the times. Some of the authors of the literary accounts were stalwart intellectuals of Delhi society. Among the many works I found insightful in understanding *haveli*-life and its fragmentation are: Farhatullah Baig, *Dihli ki akhiri shama'* (The Last Soiree of Poetry in Delhi). New Delhi: Urdu Akadmi, 1986. First published, 1949; Salahuddin Dehlavi, *Dilli vale* (The People of Delhi). New Delhi: Urdu Akadmi, 1988; Maulvi Sayyid Ahmed Dihlavi (ed.), *Rasum-i dihli* (Customs of Delhi). New Delhi: Urdu Akadmi, 1986. First published, 1890; Intizar Mirza (ed.), *Dilli ki tahzib: Seminar men parhe ga'e maqalat ka majmu'ah* (Delhi's Culture: A Collection of Papers presented at the Seminar). New Delhi: Urdu Akadmi, 1991.

30 Mirza Mahmud Beg, 'Mumani Jan aur Badi Haveli' (My Aunt [wife of mother's brother] and the Large *Haveli*. In *Mirza Mahmud Beg ke mazamin ka intikhab* (Selected Writings of Mirza Mahmud Beg, 1908–75). Edited by Kamil Quraishi. New Delhi: Urdu Akadmi, 1987.

31 Ibid., translation from the Urdu by author.

32 For a thorough discussion of the rise of the mercantile class in North India, see Bayly, op. cit.

33 Bernier, op. cit., p. 252.

34 Local history has it that Pucca Katra in Katra Kushal Rai once housed elephants on the ground floor and living quarters for the staff above. Today Pucca Katra is a neighborhood of petty traders and office workers. I found several structures in Delhi that continued to be called '*Mahal-sarā'i*' (or women's quarters) but now housing 'tenements' and workshops, with many of the residents claiming domicile of over five generations.

35 Archaeological Survey of India, *Mohammadan and Hindu Monuments*, 1916.

36 Sir Sayyid Ahmad Khan. *Asarussanadid* (Description of Historical Buildings and Monuments of Delhi). Edited by Khaliq Anjum. New Delhi: Urdu Akadmi, Delhi, 1990. First published Delhi: Matba-'yi Sultani, 1954. 2 Volumes.

37 Beg, op. cit.

38 The Cantonment was the encampment of the British military troops, while the civil station was the enclave of British and European civilians. In Delhi the civil station was called the Civil Lines. While military encampments had been around for a while, the segregation of European civilians into an enclave removed from the native city was deliberately pronounced after the 1857 insurgency. See Anthony. D. King, *Colonial Urban Development: Culture, Social Power and Environment*. London: Routledge and Kegan Paul, 1976.

39 For an excellent discussion and analysis of bungalows see Anthony D. King, *The Bungalow: The Production of a Global Culture*. London: Routledge and Kegan Paul, 1984.

40 Sabuhi, 'Khwaja Anis,' in *Dilli ki cand 'ajib hastiyan*, op. cit.

41 The 'Delhi Renaissance,' as scholars refer to it, was primarily an intellectual movement and artistic upheaval of the nineteenth century.

42 Gail Minault, 'Sayyid Ahmad Dehlavi and the Delhi Renaissance.' In *Delhi Through the*

Ages: Essays in Urban History, Culture and Society. Edited by Robert E. Frykenberg. Delhi: Oxford University Press, 1986.

43 Deputy Nazir Ahmad, *Ibnulvaqt* (The Opportunist). Delhi: Makhtab-e-jamia, 1989. First published 1888. The central theme of the novel is a debate on the reform of Muslim society that the author was deeply involved with. The two central opposing characters in the book represent the positions of the author and those of Sir Sayyid Ahmad, a noted intellectual and social reformer of the time.

44 Ahmad, op. cit., p. 92. A *galī* is a narrow lane. *Sāhib* is a term of respectful address, and in the colonial period referred to the British administrators. Translation from the Urdu.

45 The accounts of several European travelers to India during the latter part of the nineteenth century testify to this orientalist perception and representation of indigenous landscapes. The introverted *haveli* located in a maze of narrow winding lanes were threatening and inaccessible to the British. In their perception the streets were unclean and the houses, though lavish, lacked items of comfort basic to civilized life. The bungalows and the layout of the Civil Lines was meant to create salubrious surroundings in the otherwise 'dangerous tropics.'

46 Muslims in Delhi (as well as many Hindus) believed that dogs as pets should not be let inside the house.

47 Dell Upton has discussed this idea in a very different historical and cultural context in his powerful essay, 'White and Black Landscapes in Eighteenth Century Virginia.' In *Material Life in America, 1600–1860*. Edited by Robert Blair St. George. Boston: Northeastern University Press, 1988. pp. 357–370. Swati Chattopadhyay has discussed the extensive presence of servants in the European quarter of Calcutta. Swati Chattopadhyay, 'Blurring Boundaries: The Limits of "White Town" ' in Colonial Calcutta. In the *Journal of the Society of Architectural Historians*, 2000 June, vol. 59.

48 Based on the *Proceedings of the weekly meetings of the Delhi Municipal Committee* (MCD). Various volumes from 1864 to 1910; *Report on the Working of the Delhi Municipality*. From 1879 to 1912. Lahore: Superintendent of Government Printing. Various volumes. Published annually; and Rai Sahib Madho Pershad. *History of the Delhi Municipality 1863–1921*. Allahabad, India: Pioneer Press, 1921.

49 Based on various files of official correspondence from the Deputy Commissioner's Office, Delhi Division, for the period 1857–1912 (DSA); *History of Indian Railways Constructed and in Progress, Corrected up to 31st March, 1923*. Simla: Government of India Press, 1923.

50 Recounted by the residents of Katra Kushal Rai in interviews by author, March 1993.

51 Jain, op. cit. Delhi, at the time, was under the Punjab provincial administration.

3 NEGOTIATING STREETS AND SQUARES: SPATIAL CULTURE IN THE PUBLIC REALM

1 Dargah Quli Khan belonged to the royal entourage of a southern Indian kingdom. He traveled to Delhi and stayed there 1739–41. Extracts from his memoirs were published for the first time in 1926 by Mirza Muzaffar Husain. For an English translation

see *Muraqqa'-e-Dehli: The Mughal Capital in Muhammad Shah's time*. Edited and translated from the Persian by Chandra Shekhar and Shama Mitra Chenoy. Delhi: Deputy Publications, 1989.

2   Emily Eden, *Up the Country: Letters Written to Her Sister from the Upper Provinces of India*. Edited by Elizabeth Claridge. London: Virago, 1983. First published 1866; Reginald Heber, *Narrative of a Journey through the Upper Provinces of India from Calcutta to Bombay, 1824–1825: With Notes upon Ceylon, and an Account of a Journey to Madras and the Southern Provinces, 1826, and Letters Written in India*. Delhi: B.R. Pub. Corp. 1985. First published 1827.

3   Jurgen Habermas has referred to the 'public sphere' as a domain of social life in which such a thing as public opinion can be formed. In principle a public sphere is one where private persons come together to form a public and where access to the public sphere is open to all citizens. See Steven Seidman (ed.), *Jurgen Habermas on Society and Politics, a Reader*. Boston: Beacon Press, 1989, pp. 231–236.

4   Until 1857 British records generally referred to the Palace of the Mughal King as the 'King's Palace.' See, for instance, the map of Delhi surveyed by Lieut. F. J. Burgess in 1849–50. Indigenous documents referred to it as Qila' Mubarak (Auspicious Fortress). See Stephen P. Blake, *Shahjahanabad: The Sovereign City in Mughal India, 1639–1739*. Cambridge, U.K.: Cambridge University Press, 1991. The name Red Fort (*Lal Qila*) became current after the establishment of British rule in 1858. In indigenous sources the congregational mosque was formally referred to as the Masjid-I-Jami' (Friday Mosque) but was popularly known as Jami' Masjid. Jama Masjid, Jumma Masjid, and Jamia Masjid are variations of the same in various colonial sources.

5   Shama Mitra Chenoy, *Shahjahanabad: A City of Delhi, 1638–1857*. New Delhi: Munshiram Manoharlal, 1998.

6   A *sarā'i* is a traveler's shelter.

7   François Bernier, *Travels in the Mogul Empire, A.D. 1656–1668*. Second edition revised by Vincent Smith, based on Archibald Constable's revision of Irving Brock's translation. New Delhi: Low Price, 1989. First published 1670, Paris, 2 volumes; Eden, op. cit.

8   For a valuable discussion of race, class and gender during British rule in India see Kenneth Ballhatchet, *Race, Sex, and Class Under the Raj: Imperial Attitudes and Policies and their Critics, 1793–1905*. London: Weidenfeld and Nicholson, 1980.

9   Government of Punjab, *Gazetteer of the Delhi District, 1883–84*. Lahore: Government of India Press, 1886.

10   Charles Theophilus Metcalfe. *Two Native Narratives of the Mutiny in Delhi*. Westminster: A. Constable, 1898; Ahmad, Deputy Nazir, *Ibnulvaqt* (The Opportunist). Delhi: Makhtab-e-jamia, 1989, p. 57. First published 1888.

11   I. H. Taunton, Municipal Commissioner of Bombay, 'Some Aspects of Municipal Administration.' In the *Journal of the Indian Institute of Architects*, Vol. 3, No. 4, April 1937, pp. 234–235. Municipal corporations of English cities had actively engaged in public works for improving the health and comfort of the inhabitants since the 1830s.

12   See Rai Sahib Madho Pershad, *History of the Delhi Municipality 1863–1921*. Allahabad, India: Pioneer Press, 1921.

13   Andrew Lees, *Cities Perceived: Urban Society in European and American Thought, 1820–1940*. New York: Columbia University Press, 1985.

14   In her history of Delhi, Narayani Gupta has noted that the Town Hall was not 'an imperial undertaking' but was built with local funds and citizen subscriptions. However, quite apart from citizen subscriptions accounting for only a part of the total cost, I see the rebuilding of the square as products of colonial culture and modernist imperatives as they were prevalent in Delhi at the time. That the building was based partly on local funds and participation demonstrates that urban interventions by the colonial state were not simply imposed on a passive subject population. See Narayani Gupta, *Delhi Between Two Empires*. Delhi: Oxford University Press, 1981.

15   W. S. Caine, *Picturesque India: A Handbook for European Travellers*. London: George Routledge and Sons, 1890, p. 128. For a discussion of *durbar* rooms, see Jyoti Hosagrahar, 'City as *Durbar*: Theater and Power in Imperial Delhi.' In *Forms of Dominance: On the Architecture and Urbanism of the Colonial Enterprise*. Edited by Nezar Alsayyad. London: Avebury and Gower House, 1992, pp. 83–106.

16   On the death of Queen Victoria, James Skinner, grandson of the Col. James Skinner, erected at his own expense, her statue in marble facing Chandni Chowk. Col. James Skinner (1778–1841), held in high regard in the Colonial Service, was the son of a British army colonel and an Indian (Rajput) mother.

17   Musicians in the *naqqārkhānā* or spaces for offices and also music, played martial music during audiences and rang out the time of day. Many mansions of the nobility had a *naqqārkhānā*.

18   Letter # 536 to D. Murree, the Secretary, Government of Punjab. Dated October 11, 1860. Commissioner's Office, Delhi Division, *File # 76A*, Carton Box # 5. (DSA).

19   For further discussion see Hosagrahar, op. cit.

20   Docket # 1937 from the Secretary, Government of Punjab. Dated October 11, 1860. Commissioner's Office, Delhi Division, *File # 76A*, Carton Box # 5, 1860. (DSA).

21   In postcolonial Delhi the square is locally known as 'Ghantaghar' (bell-tower). The statue of Queen Victoria has been replaced by one of Swami Shraddhanand to mark his significant role in India's freedom struggle.

22   The glacis around the fort was later reduced to four hundred and fifty yards. Douglas Goodfriend believes that a lack of adequate gunpowder saved the city from total destruction. Douglas E. Goodfriend, 'A Chronology of Delhi's Development, 1803–1982.' *Design*, October–December, 1982, pp. 36–50.

23   Delhi Municipal (W. A. J.) Wilson Committee, 'Survey of Delhi City.' Delhi: Unpublished, 1910–12.

24   For a detailed study of the Red Fort, see Anisha Shekhar Mukherji. *The Red Fort of Shahjahanabad*. New Delhi: Oxford University Press, 2003.

25   Papers and Files from the *Clearance of Chandni Chowk Papers Series*, Commissioner's Office, Delhi Division, Carton Box # 5, 1859–89. (DSA).

26   Custom demanded that women (especially of Muslim households) seclude themselves from any contact with men other than their spouse and immediate family. Women who followed the *purdāh* custom wore long veils and inhabited a separate part of the

dwelling to shield themselves from the view of men outside the family. Women in *purdāh* from wealthy families traveled in curtained palanquins, as did some *rais* men.

27 Lord Northbrook fountain for instance was built to honor the visit of the Governor General of India.

28 Hamilton Road, Elgin Road, Lord Northbrook Fountain, and Dufferin Bridge were all named after significant figures in the colonial empire. Some, such as Nicholson Gardens, were named after key military figures who died fighting for the British during the 1857 revolt.

29 Pershad, op. cit., p. 17.

30 Delhi Municipal Committee. *Report on the Working of the Delhi Municipality, 1882–83*. Lahore: Superintendent of Government Printing, 1883.

31 Both European and Indian investors were active in financing banks and hotels.

32 Emma Roberts, *Scenes and Characteristics of Hindustan*. London: Allen, 1837, p. 32.

33 Some adopted British elements and motifs to ingratiate themselves with the British and some simply to be abreast with the fashions of the day.

34 During the year 1878–79 the municipal expense on maintaining a police force had risen to a third of the annual expenditure of the Municipality. Pershad, op. cit.

35 Adopted in 1886, the building by-laws were also meant to embody scientific principles and technological progress. The maximum heights of buildings were calculated in relation to the width of street and the angle of light penetration. Similarly, the size of sidewalks, the heights of overhead projections on to streets, the location of benches and stairs on shop fronts were all related to the width of the street and the height of the buildings. The optimum size and number of drains were calculated for efficient flow and designed for easy cleaning. See *Rules of Business adopted by the Delhi Municipal Committee on 9th December 1886, Appendix I, Rules for Erection or Re-erection of buildings*. In Commissioner's Office, Delhi Division, *File # B-6*, Carton Box. # 37, 1886. (DSA). Official documents of the period refer to by-laws as 'Byelaws'.

36 The master-masons in Delhi, known as *mistri*, drew up rough plans showing the arrangement of rooms, and sometimes a front elevation. They organized the construction by passing on daily instructions to the masons and stoneworkers who in turn may have had a group of assistants. Those engaged in designing and building were skilled craftsmen and not technically educated professionals. As one British official observed in frustration and admiration: 'Let me add that it has been extremely difficult to ascertain any of the names of the craftsmen engaged on the work of these buildings. They are of the humblest class, and several officials, who showed me over these modern buildings, ridiculed the idea of asking for their names and address . . .' Gordon Sanderson and J. Begg. *Types of Modern Indian Buildings at Delhi, Agra, Allahabad, Lucknow, Ajmer, Bhopal, Bikanir, Gwalior, Jaipur, Jodhpur, and Udaipur with Notes on the Craftsmen Employed on their Design and Execution*. Allahabad: Government Press, United Provinces, 1913, p. 6.

37 Bernier, op. cit.; Dargah Quli Khan, op. cit.

38 A *chattā* is a roofed lane or a covered passage. Since the streets were narrow, a common practice in the city was to build a room, pavilion, or walkway at the upper

level connecting buildings on both sides of the streets while allowing free passage underneath.

39 The structure posed a problem as it would extend beyond the boundaries of Munshi Jamaluddin's private property on to a common thoroughfare.

40 Delhi Municipal Committee, *Proceedings of an Ordinary Meeting of the Delhi Municipal Committee*. In Commissioner's Office, Delhi Division, *File # 49*, Carton Box # 53 (213), B-2, 1897, p. 5.

41 Prior to municipalization, *patvāri's* records had been more carefully maintained for agricultural land and taxation than for urban properties.

42 For different theories on the design and layout of Shahjahanabad, see Blake, op. cit.; Chenoy, op. cit.; and Samuel V. Noe, 'Shahjahanabad: Geometrical Bases for the Plan of Mughal Delhi.' In *Delhi: The Deepening Urban Crisis*. Edited by Patwant Singh and Ram Dhamija. New Delhi: Sterling, 1989, pp. 19–26.

43 Delhi Municipal Committee, *Proceedings of the Municipal Committee Delhi for 1895–96*. Commissioner's Office, Delhi Division, Carton Box. # 53, Vols VI & III, 1895–96 and 1896–99, p. 50.

44 Ibid.

45 Delhi Municipal Committee, *Proceedings of an Ordinary Meeting of the Delhi Municipal Committee, 1897*. Commissioner's Office, Delhi Division, Carton Box. # 53, 1895–96 and 1896–97, p. 5.

46 Delhi Municipal Committee, *Report on the Working of Delhi Municipality, 1872–73*. Lahore: Superintendent of Government Printing, 1874.

47 The proceedings of the Delhi Municipal Committee's weekly meetings reveal the different outcomes of offenses. See Delhi Municipal Committee, 1897.

48 Ibid.

49 Letter # 164, H-7, from Deputy Commissioner, Delhi Division to Lieutenant Governor, Punjab Government, dated 10.8.97. Commissioner's Office, Delhi Division, *File # 49*, Carton Box # 53 (213), B-2, 1897. (DSA).

50 Ibid.

51 Letter # 69 from the Commissioner and Superintendent Delhi Division to the Secretary, Municipal Committee. Dated 31 August, 1897. Commissioner's Office, Delhi Division, *File # 49*, Carton Box # 53 (213) B-2, 1897. (DSA).

52 *Rules of Business Adopted by the Delhi Municipal Committee on 9th December 1886, Appendix I, Rules for Erection or Re-erection of Buildings Passed at a Special Meeting Held on 2nd September, 1889*. Commissioner's Office, Delhi Division.˜ *File # B-6*, Carton Box. # 37, 1886. (DSA). A *takhta* was a wooden bench or platform placed outside the shop front protruding on to the street.

53 Delhi Municipal Committee, *Proceedings of the Municipal Committee Delhi for 1895–96*. In Carton Box. # 53, Vols VI & III, 1895–96 and 1896–99, p. 52. (DSA).

54 Ibid.

55 Ibid.

56 The official correspondence of the government reveals their anxiety over the arrangements to maintain peace on the two occasions. See papers in *File # 30*, Carton Box # 46, 1890, Commissioner's Office records, Delhi State Archives. Also see, Letter # 1635

from W. W. Young, the Secretary, Government of Punjab to the Commissioner and Superintendent, Delhi Division. Commissioner's Office Delhi, Carton Box # 40, 1886.

57 *Fairs and Processions – Arrangements for (Saraogi) procession on 20.7.1877.* Commissioner's Office Delhi, *File # 5,* 1877.

58 R. Aitchison, Commissioner, Delhi Division, 'Note' in Commissioner's Office Records, *File # 1,* 1878. (DSA).

59 Ibid., p. 71.

60 Letter to the Under Secretary to the Government of India, Camp Dehlie from Ricksh Lall, Agent of the Jaini Sect of Delhi, Dated, March 16, 1875. In Commissioner's Office records. *File # 1,* 1878. (DSA).

61 For an insightful discussion of British public rituals in India see Bernard Cohn, 'Representing Authority in Victorian India.' In the *Invention of Tradition.* Edited by Eric Hobsbawm and Terence Ranger. Cambridge: Cambridge University Press, 1983, pp. 165–210.

62 The description of British processions is based on official descriptions and images of the visits of Lord Curzon, Viceroy of India, in 1877, the Prince of Wales in 1902, as well as other dignitaries. See for instance, John Fortescue, *Narrative of the Visit to India of their Majesties King George V and Queen Mary and the Coronation Durbar Held at Delhi, 12th December 1911.* London: Macmillan, 1912. Descriptions of the Indian processions are based on a variety of sources including official records of the Municipality, oral histories of residents, fictional and non-fictional works in Urdu describing Delhi's cultural life. For an English woman's account see Mrs. Mir Hassan Ali, *Observations on the Mussulmauns of* India, 1832.

63 Hobsbawm and Ranger have discussed this point most eloquently in the *Invention of Tradition.*

64 Raymond Williams, *The Country and the City.* New York: Oxford University Press, 1973.

65 Peter Stallybrass and Allon White, *The Politics and Poetics of Transgression.* Ithaca, NY: Cornell University Press, 1986.

4 SANITIZING NEIGHBORHOODS; GEOGRAPHIES OF HEALTH

1 Cholera outbreaks occurred in Europe in 1848, 1861, and 1865. They altered both popular and professional perceptions of society, space, and the body. Paul Rabinow and François Delaporte offer different perspectives on the relationship of medicine and modern society. Paul Rabinow, *French Modern: Norms and Forms of the Social Environment.* Cambridge, MA: MIT Press, 1989; and François Delaporte, *Disease and Civilization: The Cholera in Paris, 1832.* Cambridge, MA: MIT Press, 1986.

2 For a good account of the public-health movement in Britain see Royston Lambert, *Sir John Simon, 1816–1904, and English Social Administration.* London: MacGibbon and Kee, 1963. See also Anthony S. Wohl, *Endangered Lives: Public Health in Victorian Britain.* Cambridge, MA: Harvard University Press, 1983.

3 Haussmann's rebuilding of Paris was one of the earliest such projects. This was followed by efforts to redevelop other European cities including Vienna and London.

4   Alan Mayne, *The Imagined Slum: Newspaper Representation in Three Cities, 1870–1914.* Leicester, London: Leicester University Press, 1993.

5   Banister Fletcher and Phillips H. Fletcher, *Architectural Hygiene or Sanitary Science as Applied to Buildings.* Ninth Edition. London: Sir Isaac Pitman and Sons, 1954. First published 1921.

6   Benjamin Ward Richardson, 'Modern Sanitary Science: A City of Health.' In *Van Nostrand's Eclectic Engineering Magazine,* Vol. 14 (January 1876), pp. 31–42. Reprinted from *Nature,* Vol. 12 (October 14, 1875), pp. 523–525 and (October 21, 1875), pp. 542–545.

7   Ibid.

8   Studies by Gyan Prakash and David Arnold on the cultural authority of science and its relationship to colonialism are illuminating on this point. Gyan Prakash, *Another Reason: Science and the Imagination of Modern India.* Princeton: Princeton University Press, 1999. David Arnold, *Science, Technology, and Medicine in Colonial India.* The Cambridge History of India. Vol. III. Cambridge: Cambridge University Press, 2000.

9   David Arnold, 'Introduction: Disease, Medicine and Empire.' In *Imperial Medicine and Indigenous Societies.* Edited by David Arnold. Manchester, U.K.: Manchester University Press, 1988, pp. 1–26.

10 Official papers during this time repeatedly refer to the need to contain and minimize the influence of neighborhoods in the walled city they perceived as being crowded, morally debased, and harboring disease. The fundamental premise of the *cordon sanitaire* the French adopted in Morocco was a cordoning off of diseased urban areas to keep them from 'infecting' the other. See papers related to the clearance of Chandni Chowk and Ellenborough Tank.

11 See for instance, George Sims, *How the Poor Live and Horrible London.* New York, London: Garland Publishing, 1984, pp. 45–46. First published 1889. Sims describes London's slums as comparable to 'Cities of the East.' Asa Briggs has observed, 'The "dark city" and the "dark continent" were alike mysterious, and it is remarkable how often the exploration of the unknown city was compared with the exploration of Africa and Asia.' Asa Briggs, *Victorian Cities.* London: Odhams, 1964.

12 Surgeon Major C. J. McNally, *The Elements of Sanitary Science: A Hand-Book.* Madras, India: Superintendent, Government Press, 1889.

13 Veena Oldenburg, *The Making of Colonial Lucknow,* Princeton, NJ: Princeton University Press, 1984.

14 To facilitate the policing of those suspected in participating in the rebellion, sometimes surrounding structures around were also demolished. Hamid Ali Khan, for instance, was arrested as a 'mutineer,' his house confiscated, and the houses around his were demolished. (See papers in *Clearance of Ellenborough Tank Series.* Commissioner's Office, Delhi Division, Carton Box # 5. (DSA)).

15 Government of Punjab, *Gazetteer of the Delhi District, 1883–84.* Lahore: Government of India Press, 1886.

16 Among the prominent buildings lost to Delhi were the Akbarabadi Masjid (mosque), and the mansions of the Nawab Wazir and the Nawabs of Jajjhar, Ballabgarh, Farrucknagar and Bahadurgarh. See Vernacular map of Delhi in the British Library, OIOC

X/1659. Narayani Gupta has also listed in her book some of the prominent buildings destroyed. Narayani Gupta, op. cit.

17 Letter from Executive Engineer, Delhi Department of Public Works to C. B. Saunders, Commissioner and Superintendent, Delhi Division, Dated January 17, 1859. Commissioner's Office, Delhi Division, *File # 9, Clearance of Chandni Chowk Papers Series,* Carton Box # 5, 1859–89. 'Huts,' probably refers to the general state of dilapidation that the buildings had fallen into after the siege as well as the numerous temporary structures. (DSA).

18 Letter # 61, To the Secretary, Punjab Government, Dated November 15, 1859. Commissioner's Office, Delhi Division, *File # 2, Clearance of Chandni Chowk Papers Series,* Carton Box # 5, 1859–89. (DSA).

19 Papers and Files from the *Clearance of Ellenborough Tank Papers Series,* Commissioner's Office, Delhi Division, Carton Box # 5, 1859–89. (DSA).

20 Letter # 6, from Executive Engineer, Delhi Division, to C. B. Saunders, Commissioner and Superintendent, Delhi Division, Dated May 6, 1859. Commissioner's Office, Delhi Division, *File # 9, Clearance of Chandni Chowk Papers Series,* Carton Box # 5, 1859–89, pp. 81–1 to 81–4. (DSA).

21 See, for instance, James W. Moore, *Health in the Tropics or Sanitary Art Applied to Europeans in India.* London: Churchill, 1862. Colonel David B. Smith, Civil Assistant Surgeon of Delhi, recommended James Moore as one of the most approved authors on sanitation and hygiene. Letter # 174 from Colonel David B. Smith, Civil Assistant Surgeon of Delhi, Dated October 26, 1863. Commissioner's Office, Delhi Division, *File # 163,* Carton Box # 10, 1863, pp. 49–55.

22 *Report of Royal Commission on the Sanitary State of the Army in India.* London: Her Majesty's Stationary Office, 1863.

23 Gupta and Oldenburg have both discussed in detail the creation of a green belt to separate the European quarters from the 'native.' Narayani Gupta, *Delhi Between Two Empires.* Delhi: Oxford University Press, 1981; Oldenburg, op. cit.

24 I also agree with Shirine Hamadeh's analysis that the *cordon sanitaire* served to construct opposing identities of native subject and European colonizer. See Shirine Hamadeh, 'Creating the Traditional City: A French Project.' In *Forms of Dominance: On the Architecture and Urbanism of the Colonial Enterprise.* Edited by Nezar Alsayyad. London: Avebury and Gower House, 1992, pp. 241–260. For discussions of French colonization of Algeria and Morocco see also Rabinow, op. cit.; Janet L. Abu-Lughod, *Rabat: Urban Apartheid in Morocco.* Princeton, NJ: Princeton University Press, 1980; Gwendolyn Wright, *Politics of Design in French Colonial Urbanism.* Chicago: University of Chicago Press, 1991.

25 See, for instance, 'Letter # 6 from Executive Engineer,' op. cit.

26 See, for instance, Letter # 325 from B. W. Egerton, Deputy Commissioner, Delhi to C. B. Saunders, Commissioner and Superintendent, Delhi Division, Dated May 20, 1859. Commissioner's Office, Delhi Division, *File # 14, Clearance of Chandni Chowk Papers Series,* Carton Box # 5, 1859–89. (DSA).

27 Official correspondence in the files record in detail the methods and amount of com-

pensation, and the auctions. Commissioner's Office, Delhi Division, *File # 2, Clearance of Chandni Chowk Papers Series*, Carton Box # 5, 1859–89. (DSA).

28   See, for instance, Letter # 136–1875, from G. K. Smith, Deputy Commissioner Delhi, to J. W. Smyth, Commissioner and Superintendent, Delhi Division, Dated, May 7, 1875. Commissioner's Office, Delhi Division, *File # 93A*, 1875; and Memorandum from C. H. Aitchison, Punjab Government, Dated September 23, 1863. Commissioner's Office, Delhi Division, *File # 92-B*, Carton Box # 5, 1864. Also, see Minutes in *File # 92-B*, Carton Box # 5, 1864. (DSA).

29   A caste-group specializing in trade.

30   Letter # 1472, from the Chief Engineer, Punjab Government to the Secretary, Punjab Government, Dated July 13, 1860. Commissioner's Office, Delhi Division, *File # 72, Clearance of Chandni Chowk Papers Series*, Carton Box # 5, 1859–89. (DSA).

31   Letter #7, from W. C. Plowden, Commissioner and Superintendent, Delhi Division to the Military Secretary the Punjab Government, Dated March 28, 1860. Commissioner's Office, Delhi Division, *File # 49A, Clearance of Chandni Chowk Papers Series*, Carton Box # 5, 1859–89. (DSA). Urdu petitions and other papers in the file also support this.

32   Ibid.

33   Chief Engineer, Punjab Government, op. cit., all emphasis in original.

34   The view of 'dangerous' disease comes up in descriptions of the time of both industrial slums and the walled city of Delhi in the aftermath of the rebellion. Official correspondence indicates that the danger in Delhi came more from the potential for rebellion than the potential for epidemics. See official correspondence and reports related to the Clearance of Chandni Chowk and Ellenborough Tank, Commissioner's Office, Delhi Division (DSA).

35   The Tughluq Kings in Delhi channeled water to their fort from Hissar, around 100 miles north-west of Delhi during the fourteenth century.

36   *Ba'oli* are tanks with steps leading down to the water. Wells in most *havelis* and temples are now covered up and in disuse. Local history suggests that well-water was declared polluted and wells became disused in the latter part of the nineteenth century. Khari Baoli, one of the largest and busiest bazaars today, derived its name from the peculiar taste of the water in a *baoli* along the street. Hauz Khazi, the second biggest square in Old Delhi (after Chandni Chowk), also had a well which was the principal source of water for the area. Chandni Chowk also had an octagonal pool of water from the Faiz *nahar*.

37   Lord Ellenborough was the Governor General of India from 1841 to 1844.

38   Samuel Noe has suggested that the canals represented a considerable engineering achievement and that their pattern is central to understanding the form and structure of Shahjahan's Delhi. Noe also suggests that the entire city was originally designed as a paradise garden in the tradition of Islamic design in medieval Persia. Although one may question his assertion that geometry was the primary determinant of Delhi's form, Noe's analysis is valuable in pointing out the significance of engineering in the planning of Delhi. See Samuel V. Noe, 'Shahjahanabad: Geometrical Bases for the Plan of Mughal Delhi.' In *Delhi: The Deepening Urban Crisis*. Edited by Patwant Singh and Ram Dhamija. New Delhi: Sterling, 1989, pp. 19–26.

39 W. H. Greathed, *Report on the Drainage of the City of Delhi (and on the Means of Improving It)*. Agra: Secundra Orphan Press, 1852.

40 By extension of the Improvement of Towns Act of 1850. Punjab Government Notification No. 237U, Dated December 13, 1862 declares Act XXVI of 1850 to be in force in Delhi.

41 While some members of the Municipal Committee were elected by popular vote, only those voters furnished with voting certificates were allowed to vote. Since the voting areas included the Civil Lines, Europeans were also voting for the appointment of native members.

42 Delhi Municipal Committee, *Report on the Working of Delhi Municipality, 1904–1905*, Vol. I. Lahore: Superintendent of Government Printing, 1906.

43 Besides these improvements the Committee took an interest in everything else that required its attention for the 'welfare of the citizens.' For instance, lime kilns were removed to the Ajmere Gate corner of the city owing to their smoke nuisance and in a like manner other offensive trades, such as trade in hides, did not escape the Committee's notice. Rai Sahib Madho Pershad, *History of the Delhi Municipality 1863–1921*. Allahabad, India: Pioneer Press, 1921, p. 11.

44 Letter from Major C. A. M. Mahon, Deputy Commissioner, Delhi to Lieutenant W. M. Wiley, Commissioner and Superintendent, Delhi Division, Commissioner's Office, Delhi Division, *File # 206*, Carton Box # 11, 1869–82. (DSA).

45 Ibid.

46 Note by Chief Engineer, Major General C. Pollard, Dated Feb. 2, 1882. Commissioner's Office, Delhi Division, *File # 206*, 1869–82. (DSA).

47 'Rules of Business adopted by the Delhi Municipal Committee on 9th December 1886, Appendix I, Rules for Erection or Re-erection of Buildings.' Commissioner's Office, Delhi Division. *File # B-6*, Carton Box. # 37, 1886. (DSA).

48 An examination of the annual reports of the Municipality reveals that the introduction of each measure was chronicled with pride. Delhi Municipal Committee, *Report on the Working of the Delhi Municipality*. Published annually from 1879 to 1912. Lahore: Superintendent of Government Printing.

49 Pershad, op. cit.

50 Reply by His Honor Sir Charles Montgomery Rivis, Lieutenant Governor of the Punjab and its Dependencies to the address presented by the Municipal Committee of Delhi on April 17, 1902. See Delhi Municipal Committee, *Report on the Working of Delhi Municipality, 1902–1903*. Lahore: Superintendent of Government Printing, 1903.

51 Patrick Geddes, *Town Planning Towards City Development. A Report to the Durbar of Indore*. Part I. Indore, India: Holkar State Printing Press, 1918, p. 72.

52 Gupta, op. cit., has discussed the politics and burdens of taxation in detail.

53 The census of 1911 records a population of 413,851.

54 J. Robertson, Sanitary Commissioner, Government of India. *Note on the Sanitation of Delhi City*, 1912. Commissioner's Office, Delhi Division. *New File # 22*, Carton Box # 69, 1912. (DSA).

55 Narayani Gupta and Anthony King also observed the bias towards improving European areas in Delhi's urban development. Gupta, op. cit.; Anthony D. King, *Colonial*

Urban Development: Culture, Social Power and Environment. London: Routledge and Kegan Paul, 1976.

56 Pershad, 1921; *Report on the Working of the Delhi Municipality, 1879–1912*. Lahore: Superintendent of Government Printing.

57 Letter # 99, from H. P. Tollinton, Secretary, Punjab Government and its Dependencies to General Officer Commanding, 7th Division, Dated Lahore, March 1, 1910; Commissioner's Office, Delhi Division, *File # 610*, Vol. III, Carton Box # 16, 1889, p. 125. (DSA). For discussion on the clearance of swampy vegetation see the discussion on the improvement of Bela Plantation in *File # 610*, Vol. III, Carton Box # 16, 1889, Commissioner's Office, Delhi Division. (DSA).

58 Bernard Cohn's seminal work on imperial rituals in the colonies offers valuable insights on the meanings of the grand Imperial Assemblages. See Bernard S. Cohn. 'Representing Authority in Victorian India.' In *The Invention of Tradition*. Edited by Eric Hobsbawm and Terence Ranger. Cambridge University Press, 1983, pp. 165–209. On the representation of Empire, see also Francis G. Hutchins, *Illusion of Permanence: British Imperialism in India*. Princeton, NJ: Princeton University Press, 1967.

59 Gupta, op. cit., has made similar observations. Gupta has also observed that many of the new roads and electricity came to Delhi to impress visitors at the 1877 and 1902 durbars. For a discussion of imperial assemblages or durbars also see Jyoti Hosagrahar, 'City as *Durbar*: Theater and Power in Imperial Delhi.' In *Forms of Dominance: On the Architecture and Urbanism of the Colonial Enterprise*. Edited by Nezar Alsayyad. London: Avebury and Gower House, 1992, pp. 83–106.

60 Delhi Municipal Committee, *Report on the Working of Delhi Municipality, 1904–1905*, Vol. I. Lahore: Superintendent of Government Printing, 1905, p. 9.

61 'Conservancy' was a term widely used in British documents. Conservancy works included cleaning of streets, disposal of refuse from pit latrines in homes, garbage disposal, maintenance of public urinals and toilets, and flushing of public drains. Pershad, op. cit., p. 141.

62 Benjamin Ward Richardson, *Hygeia: A City of Health*. London: Macmillan, 1876.

63 As early as 1861, prominent citizens such as Rai Chunnamal, a wealthy banker, and Rai Jeewan Lal Bahadur, once Honorary Magistrate of Delhi, mediated on behalf of the colonial government to allay people's fear of taxation and to dispel their opposition to it. See Anonymous, *A Brief History of the Family of Rai Chhunna Mal*. Delhi: Oxford Printing Works, 1930; Anonymous, *A Short Account of the Life and Works of Rai Jeewan Lal Bahadur Late Honorary Magistrate, Delhi with Extracts from his Diary Relating to the Time of Mutiny, 1857*. Lahore: The Tribune Steam Press, 1911. Four decades later, the local government still had to contend with opposition to taxation to achieve sanitary reform.

64 In Deputy Nazir Ahmad's novel *Ibnulvaqt*, the main character, Ibnulvaqt, extols the virtues of living in a well-ventilated bungalow. After being appointed a senior official in the British service, Ibnulvaqt moves out of his family home in the dense, narrow alleyways of the old city into a substantial bungalow in the civil lines situated on a wide road complete with a garden and a Western-style toilet. Deputy Nazir Ahmad, Ibnulvaqt (The Opportunist). Delhi: Makhtab-e-jamia, 1989. First published 1888.

65 Gupta, op. cit., p. 100.

66 Letter in English from Abbas Hussain, Haider Hasan, and Hazi Abdul Samed to the Commissioner and Superintendent Delhi Division, Dated February 16, 1907. Commissioner's Office, Delhi Division. *New File # 60*, Carton Box # 62, 1907. (DSA).

67 Ibid.

68 Included in the category of 'nuisance' were *jhaps, chapars* (temporary shelters and lean-tos), encroachments on public lands, the construction of new privies opening onto public streets, dilapidated houses and walls endangering the lives of occupants or passers by, and cremation grounds. All burials within 500 yards of the city walls were prohibited. See Pershad, op. cit., p. 8.

69 Local businesses, in particular, found the urinals detrimental to their business. Inferred from weekly proceedings of the Municipal Committee where protests were frequently noted. Proceedings of the weekly meetings of the Delhi Municipal Committee located at the Delhi Municipal Corporation, Record Office, Delhi.

70 The absence of facilities for women (for a discussion of them) is indicative of the continued exclusion of women from the public arena and of the gender bias in the provision of infrastructure services. Clearly, with the increase in male migrant workers from the surrounding countryside, and the local practice of excluding middle- and upper-income women from the public arena, both justified the bias in the provision of services. However, it is interesting that while seeking to modernize, municipal policies made no effort to transform women's access and use of space but rather deferred to 'tradition' in this regard.

71 In this instance, officials ordered Azimuddin to remove the *malba* and repair the urinal within fifteen days or face further action. Delhi Municipal Committee, *Proceedings of the Municipal Committee Delhi for 1895–96*. Commissioner's Office, Delhi Division, Vol. VI & III, Carton Box. # 53, 1895–96. (DSA).

72 Ibid., p. 169. Urination was considered a profane activity and its formal inclusion on the street offended the residents' sensibilities. Public facilities were particularly useful for the laboring and menial classes who plied the streets. The gathering of such people around the urinals might threaten both the shopkeepers and their customers.

73 Ibid.

74 Ibid.

75 Charles John Griffiths, *A Narrative of the Siege of Delhi with an Account of the Mutiny at Ferozepore in 1857*. London: John Murray, 1910.

76 Most returned to the city on the payment of a tax in January of 1858. Foreign Special Consultations, # 2–8, March 26, 1858. Carton box # 5. (DSA).

77 Griffiths, op. cit.

78 For instance I observed that the spatial arrangement of Hindu homes in Delhi could be understood in terms of profane and sacred uses. Kitchens and shrines were in the most sacred part of the dwelling, facing north or east, while privy pits were in the most profane. The interior of the dwelling itself was sacred compared to the outside. Water containers were usually placed near entrance areas for a required wash before proceeding to the sacred interiors. The *tūlsī* plant, revered for its medicinal and sanitizing properties, was an essential presence in the courtyard. Burial, cremation, and

slaughter-houses had been located just outside the city walls and hence the city limits.

79 'Sweeper' is a term that colonial officials used to refer to those who collected refuse and cleaned toilets and streets. Such people were considered untouchable according to local caste divisions.

80 In her insightful discussion of Chinese medicine and British sanitary reform in Singapore, Brenda Yeoh has noted that a similar distinction existed between traditional Chinese medicine and Western medical theories. Brenda Yeoh, *Municipal Sanitary Surveillance, Asian Resistance and the Control of the Urban Environment in Colonial Singapore.* Research Paper # 47. Oxford: University of Oxford, School of Geography, 1991. Also Brenda Yeoh, 'Sanitary Ideology and the Control of the Urban Environment.' In *Ideology and Landscape.* Edited by Alan R. H. Baker. Cambridge: Cambridge University Press, 1992, pp. 148–172.

81 The Delhi Municipality was formed in February 1863 by extension of the Police Act of 1861. Fifty other municipalities had been set up in Punjab before 1864 – all as extensions of the Police Act of 1861. The stated missions of the municipalities were to raise funds for police and 'conservancy' and to spend on works of improvement, education, and others that the members saw fit. But the expense of maintaining an adequate police force was to have the first call on all such funds. See *Gazette of India Extraordinary*, Dated September 14, 1864.

82 Pershad, op. cit.

83 Brenda Yeoh observed a similar policing of reform and the importance of sanitary inspectors in colonial Singapore. See Yeoh, op. cit.

84 Pershad, op. cit., p. 34.

85 Based on local history of sweepers' quarters as narrated during an interview with Kishen Chand, resident of a sweeper community, Delhi, November, 1992.

86 Ibid.

87 Anthony King observes that this was true also of early colonial bungalows. Personal communication, 2004.

88 In the absence of piped sewage disposal, sweepers removed material from latrines and carried them in baskets on their head. One effort to improve this traditional system was to develop a cart in which the offensive material could be carried.

89 Dell Upton has discussed a similar interpenetration of the landscapes of slaves and plantation owners despite obvious segregation in eighteenth-century Virginia. See Dell Upton, 'White and Black Landscapes in Eighteenth Century Virginia.' In *Material Life in America, 1600–1860*. Edited by Robert Blair St. George. Boston: Northeastern University Press, 1988, pp. 357–370.

90 Pershad, op. cit., p. 48.

91 Letter # 219/m7, from S. M. Jacob, Deputy Commissioner, Delhi District to A. Meredith, Commissioner and Superintendent, Delhi Division, Commissioner's Office, Delhi Division. *New File # 22*, Carton Box # 69, 1912. (DSA).

92 Pershad, op. cit., p. 47.

93 While the stated purpose of the numbering was for collection of census information, later it also aided in the collection of house-tax.

94 Pershad, op. cit., p. 21.

95 Mark Harrison, 'Towards a Sanitary Utopia? Professional Visions and Public Health in India, 1880–1914.' In *South Asia Research*, Vol. 10, No. 1, May 1990, pp. 19–40.

96 For a detailed discussion of conflicts between followers of indigenous medicine and Western medicine, see Barbara Metcalf, 'Hakim Ajmal Khan: *Rais* of Delhi and Muslim leader.' In *Delhi Through the Ages: Essays in Urban History, Culture and Society*. Edited by R. E. Frykenberg. Delhi: Oxford University Press, 1986, pp. 299–315.

97 Letter # 55, from Captain H. S. P. Davies, Deputy Commissioner Delhi, to Robert Clarke, Commissioner and Superintendent, Delhi Division, Dated March 5, 1898. Commissioner's Office, Delhi Division, *New File*, Carton Box # 54 (49-E(3)), Vol. III, 1898, p. 75. (DSA).

98 For instance, the number of deaths from cholera in Delhi were 44 persons in 1878 but 416 in 1879 or from smallpox was 12 in 1879 but 72 in 1881. Punjab Government. *A Gazetteer of the Delhi District (1883–4)*. Gurgaon, India: Vintage Books, 1988. First published 1884.

99 Brenda Yeoh makes similar observations in her work on Singapore. Brenda S. A. Yeoh, *Contesting Space: Power Relations and the Urban Built Environment in Colonial Singapore*. Kuala Lumpur: Oxford University Press, 1996.

100 Perceval Landon, *Under the Sun: Impression of Indian Cities*. London: Hurst and Blackett, 1906, pp. 52–53.

101 Despite the rhetoric of improvement, the primary charge of municipalities in northern India was to maintain an adequate police force.

5 BEYOND THE WALLS: COMMERCE OF URBAN EXPANSION

1 *Illustrated London News*, September 18, 1858, p. 254. (OIOC).

2 Letter # 64, from Robert Clarke, Deputy Commissioner, Delhi, to Colonel L. I. H. Grey, Commissioner and Superintendent, Delhi Division, Dated April 18, 1888. Commissioner's Office records, *New File # 10(a)*, Carton Box # 41, 1888. (DSA).

3 *Report on the Census of the Punjab taken on the 17th of February 1881 by Denzil Charles Ibbetson*. Calcutta: Superintendent of Government Printing, 1883.

4 In 1861, the Commander-in-Chief of the British Army in India wanted the city walls to be dismantled but was unable to achieve this due to the expense involved in the demolition. He had, however, insisted that a space of 500 yards from the walls be retained under military control all around the city. Subsequently, in 1863, the jurisdiction of the walls, moat, and glacis of the city was transferred to the Civil Department with the stipulation that no additions or alterations of any sort, nor any building operations, be permitted without permission from the Military Department.

5 Office of the Registrar General of India. 'Delhi [1857].' Trevelyanganj and Kishenganj had previously been established as market squares and small private developments to the west of the city, named after the personages who established them. C. E. Trevelyan, Cantonment Magistrate and Superintendent, established Trevelyanganj, and Diwan Kishan Lal, Deputy Collector to Thomas Metcalfe, founded Kishanganj.

Trevelyanganj was laid out on a grid pattern with streets ninety-feet wide, public gardens, and a central colonnaded market. Since the sanitary planning of the city was not of overwhelming concern at the time, and prominent members of the Mughal court often founded enclaves, these small settlements were probably meant to celebrate the benevolence of the individuals who established them. I agree with Goodfriend that these settlements were more in the nature of personal fiefdoms than as solutions for planned extensions. They were not meant to be new models for development. While these were commercial enterprises, I see Clarkegunj as being the earliest official effort at developing a planned extension to the walled city. Douglas Goodfriend, 'The Tyranny of the Right Angle,' In *Delhi: The Deepening Crisis*. Patwant Singh and Ram Dhamija (eds). New Delhi: Sterling Publishers, 1989.

6 Major Charles Trevelyan (different from C. E. Trevelyan) issued a proclamation in 1858 inviting shopkeepers to settle on government lands that officials regarded as 'waste lands' in Jahan Numah, Sadar Bazaar. In 1881, the occupants acquired the right to permanence on the sites they had purchased subject to payment of rent. Officials later came to regard these people as 'Major Trevelyan's Squatters.' For discussion of the case see, R. B. Whitehead, *Report on the Administration of the Delhi Crown Lands*. Delhi: Oxford Printing Works, 1933. Appendix V.

7 Clarke, 'Letter # 64,' 1888.

8 Robert Clarke was later appointed as Commissioner, Delhi District.

9 Clarke, 'Letter # 64,' 1888.

10 Letter # 146, from Robert Clarke, Deputy Commissioner, Delhi to Colonel L. I. H. Grey, Commissioner and Superintendent, Delhi Division, Dated March 25, 1889. Commissioner's Office, Delhi Division. *File # 10(a)*, Carton Box # 41, 1888. (DSA).

11 Ibid.

12 Memorandum from Robert Clarke, Deputy Commissioner, Delhi, and President, Delhi Municipal Committee to Members of the Delhi Municipal Committee (undated, but likely to be 1889). Commissioner's Office, Delhi Division. *File # 10(a)*, Carton Box # 41, 1888. (DSA).

13 Letter # 772, from C. L. Tipper, Secretary, Government of Punjab to L. I. H. Grey, Commissioner and Superintendent, Delhi Division, Dated May 2, 1889. Commissioner's Office, Delhi Division, *File # 10(a)*, Carton Box # 41, 1888. (DSA).

14 Lahori Darvaza was not the first gate of the city wall to be removed since Mori Darvaza (Mori Gate) and Kabuli Darvaza (Kabul Gate) had been taken down much earlier. Yet the demolition of Lahori Darvaza was significant because the purpose was to allow the city to expand out toward the west and improve the sanitary and living conditions of the inhabitants. The Kabuli Darvaza and Mori Darvaza had been removed some decades earlier to make way for the railroad tracks.

15 Tipper, op. cit.

16 Ibid. City officials used the word 'suburbs' to denote neighborhoods and settlements outside the walled city.

17 Ibid.

18 Much of the heavy trade in grain happened in the vicinity of Lahori Darvaza and to relieve traffic the grain market was being relocated outside the city walls.

19   Clarke, 'Letter # 64,' 1888.

20   Ibid.

21   I use 'landmark' here not in the monumental sense, but in the manner of Kevin
     Lynch. In this instance, I see the design of the square or *gunj* as an attempt to create
     a memorable space similar to others in the city that were significant in people's cogni-
     tive maps of Delhi. Kevin Lynch, *Image of the City*. Cambridge, MA: MIT Press, 1981.

22   Clarke, 'Letter # 64,' 1888. See also Clarke, 'Memorandum,' 1889.

23   For detailed discussions of Haussmann's rebuilding of Paris among others see
     Anthony Sutcliff, *The Autumn of Central Paris: The Defeat of Town Planning
     1850–1970*. Montreal: McGill-Queen's University Press, 1971; Howard Saalman,
     Haussmann: Paris Transformed. New York: George Braziller, 1971; David Pinkney,
     Napoleon III and the Rebuilding of Paris. Princeton, NJ: Princeton University Press,
     1958. For utopian city planning, see Robert Fishman, *Urban Utopias in the Twentieth
     Century: Ebenezer Howard, Frank Lloyd Wright, and Le Corbusier*. New York: Basic
     Books, 1977; Charles Fourier, *Design for Utopia: Selected Writings of Charles Fourier*.
     New York: Schocken Books, 1971; Sir Ebenezer Howard, *Garden Cities of To-morrow*.
     London: Faber and Faber, 1946. (First published in 1898 as 'Tomorrow: A Peaceful
     Path to Real Reform.'); and Benjamin Ward Richardson, *Hygeia: a City of Health*.
     London: Macmillan, 1876.

24   One major difference between Howard's vision and that of Clarke's was that in
     Howard's Garden City land was communally owned.

25   Letter # 452, from Robert Clarke, Deputy Commissioner, Delhi to Colonel L. J. H.
     Grey, Commissioner and Superintendent, Delhi Division, Dated July 15, 1890. Com-
     missioner's Office, Delhi Division, *File # 10(a)*, Carton Box # 41, 1888. (DSA).

26   James Mill (1773–1836) served in the East India Company from 1819 to 1836 and is
     best known for his *magnum opus*, *History of British India*. He accepted Jeremy
     Bentham and David Ricardo as his mentors and argued for private property as a
     necessary pre-condition to civilization. James Mill, *The History of British India*. Notes
     by Horace Hayman Wilson. Introd. by John Kenneth Galbraith, Vols 1–6. New York:
     Chelsea, 1968. First published 1817.

27   The symbolism of the mosque's location is particularly significant in view of Jamal
     Malik's observations. He argues that the size and location of the mosque have a rela-
     tionship to its importance in the city and society. Jamal Malik, 'Islamic Institutions and
     Infrastructure in Shahjahanabad.' In *Shahjahanabad/Old Delhi: Tradition and Colonial
     Change*. Edited by Eckhart Ehlers and Thomas Krafft. Stuttgart: Franz Steiner Verlag,
     1993.

28   Clarke, 'Memorandum,' 1888.

29   Ibid.

30   Ibid.

31   As Clarke noted, Clarke, 'Letter # 64,' 1888.

32   Clarke, 'Letter # 452,' 1888.

33   Ibid.

34   Whitehead, op. cit.

35   Ibid. At the exact location of the Clarkegunj project, the Bombay Baroda and Central

India Railway Company had decided to construct a railroad siding and local goods station. The Municipal Committee decided to postpone development on the city side of the canal until after the railroad siding had been built and the railways had taken all the land they needed. Despite having to alter their plans, the Municipality was encouraged by the predicted increase in land values with the construction of the goods station and siding.

36 Ibid.

37 Government of Punjab, *District Gazetteer of Delhi*. Lahore: Government of India Press, 1912, p. 221.

38 Delhi Municipal Committee, *Report on the Working of Delhi Municipality, 1905–1906*. Lahore: Superintendent of Government Printing, 1906, p. 11.

39 A comparison of annual octroi income clearly shows that the importance of Delhi as a trade center had increased considerably 1892–97. See Letter # 338, from Major H. S. P. Davies, Deputy Commissioner Delhi, to Robert Clarke, Commissioner and Superintendent, Delhi Division, Dated October 18, 1898. Commissioner's Office, Delhi Division, *New File # 558*, Carton Box # 54 (49-E(2)), Vol. II, 1898. (DSA).

40 List of Assessees of the Delhi City under Section 16 and 17 of Income Tax Act II of 1886 included the following companies: Delhi Cloth and General Mills, Krishan Mills, Ganesh Flour Mills, and Hindu Biscuit, in Sabzi Mandi; Diamond Jubilee Flour Mills, in Mori Gate; Hindu Ice and General Mills, in Kuriapul; Native Commercial Bank, Chandni Chowk; and Kayasth Mercantile Banking, in Dariba Khurd. (Source: Letter # 62, from Major M. W. Douglas, Deputy Commissioner, Delhi to T. Gordon Walker, Commissioner and Superintendent Delhi Division, Dated August 12, 1902. Commissioner's Office, Delhi Division, *New File # 558*, Carton Box # 54 (49-E(2)), Vol. II, 1898). (DSA).

41 Whitehead, op. cit.

42 The reason that the city was most likely to expand towards the west was that the city was bounded on the east by the river, the British Cantonment and the Civil Lines lay immediately to the north, and the residents of the city had exhibited little inclination to settle the rocky lands to the south. After 1911, the colonial government's acquisition of land for the new capital of New Delhi also ruled out expansion of the walled city of the south.

43 Letter # 35/m7, from Major H. C. Beadon, Deputy Commissioner, Delhi District to Lieutenant Colonel C. M. Dallas, Commissioner and Superintendent, Delhi Division, Dated March 7, 1912. Commissioner's Office, Delhi Division. *New File # 1*, Carton Box # 64, 1908. (DSA).

44 Ibid., p. 15.

45 For instance, Deputy Commissioner Humphreys observed, 'The government does not like to own isolated pieces of property ordinarily since the trouble of managing them is not worth it. But the isolated plots of Nazul land inside the city walls are very valuable and bring in a handsome revenue to the Municipality which it cannot afford to forego.' Letter # 234/M. F., from R. Humphreys, Deputy Commissioner, Delhi District to A. Meredith, Commissioner and Superintendent, Delhi Division, dated August 14, 1908. Commissioner's Office, Delhi Division. *File # 18*, 1908. (DSA).

46 Whitehead, R. B., Assistant Commissioner, Delhi District. *Nazul Lands Administered by the Delhi Municipality.* Unpublished note, Dated December 14, 1909. Punjab Government Consolidated Circular # 27, p. 2. (DSA).

47 Ibid., p. 33.

48 Ibid.

49 Whitehead, 1933, p. 39.

50 Ibid., p. 48.

51 The bulky appendix of the Whitehead report contained several prototypes of lease forms and property records he had suggested.

52 Whitehead, 1933, Whitehead's observation was of an area that was once a small colony occupied by stone quarries and *thelawala* who carted the stone away. *Thelawala* was a hand-cart puller, and a *faqir* referred to a mendicant who lived on charity.

53 Ibid., p. 39.

54 Municipal income came from returns on government owned Nazul lands and buildings, *teh-bazari* or the rents paid for the temporary occupation of road-sides and foot paths; and income from Municipal buildings and lands. The total income derived from Nazul lands in the year 1907–08 was Rs.36, 633. Whitehead, *Nazul Lands Administered by the Delhi Municipality*, 1909, appendix table 6.

55 The rents from each of the vendors, hawkers, and lessees was too small to justify the costs of collection. Whitehead observed in his report: 'Great difficulties are experienced in the collection of Nazul income. Out of the eighteen hundred bills issued every month, about one thousand are for sums of eight annas and under. There is a large number of small squatters holding by virtue of proclamations who pay monthly rents of one anna and two annas only. They are a floating population and a civil suit would have no terrors for them. A decree even when obtained could not be carried into effect, as they have no belongings which could be profitably attached. Yet this is the only legal coercive process to which the Committee can resort.' Whitehead, 1933, p. 39. Before a metric currency was adopted 6 'paise' made an 'anna;' 16 'annas' a Rupee.

56 Humphreys, 'Letter # 234/M. F,' 1908, p. 3.

57 Col. Parsons, then Deputy Commissioner of Delhi, had raised the issue but the Survey of India could not take it up because they did not have staff available for the job. The map of Delhi that was in use in 1910 had been prepared by the Survey of India during 1865–66.

58 Letter # 45 [name of sender illegible] to the Commissioner and Superintendent, Delhi Division, Dated Delhi, March 20, 1910. Commissioner's Office, Delhi Division. *File # 23*, 1910. (DSA).

59 The traditional system of land records and the redefined colonial ones both contained a *khata* and a *khasra*. The first was a detailed map including dimensions of the boundaries of the properties. The latter was a ledger that listed the dimensions of the properties, the structures on it, and the ownership and tenancy status. Lack of a reliable large-scale map caused much confusion in the Municipal office. As one official observed, 'I would think that at least three-fourths of the contentious business con-

nected with buildings and encroachments would disappear if the Municipality, had such a map or plan, and a properly attested khasra attached to it.' Ibid.

60 Letter # 199/T, from E. Burdon, Secretary Municipal Committee, Delhi to C. A. Barron, Deputy Commissioner, Delhi, Dated February 22, 1910. Commissioner's Office, Delhi Division. *File # 23*, 1910. (DSA).

61 In another survey, for instance, Humphreys instructed his subordinates in meticulous detail about maps that were to be updated, the specific aspects that needed further surveying, the scales that each different property and area was to be mapped in, and the location of points of reference on the lands that were to be permanently marked in stone. Humphreys, 'Letter # 234/M. F,' 1908.

62 Patrick Geddes was critical of the official efforts at urban improvement in India for their 'mere application of a standard remedy or arbitrary prescription.' Geddes reproached British sanitarians for complacently applying their English and Victorian manufacturing-town experience in India. However, Geddes and his views remained marginal to state-sponsored urban improvement in India. Patrick Geddes, *Town Planning Towards City Development: A Report to the Durbar of Indore*. Parts I and II. Indore: Holkar State Printing Press, 1918. p. xiii.

63 In a system in which liberty and security were perfectly reconciled, and laid no further restraint on individual action than was beneficial, 'Bentham believed that wealth, and hence, happiness would be "maximized." ' Eric Stokes, *The English Utilitarians and India*. Oxford: Oxford University Press, 1959, p. 67.

64 James Mill, *An Essay on Government*. Edited by Curan V. Shields. Indianapolis: Bobbs-Merrill, 1955.

65 Notes and correspondence regarding survey and preparation of Delhi city maps. Commissioner's Office, Delhi Division. *File # 23*, 1910. (DSA).

66 Mill, op. cit., p. xii. Eric Stokes has argued that British policy in India 'moved within an orbit of ideas primarily determined in Europe.' Stokes, op. cit.

6 IMAGINING MODERNITY: SYMBOLIC TERRAINS OF HOUSING

1 See Jyoti Hosagrahar, 'Fractured Plans: Real Estate, Moral Reform, and the Politics of Housing in New Delhi, 1936–1941.' In *Traditional Dwellings and Settlements Review*, Vol. 11, No. 1, Fall 1999. See also, Stephen Legg. 'Colonial Governmentality: spaces of imperialism and nationalism in India's New Capital, Delhi 1911–47.' Department of Geography, University of Cambridge, Unpublished Dissertation, 2003.

2 Delhi Town Planning Committee, *Final Report of the Delhi Town Planning Committee on the Town Planning of the New Imperial Capital*. Delhi: Superintendent of Government Printing, India, 1913, p. 2.

3 Ibid., p. 5.

4 Dr. K. S. Sethna, Medical Officer of Health of Delhi, published a report included in *Report on the Administration of the Delhi Municipality for the Year 1933–34*. Delhi: Printed at the Municipal Press, 1934.

5 'Delhi the Death-Trap,' *The Times of India*, January 15, 1934.

6 Ibid.

7   A. P. Hume, *Report on the Relief of Congestion in Delhi*. Vols I and II. Simla: Government of India Press, 1936, p. 113.

8   *Public Health Report of the Delhi Province*. Delhi: Superintendent of Government Printing, 1931, p. 9.

9   *The Statesman*, Delhi, December 4, 1934. 56.67 persons per acre is equivalent to 36,923 persons/square mile.

10 Officials blamed the entrenched traditional systems for the failure of the new: 'The Health Officer is greatly handicapped in pushing forward the introduction of the water borne system on account of the "Customary sweepers." The Municipality will have to educate public opinion, and take steps to introduce the water borne system as soon as practicable.' *Public Health Report of the Delhi Province*, op. cit., pp. 26–27.

11 *Report on the Administration of the Delhi Municipality for the Year 1927–28*. Vol. I. General Administration. Delhi: Printed at the Municipal Press, 1928, p. 12.

12 According to official reports by 1938, 'The outdoor building staff of the Committee consists of one Building Superintendent who is in charge of the staff, 4 Naib-Tahsildars, 9 Building Inspectors and 17 Building Jamadars. Of these one Inspector, 2 Jamadars and a gang of 4 persons is on constant duty of demolition.' *Report on the Administration of the Delhi Municipality 1938–39*. Vol. I. General Administration. Delhi: Printed at the Municipal Press, 1939, pp. 32–33.

13 This understanding of the building process is based on my 16 months of fieldwork in Delhi, interviews with various residents, oral histories, and my interpretation of volumes of detailed proceedings, minutes of meetings, and petitions in the records of the Delhi Municipal Committee.

14 *Report on the Administration of the Delhi Municipality 1938–39*, op. cit., p. 32.

15 Ibid., p. 32.

16 Ibid.

17 Bribes and clandestine payments were often couched under the euphemism of a gift to gain social 'goodwill.'

18 *Report on the Administration of the Delhi Municipality 1929–30*, op. cit., pp. 44–45.

19 Ibid.

20 Ibid., p. 6.

21 *Report on the Administration of the Delhi Municipality for the year 1930–31*. Vol. I. General Administration. Delhi: Printed at the Municipal Press, 1931, p. 50.

22 Ibid., p. 50.

23 *Report on the Relief of Congestion in Delhi*, 1936, Vols I and II; Delhi Improvement Trust. *Report of the First Three Year Programme of the Delhi Improvement Trust, 1936–39*. New Delhi: New India Press, 1939, p. 2.

24 *Final Report of the Delhi Town Planning Committee on the Town Planning of the New Imperial Capital*. Delhi Improvement Trust, 1913, p. 2.

25 *Report of the First Three Year Programme of the Delhi Improvement Trust*. New Delhi: Government of India Press, 1939, p. 6.

26 As far back as 1925 the Municipal Committee raised the question of extending the Town Improvement Act (Act IV of 1922) and the formation of a Town Improvement Trust in accordance with it. In so doing the stated objectives of the Committee were:

a) The improvement of certain areas in the city known as bastis in which persons belonging to an inferior social order and especially the class known as untouchables are residing. Some of these bastis are not fit for human habitation. They consist of a number of few thatched houses, from which sun and air seem to have been deliberately excluded. The lanes are narrow and no sanitary arrangements in them, under the present circumstances are possible. The Committee considered that it would be in the public interest to acquire a few of these bastis and to provide housing accommodation for this class under more congenial circumstances elsewhere.'

b) The widening of streets where necessary. There are certain lanes, which are less than 3 feet wide with double and three storyed houses abutting on either side of it. In some of them it is difficult for 2 persons to walk abreast.

c) The acquisition of certain undeveloped areas in the city to provide sanitary tenements of reasonable rent for middle classes.

d) The provision of open spaces in the interests of the residents of various localities.

e) The securing and reservation of plots of land for the grazing of milch cattle.

f) The provision of a proper system of drains and sewers.

Report on the Administration of the Delhi Municipality for the year 1935–36. Vol. I. General Administration. Delhi: Printed at the Municipal Press, 1936, p. 52.

27 Ibid., p. 48. By 1935, the idea of scientific town planning to prevent the growth of disorganized and unsanitary suburbs had taken root. In Punjab, for instance, a Town Planning Engineer was appointed for the purpose. See The Statesman, June 21, 1935.

28 A. P. Hume, 'A Preliminary Note on the Problem of Congestion in Delhi,' dated September 11, 1935, Chief Commissioner's Office, Delhi, p. 6. (DSA).

29 British officials saw some cultural/ethnic/caste groups such as Gujar and Ranghar as having a 'habit of thieving' and of 'cattle-lifting.' A Gazaetter of Delhi. Delhi: Vintage, 1988. First published as Gazeteer of the Delhi District 1883–84, Compiled and published under the authority of the Punjab Government, 1884.

30 Since the re-housing was often delayed, unserviced, inadequate (and therefore high density), and in environmentally poor locations they created new 'slums.'

31 Delhi Improvement Trust, Administration Report of the Delhi improvement Trust for the years, 1937–39. New Delhi: Author, 1940.

32 Report on the Administration of the Delhi Municipality for the year 1936–37. Vol. I. General Administration. Delhi: Printed at the Municipal Press, 1937.

33 Delhi Improvement Trust. Administration Report of the Delhi improvement Trust for the Years, 1950–51. New Delhi: Author, 1952.

34 Hume's report submitted in 1936 proved instrumental to the setting up of the Delhi Improvement Trust.

35 Hume, op. cit., Vol. I. Hume's figures for density were remarkably different from the Health Report of 1931 (see Table 6.1).

36 Hume, op. cit., Vol. II, p. 9.

37 Ibid., p. 10. Hume also notes that in a 'D'-class orthodox clerk's quarter in New Delhi the living space amounted to a fifth of the total area of the house. This was less generous than what Hume himself proposed.

38 Hume, op. cit., Vol. II.

39 A. P. Hume, 'A Preliminary Note on the Problem of Congestion in Delhi,' 1935, p. 4.

40 Ibid., pp. 2–3.

41 *Report of the First Three Year Programme of the Delhi Improvement Trust*, 1939, p. 32.

42 The DIT's architectural section prepared layouts of Basti Arakashan, the Roshanara Extension, and Shadipur town expansion layouts among others. 'On streets where a standard design and elevation was considered necessary, these were enforced by the Trust through the lease. Elsewhere, as in the purely residential parts of Daryaganj, only horizontal heights and building lines have been prescribed.' Ibid., p. 33.

43 Ibid.

44 Delhi Improvement Trust, *Building Bye-Laws for Trust Extra Municipal Areas*. New Delhi: Author, 1944.

45 *Report of the First Three Year Programme of the Delhi Improvement Trust*, 1939, pp. 33–34.

46 See papers in New File # 9/1914 at the Delhi State Archives. This law was modified for the purposes of the Trust. Under the schedule to the Trust Law an important modification of the Land Acquisition Act relates to assessment of market value, whereby market value is to be determined according to the use to which the land was being put on the date of the relevant notification. *Report of the First Three Year Programme of the Delhi Improvement Trust*, 1939, pp. 30–31.

47 *Report on the Administration of the Delhi Municipality for the Year 1936–37*, 1937.

48 *Report of the First Three Year Programme of the Delhi Improvement Trust*, 1939.

49 For instance, the total amount that the DIT expended in 1939–40 was Rs.60,897, a mere 2 percent of the annual income of Rs.32,20,014. In 1940–41 the Trust expended Rs.9,34,871, or 79 percent of an income of Rs.11,76,473. Even with several projects in full swing, the DIT spent substantially less than its income. Administration Report of the D.I.T for the years 1939–41, 1942, Annexure V.

50 Letter # 30-M from A. P. Hume, Officer on Special Duty attached to the Delhi Administration, New Delhi. Dated March 14, 1936. Chief Commissioner's Office, Delhi. New File # 122/B/1935 (DSA).

51 For details see, for instance, 'Copy of the Proceedings of the Conference held on the 13th September, 1935,' by M. W. Yeatts, Chief Commissioner, Delhi. Chief Commissioner's Office, New File # 122/B/1935 (DSA), p. 1.

That such speculation already exists is shown by the fact that some of the most suitable building land in the Khanpur village area has already been sold. For instance, a contractor of the Agricultural Institute has bought 3 bighas at Rs.100/- per bigha and has already built a shop. A contractor of the Forest Department has bought 25 bighas at the rate of about Rs.400/- an acre, and has already erected a brick wall round the area. It seems a pity, if there is any likelihood of Government agreeing to the acquisition of these lands – in my opinion most suitable for Delhi Expansion that we should allow the market to be spoiled for the sake of a simple notification under section 4.

> Letter # 4 from A. P. Hume, Officer on Special Duty attached to the Delhi Administration to the Deputy Commissioner, Delhi Division. Dated February 10/11, 1936. Commissioner's Office, Delhi Division. New File # 122/B/1935/R & A (DSA).

52 In March 1936, Hume observed:

> Already last September it was apparent that in the area covered by what is known as the Municipal Northern City Extension Scheme, as well as in other land in the immediate vicinity of the scheme and outside municipal limits, speculation in land was going on. The Northern City Extension scheme was started about 1932, since when numerous sales of land in and around the area, and also I understand some fictitious transfers have taken place. Until last year speculation was not serious, since the immediate prospect of extensive development on this side was still indefinite.
>
> Letter # 30-M from A. P. Hume, Officer on Special Duty attached to the Delhi Administration, New Delhi. Dated March 14, 1936. Chief Commissioner's Office, Delhi. New File # 122/B/1935 (DSA).

53 Ibid.

54 *Report of the First Three Year Programme of the Delhi Improvement Trust*, 1939, p. 25, also Annexure VIII.

55 In 1944 Sir Patrick Abercrombie proposed a 'Greater London Plan' for the decentralization of London.

7 RECOVERING AN URBAN PAST

1 Benjamin Ward Richardson, 'Modern Sanitary Science: A City of Health.' In *Van Nostrand's Eclectic Engineering Magazine* 14 (January 1876): 31–42. Reprinted from *Nature* 12 (October 14, 1875): 523–525 and (October 21, 1875): 542–545.

2 Ashis Nandy, *The Intimate Enemy: Loss and Recovery of Self under Colonialism.* Delhi: Oxford University Press, 1988.

3 Dipesh Chakrabarty, Gyan Prakash, and Partha Chatterjee have each, in their different essays, held the nationalists complicit in equating Europe with modernity. That Jawaharlal Nehru, the first Prime Minister of the Indian Republic, appointed Le Corbusier for the design of Chandigarh is evidence of this. See Dipesh Chakrabarty, *Provincializing Europe: Postcolonial Thought and Historical Difference*. Princeton: Princeton University Press, 2000; Partha Chatterjee, *Nation and its Fragments: Colonial and Postcolonial Histories*. Princeton: Princeton University Press, 1993; Gyan Prakash, *Another Reason: Science and the Imagination of Modern India*. Princeton, NJ: Princeton University Press, 1999. For critical discussions of Nehru and Chandigarh, see Vikramaditya Prakash, *Chandigarh's Le Corbusier: the Struggle for Modernity in Postcolonial India*. Seattle: University of Washington Press, 2002; and Madhu Sarin. *Urban Planning in the Third World: The Chandigarh Experience*. London: Mansell, 1982.

4 Gyan Prakash has talked about an internally divided modernity with reference to the nationalists' imagination of an 'Indian' modernity. Gyan Prakash, op. cit.

ABBREVIATIONS FOR ARCHIVES AND LIBRARIES

BL   British Library, London.
DDA   Delhi Development Authority, New Delhi.
DSA   Delhi State Archives, New Delhi.
MCD Municipal Corporation of Delhi.
NAI   National Archives of India.
OIOC Oriental and India Office Collections, British Library, London.

Index

Italic page numbers indicate figures and illustrations not included in the text page range. References to notes are prefixed by 'n'